THE PERSEPHONE BOOK OF SHORT STORIES

Persephone Book Nº 100
Published by Persephone Books Ltd 2012

Endpapers taken from a roller-printed cotton twill weave manufactured in 1911 at the Arnold Print Works, North Adams, Massachusetts
© Museum of Art, Rhode Island School of Design
and 'Côte D'Azure', a screen-printed cotton furnishing fabric designed by Susan Collier and Sarah Campbell for Fischbacher Ltd in 1983
© Victoria and Albert Museum

Typeset in ITC Baskerville by
Keystroke, Tettenhall, Wolverhampton

Printed and bound in Germany by
GGP Media GmbH, Poessneck

978 1903 155 905

Persephone Books Ltd
59 Lamb's Conduit Street
London WC1N 3NB
020 7242 9292

www.persephonebooks.co.uk

THE PERSEPHONE BOOK OF SHORT STORIES

PERSEPHONE BOOKS
LONDON

CONTENTS

From A to Z *Susan Glaspell (1909)* 1

The Black Cap *Katherine Mansfield (1917)* 27

The Pain *Pauline Smith (1923)* 37

Holiday Group *E M Delafield (1926)* 57

The Music Box *Malachi Whitaker (1929)* 73

Here We Are *Dorothy Parker (1931)* 87

A Lovely Time *Dorothy Whipple (1933)* 101

Roman Fever *Edith Wharton (1934)* 117

Dimanche *Irène Némirovsky (1934)* 137

The Photograph *Phyllis Bentley (1935)* 161

The Exile *Betty Miller (1935)* 175

The Rainy Day, the Good Mother and the Brown Suit *Dorothy Canfield Fisher (1937)* 193

Nine Years is a Long Time *Norah Hoult (1938)* 205

The Test *Angelica Gibbs (1940)* 223

It All Begins Again *Helen Hull (1941)* 229

Defeat *Kay Boyle (1941)* 255

Good Evening, Mrs Craven
Mollie Panter-Downes (1942) 269

Subject for a Sermon *Elizabeth Berridge (1944)* 279

Wednesday *Dorothy Whipple (1944)* 303

Spade Man from over the Water
Frances Towers (1947) 317

Minnie's Room *Mollie Panter-Downes (1947)* 329

The English Lesson *Margaret Bonham (1947)* 339

The Lottery *Shirley Jackson (1948)* 349

A View of Exmoor *Sylvia Townsend Warner (1948)* 363

The Woman Novelist *Diana Gardner (1950)* 373

What a Lovely Surprise *Penelope Mortimer (1957)* 389

The Real Thing *Diana Athill (1958)* 407

A Bad Cold *Elizabeth Spencer (1967)* 419

Worlds Apart *Penelope Fitzgerald (1983)* 427

A Few Problems in the Day Case Unit
Georgina Hammick (1986) 441

AUTHOR BIOGRAPHIES 465

PUBLICATION HISTORY 475

THE PERSEPHONE BOOK OF SHORT STORIES

FROM A TO Z

Susan Glaspell

(1909)

Thus had another ideal tumbled to the rubbish heap! She seemed to be breathing the dust which the newly fallen had stirred up among its longer dead fellows. Certainly she was breathing the dust from somewhere.

During her senior year at the university, when people would ask: 'And what are you going to do when you leave school, Miss Willard?', she would respond with anything that came to hand, secretly hugging to her mind that idea of getting a position in a publishing house. Her conception of her publishing house was finished about the same time as her class-day gown. She was to have a roll-top desk – probably of mahogany – and a big chair which whirled round like that in the office of the undergraduate dean. She was to have a little office all by herself, opening on a bigger office – the little one marked 'Private'. There were to be beautiful rugs – the general effect not unlike the library at the University Club – books and pictures and cultivated gentlemen who spoke often of Greek tragedies and the Renaissance. She was a little uncertain as to her duties, but had a general idea about getting down between nine and ten, reading the morning paper, cutting the latest magazine, and then 'writing something'.

Commencement was now four months past, and one of her professors had indeed secured for her a position in a Chicago 'publishing house'. This was her first morning and she was standing at the window looking down into Dearborn Street while the man who was to have her in charge was fixing a place for her to sit.

That the publishing house should be on Dearborn Street had been her first blow, for she had long located her publishing house on that beautiful stretch of Michigan Avenue which overlooked the lake. But the real insult was that this publishing house, instead of having a building, or at least a floor, all to itself, simply had a place penned off in a bleak, dirty building such as one who had done work in sociological research instinctively associated with a box factory. And the thing which fairly trailed her visions in the dust was that the partition penning them off did not extend to the ceiling, and the adjoining room being occupied by a patent medicine company, she was face to face with glaring endorsements of Dr Bunting's Famous Kidney and Bladder Cure. Taken all in all, there seemed little chance for Greek tragedies or the Renaissance.

The man who was 'running things' – she buried her phraseology with her dreams – wore a skull cap, and his moustache dragged down below his chin. Just at present he was engaged in noisily pulling a most unliterary pine table from a dark corner to a place near the window. That accomplished, an ostentatious hunt ensued, resulting in the triumphant flourish of a feather duster. Several knocks at the table, and the dust of many months – perhaps likewise of many dreams – ascended to a resting place on the endorsement of Dr Bunting's Kidney and Bladder Cure. He next produced a short, straight-backed chair which she recognised as brother to the one which used to stand behind their kitchen stove. He gave it a shake, thus delicately indicating that she was receiving special favours in this matter of an able-bodied chair, and then announced with brisk satisfaction: 'So! Now we are ready to begin.' She murmured a 'Thank you', seated herself and her buried hopes in this chair which did not whirl round, and leaned her arms upon a table which did not even dream in mahogany.

In the *other* publishing house, one pushed buttons and uniformed menials appeared – noiselessly, quickly and deferentially. At this moment a boy with sandy hair brushed straight back in a manner either statesmanlike or clownlike – things were too involved to know which – shuffled in with an armful of yellow paper which he flopped down on the pine table. After a minute he returned with a warbled 'Take Me Back to New York Town' and a paste-pot. And upon his third appearance he was practising gymnastics with a huge pair of shears, which he finally presented, grinningly.

There was a long pause, broken only by the sonorous voice of Dr Bunting upbraiding someone for not having billed out that stuff to Apple Grove, and then the sandy-haired boy appeared bearing a large dictionary, followed by the man in the skull cap behind a dictionary of equal unwieldiness. These were set down on either side of the yellow paper, and he who was filling the position of cultivated gentleman pulled up a chair, briskly.

'Has Professor Lee explained to you the nature of our work?' he wanted to know.

'No,' she replied, half grimly, a little humorously, and not far from tearfully, 'he didn't – explain.'

'Then it is my pleasure to inform you,' he began, blinking at her importantly, 'that we are engaged here in the making of a dictionary.'

'A *dic* –?' but she swallowed the gasp in the laugh coming up to meet it, and of their union was born a saving cough.

'Quite an overpowering thought, is it not?' he agreed pleasantly. 'Now you see you have before you the two dictionaries you will use most, and over in that case you will find other references. The main thing' – his voice sank to an impressive whisper – 'is *not* to infringe the copyright. The publisher was in yesterday and made a little talk to the force, and he said that anyone who handed in a piece of copy infringing the copyright simply employed that means of writing his own resignation. Neat way of putting it, was it not?'

'Yes, *wasn't* it – neat?' she agreed, wildly.

She was conscious of a man's having stepped in behind her and taken a seat at the table next to hers. She heard him opening his dictionaries and getting out his papers. Then the man in the skull cap had risen and was saying genially: 'Well, here is a piece of old Webster, your first "take" – no copyright on this, you see, but you must modernise and expand. Don't miss any of the good words in either of these dictionaries. Here you have dictionaries, copy-paper, paste, and Professor Lee assures me you have brains – all the necessary ingredients for successful lexicography. We are to have some rules printed tomorrow, and in the meantime I trust I've made myself clear. The main thing' – he bent down and spoke it solemnly – 'is *not* to infringe the copyright.' With a cheerful nod he was gone, and she heard him saying to the man at the next table: 'Mr Clifford, I shall have to ask you to be more careful about getting in promptly at eight.'

She removed the cover from her paste-pot and dabbed a little on a piece of paper. Then she tried the unwieldy shears on another piece of paper. She then opened one of her dictionaries and read studiously for fifteen minutes. That accomplished, she opened the other dictionary and perused it for twelve minutes. Then she took the column of 'old Webster', which had been handed to her pasted on a piece of yellow paper, and set about attempting to commit it to memory. She looked up to be met with the statement that Mrs Marjory Van Luce De Vane, after spending years under the so-called best surgeons of the country, had been cured in six weeks by Dr Bunting's Famous Kidney and Bladder Cure. She pushed the dictionaries petulantly from her, and leaning her very red cheek upon her hand, her hazel eyes blurred with tears of perplexity and resentment, her mouth drawn in pathetic little lines of uncertainty, looked over at the sprawling warehouse on the opposite side of Dearborn Street. She was just considering the direct manner of writing one's resignation – not knowing how to infringe the copyright

– when a voice said: 'I beg pardon, but I wonder if I can help you any?'

She had never heard a voice like that before. Or, *had* she heard it? – and where? She looked at him, a long, startled gaze. Something made her think of the voice the prince used to have in long-ago dreams. She looked into a face that was dark and thin and – different. Two very dark eyes were looking at her kindly, and a mouth which was a baffling combination of things to be loved and things to be deplored was twitching a little, as though it would like to join the eyes in a smile, if it dared.

Because he saw both how funny and how hard it was, she liked him. It would have been quite different had he seen either one without the other.

'You can tell me how *not* to infringe the copyright,' she laughed. 'I'm not sure that I know what a copyright is.'

He laughed – a laugh which belonged with his voice. 'Mr Littletree isn't as lucid as he thinks he is. I've been here a week or so, and picked up a few things you might like to know.'

He pulled his chair closer to her table then and gave her a lesson in the making of copy. Edna Willard was never one-half so attractive as when absorbed in a thing which someone was showing her how to do. Her hazel eyes would widen and glisten with the joy of comprehending; her cheeks would flush a deeper pink with the coming of new light, her mouth would part in a childlike way it had forgotten to outgrow, her head would nod gleefully in token that she understood, and she had a way of pulling at her wavy hair and making it more wavy than it had been before. The man at the next table was a long time in explaining the making of a dictionary. He spoke in low tones, often looking at the figure of the man in the skull cap, who was sitting with his back to them, looking over copy. Once she cried, excitedly: 'Oh – I *see*!' and he warned, 'S–h!' explaining, 'Let him think you got it all from him. It will give you a better stand-in.' She nodded, appreciatively, and felt very well acquainted with this kind man whose voice made her think of something – called to something – she did not just know what.

After that she became so absorbed in lexicography that when the men began putting away their things it was hard to realise that the morning had gone. It was a new and difficult game, the evasion of the copyright furnishing the stimulus of a hazard.

The man at the next table had been watching her with an amused admiration. Her childlike absorption, the way every emotion from perplexity to satisfaction expressed itself in the poise of her head and the pucker of her face, took him back over years emotionally barren to the time when he too had those easily stirred enthusiasms of youth. For the man at the next table was far from young now. His mouth had never quite parted with boyishness, but there was more white than black in his hair, and the lines about his mouth told that time, as well as forces more ageing than time, had laid a heavy hand upon him. But when he looked at the girl and told her with a smile that it was time to stop work, it was a smile and a voice to defy the most tell-tale face in all the world.

During her luncheon, as she watched the strange people coming and going, she did much wondering. She wondered why it was that so many of the men at the dictionary place were very old men; she wondered if it would be a good dictionary – one that would be used in the schools; she wondered if Dr Bunting had made a great deal of money, and most of all she wondered about the man at the next table whose voice was like – like a dream which she did not know that she had dreamed.

When she had returned to the straggling old building, had stumbled down the narrow, dark hall and opened the door of the big bleak room, she saw that the man at the next table was the only one who had returned from luncheon. Something in his profile made her stand there very still. He had not heard her come in, and he was looking straight ahead, eyes half closed, mouth set – no unsurrendered boyishness there now. Wholly unconsciously she took an impulsive step forward. But she stopped, for she saw, and felt without really understanding, that it was not just the moment's pain, but the revealed pain of years. Just then he began to cough, and it seemed the cough, too, was more than of the moment. And then he turned and saw her, and smiled, and the smile changed all.

As the afternoon wore on the man stopped working and, turning a little in his chair, sat there covertly watching the girl. She was just typically girl. It was written that she had spent her days in the happy ways of healthful girlhood. He supposed that a great many young fellows had fallen in love with her – nice, clean young fellows, the kind she would naturally meet. And then his eyes closed for a minute and he put up his hand

and brushed back his hair; there was weariness, weariness weary of itself, in the gesture. He looked about the room and scanned the faces of the men, most of them older than he, many of them men whose histories were well known to him. They were the usual hangers-on about newspaper offices; men who, for one reason or other – age, dissipation, antiquated methods – had been pitched over, men for whom such work as this came as a godsend. They were the men of yesterday – men whom the world had rushed past. She was the only one there, this girl who would probably sit here beside him for many months, with whom the future had anything to do. Youth! – Goodness! – Joy! – Hope! – strange things to bring to a place like this. And as if their alienism disturbed him, he moved restlessly, almost resentfully, bit his lips nervously, moistened them, and began putting away his things.

As the girl was starting home along Dearborn Street a few minutes later, she chanced to look in a window. She saw that it was a saloon, but before she could turn away she saw a man with a white face – white with the peculiar whiteness of a dark face, standing before the bar drinking from a small glass. She stood still, arrested by a look such as she had never seen before: a panting human soul sobbingly fluttering down into something from which it had spent all its force in trying to rise. When she recalled herself and passed on, a mist which she could neither account for nor banish was dimming the clear hazel of her eyes.

The next day was a hard one at the dictionary place. She told herself it was because the novelty of it was wearing away, because her fingers ached, because it tired her back to sit in that horrid chair. She did not admit of any connection between her flagging interest and the fact that the place at the next table was vacant.

The following day he was still absent. She assumed it was nervousness occasioned by her queer surroundings that made her look round whenever she heard a step behind her. Where was he? Where had that look carried him? If he were in trouble, was there no one to help him?

The third day she did an unpremeditated thing. The man in the skull cap had been showing her something about the copy. As he was leaving, she asked: 'Is the man who sits at the next table coming back?'

'Oh yes,' he replied grimly, 'he'll be back.'

'Because,' she went on, 'if he wasn't, I thought I would take his shears. These hurt my fingers.'

He made the exchange for her – and after that things went better.

He did return late the next morning. After he had taken his place he looked over at her and smiled. He looked sick and shaken – as if something that knew no mercy had taken hold of him and wrung body and soul.

'You have been ill?' she asked, with timid solicitude.

'Oh no,' he replied, rather shortly.

He was quiet all that day, but the next day they talked about the work, laughed together over funny definitions they found. She felt that he could tell many interesting things about himself, if he cared to.

As the days went on he did tell some of those things – out of the way places where he had worked, queer people whom he had known. It seemed that words came to him as gifts, came freely, happily, pleased, perhaps, to be borne by so sympathetic a voice. And there was another thing about him. He seemed always to know just what she was trying to say; he never missed the unexpressed. That made it easy to say things to him; there seemed a certain at-homeness between his thought and hers. She accounted for her interest in him by telling herself she had never known anyone like that before. Now Harold, the boy whom she knew best out at the university, why one had to *say* things to Harold to make him understand! And Harold never left one wondering – wondering what he had meant by that smile, what he had been going to say when he started to say something and stopped, wondering what it was about his face that one could not understand. Harold never could claim as his the hour after he had left her, and was one ever close to anyone with whom one did not spend some of the hours of absence? She began to see that hours spent together when apart were the most intimate hours of all.

And as Harold did not make one wonder, so he did not make one worry. Never in all her life had there been a lump in her throat when she thought of Harold. There was often a lump in her throat when the man at the next table was coughing.

One day, she had been there about two months, she said something to him about it. It was hard; it seemed forcing one's way into a room that had never been opened to one – there were several doors he kept closed.

'Mr Clifford,' she turned to him impetuously as they were putting away their things that night, 'will you mind if I say something to you?'

He was covering his paste-pot. He looked up at her strangely. The closed door seemed to open a little way. 'I can't conceive of "minding" anything you might say to me, Miss Noah,' – he had called her Miss Noah ever since she, by mistake, had one day called him Mr Webster.

'You see,' she hurried on, very timid, now that the door had opened a little, 'you have been so good to me. Because you have been so good to me it seems that I have some right to – to –'

His head was resting upon his hand, and he leaned a little closer as though listening for something he wanted to hear.

'I had a cousin who had a cough like yours' – brave now that she could not go back – 'and he went down to New Mexico and stayed for a year, and when he came back – when he came back he was as well as any of us. It seems so foolish not to' – her voice broke, now that it had so valiantly carried it – 'not to –'

He looked at her, and that was all. But she was never wholly the same again after that look. It enveloped her being in something which left her richer – different. It was a look to light the dark place between two human souls. It seemed for the moment that words would follow it, but as if feeling their helplessness – perhaps needlessness – they sank back unuttered, and at the last he got up, abruptly, and walked away.

One night, while waiting for the elevator, she heard two of the men talking about him. When she went out on the street it was with head high, cheeks hot. For nothing is so hard to hear as that which one has half known, and evaded. One never denies so hotly as in denying to one's self what one fears is true, and one never resents so bitterly as in resenting that which one cannot say one has the right to resent.

That night she lay in her bed with wide open eyes, going over and over the things they had said. '*Cure*?' – one of them had scoffed, after telling how brilliant he had been before he 'went to pieces' – 'why all the cures on earth couldn't help him! He can go just so far, and then he can no more stop himself – oh, about as much as an ant could stop a prairie fire!'

She finally turned over on her pillow and sobbed; and she wondered why – wondered, yet knew.

But it resulted in the flowering of her tenderness for him. Interest mounted to defiance. It ended in blind, passionate desire to 'make it up' to him. And again he was so different from Harold; Harold did not impress himself upon one by upsetting all one's preconceived ideas.

She felt now that she understood better – understood the closed doors. He was – she could think of no better word than sensitive.

And that is why, several mornings later, she very courageously – for it did take courage – threw this little note over on his desk – they had formed a habit of writing notes to each other, sometimes about the words, sometimes about other things.

'IN-VI-TA-TION, *n*. That which Miss Noah extends to Mr Webster for Friday evening, December second, at the house where she lives – hasn't she already told him where that is? It is the wish of Miss Noah to present Mr Webster to various other Miss Noahs, all of whom are desirous of making his acquaintance.'

She was absurdly nervous at luncheon that day, and kept telling herself with severity not to act like a high-school girl. He was late in returning that noon, and though there seemed a new something in his voice when he asked if he hadn't better sharpen her pencils, he said nothing about her new definition of invitation. It was almost five o'clock when he threw this over on her desk:

'AP-PRE-CI-ATION, *n.* That sentiment inspired in Mr Webster by the kind invitation of Miss Noah for Friday evening.

'RE-GRET, *n.* That which Mr Webster experiences because, for reasons into which he cannot go in detail, it is impossible for him to accept Miss Noah's invitation.

'RE-SENT-MENT, *n.* That which is inspired in Mr Webster by the insinuation that there are other Miss Noahs in the world.'

Then below he had written: 'Three hours later. Miss Noah, the world is queer. Some day you may find out – though I hope you never will – that it is frequently the things we most want to do that we must leave undone. Miss Noah, won't you go on bringing me as much of yourself as you can to Dearborn Street, and try not to think much about my not being able to know the Miss Noah of Hyde Park? And little Miss Noah – I thank you. There aren't words enough in this old book of ours to tell you how much – or why.'

That night he hurried away with never a joke about how many words she had written that day. She did not look up as he stood there putting on his coat.

It was spring now, and the dictionary staff had begun on W.

They had written of Joy, of Hope and Life and Love, and many other things. Life seemed pressing just behind some of those definitions, pressing the harder, perhaps, because it could not break through the surface.

For it did not break through; it flooded just beneath.

How did she know that he cared for her? She could not possibly have told. Perhaps the nearest to actual proof she could bring was that he always saw that her overshoes were put in a warm place. And when one came down to facts, the putting of a girl's galoshes near the radiator did not necessarily mean love.

Perhaps then it was because there was no proof of it that she was most sure. For some of the most sure things in the world are things which cannot be proved.

It was only that they worked together and were friends; that they laughed together over funny definitions they found, that he was kind to her, and that they seemed remarkably close together.

That is as far as facts can take it.

And just there – it begins.

For the force which rushes beneath the facts of life, caring nothing for conditions, not asking what one desires or what one thinks best, caring as little about a past as about a future – save its own future – the force which can laugh at man's institutions and batter over in one sweep what he likes to call his wisdom, was sweeping them on. And because it could get no other recognition it forced its way into the moments when he asked her for an eraser, when she wanted to know how to spell a word. He could not so much as ask her if she needed more copy-paper without seeming to be lavishing upon her all the love of all the ages.

And so the winter had worn on, and there was really nothing whatever to tell about it.

She was quiet this morning, and kept her head bent low over her work. For she had estimated the number of pages there were between W and Z. Soon they would be at Z; – and then? Then? Shyly she turned and looked at him; he too was bent over his work. When she came in she had said something about its being spring, and that there must be wild flowers in the woods. Since then he had not looked up.

Suddenly it came to her – tenderly, hotly, fearfully yet bravely, that it was she who must meet Z. She looked at him again, covertly. And she felt that she understood. It was the lines in his face made it clearest. Years, and things blacker, less easily surmounted than years – oh yes, that too she faced fearlessly – were piled inbetween. She knew now that it was she – not he – who could push them aside.

It was all very unmaidenly, of course; but maidenly is a word love and life and desire may crowd from the page.

Perhaps she would not have thrown it after all – the little note she had written – had it not been that when she went over for more copy-paper, she stood for a minute looking out of the window. Even on Dearborn Street the seductiveness of spring was in the air. Spring, and all that spring meant, filled her.

Because, way beyond the voice of Dr Bunting she heard the songs of far-away birds, and because beneath the rumble of a printing press she could get the babble of a brook, because Z was near and life was strong, the woman vanquished the girl, and she threw this over to his desk:

'CHAFING-DISH, *n*. That out of which Miss Noah asks Mr Webster to eat his Sunday-night lunch tomorrow. All the other Miss Noahs are going to be away, and if Mr Webster does not come, Miss Noah will be all alone. Miss Noah does not like to be lonely.'

She ate no lunch that day; she only drank a cup of coffee and walked around.

He did not come back that afternoon. It passed from one to two, from two to three, and then very slowly from three to four, and still he had not come.

He too was walking about. He had walked down to the lake and was standing there looking out across it.

Why not? – he was saying to himself – fiercely, doggedly. Over and over again – Well, *why not*?

A hundred nights, alone in his room, he had gone over it. Had not life used him hard enough to give him a little now? – longing had pleaded. And now there was a new voice – a more prevailing voice – the voice of *her* happiness. His face softened to an almost maternal tenderness as he listened to that voice.

Too worn to fight any longer, he gave himself up to it, and sat there dreaming. They were dreams of joy rushing in after lonely years, dreams of stepping into the sunlight after long days in fog and cold, dreams of a woman before a fireplace – her arms about him, her cheer and her tenderness, her comradeship and her passion – all his to take! Ah, dreams which even thoughts must not touch – so wonderful and sacred they were.

A long time he sat there, dreaming dreams and seeing visions. The force that rules the race was telling him that the one crime was the denial of happiness – his happiness, her happiness; and when at last his fight seemed but a puerile fight against forces worlds mightier than he, he rose, and as one who sees a great light, started back towards Dearborn Street.

On the way he began to cough. The coughing was violent, and he stepped into a doorway to gain breath. And after he had gone in there he realised that it was the building of Chicago's greatest newspaper.

He had been city editor of that paper once. Facts, the things he knew about himself, talked to him then. There was no answer.

It left him weak and dizzy and crazy for a drink. He walked on slowly, unsteadily, his white face set. For he had vowed that if it took the last nerve in his body there should be no more of that until after they had finished with Z. He knew himself too well to vow more. He was not even sure of that.

He did not turn in where he wanted to go; but resistance took the last bit of force that was in him. He was trembling like a sick man when he stepped into the elevator.

She was just leaving. She was in the little cloakroom putting on her things. She was all alone in there.

He stepped in. He pushed the door shut, and stood there leaning against it, looking at her, saying nothing.

'Oh – you are ill?' she gasped, and laid a frightened hand upon him.

The touch crazed him. All resistance gone, he swept her into his arms; he held her fiercely, and between sobs kissed her again and again. He could not let her go. He frightened her. He hurt her. And he did not care – he did not know.

Then he held her off and looked at her. And as he looked into her eyes, passion melted to tenderness. It was she now – not he; love – not hunger. Holding her face in his two hands, looking at her as if getting something to take away, his white lips murmured words too inarticulate for her to hear. And then again he put his arms around her – all differently. Reverently, sobbingly, he kissed her hair. And then he was gone.

He did not come out that Sunday afternoon, but Harold dropped in instead, and talked of some athletic affairs over at the university. She wondered why she did not go crazy in listening to him, and yet she could answer intelligently. It was queer – what one *could* do.

They had come at last to Z. There would be no more work upon the dictionary after that day. And it was raining – raining as in Chicago alone it knows how to rain.

They wrote no notes to each other now. It had been different since that day. They made small effort to cover their raw souls with the mantle of commonplace words.

Both of them had tried to stay away that last day. But both were in their usual places.

The day wore on eventlessly. Those men with whom she had worked, the men of yesterday, who had been kind to her, came up at various times for little farewell chats. The man in the skull cap told her that she had done excellent work. She was surprised at the ease with which she could make decent reply, thinking again that it was queer – what one could do.

He was moving. She saw him lay some sheets of yellow paper on the desk in front. He had finished with his 'take'. There would not be another to give him. He would go now.

He came back to his desk. She could hear him putting away his things. And then for a long time there was no sound. She knew that he was just sitting there in his chair.

Then she heard him get up. She heard him push his chair up to the table, and then for a minute he stood there. She wanted to turn towards him; she wanted to say something – do something. But she had no power.

She saw him lay an envelope upon her desk. She heard him walking away. She knew, numbly, that his footsteps were not steady. She knew that he had stopped; she was sure that he was looking back. But still she had no power.

And then she heard him go.

Even then she went on with her work; she finished her 'take' and laid down her pencil. It was finished now – and he had gone. Finished? – *Gone*? She was tearing open the envelope of the letter.

This was what she read:

'Little dictionary sprite, sunshine vendor, and girl to be loved, if I were a free man I would say to you – Come, little one, and let us learn of love. Let us learn of it, not as one learns from dictionaries, but let us learn from the morning glow and the evening shades. But Miss Noah, maker of dictionaries and creeper into hearts, the bound must not call to the free. They might fittingly have used my name as one of the synonyms under that word Failure, but I trust not under Coward.

'And now, you funny little Miss Noah from the University of Chicago, don't I know that your heart is blazing forth the assurance that you don't *care* for any of those things – the world, people, common sense – that you want just love? They made a grand failure of you out at your university; they taught you philosophy and they taught you Greek, and they've left you just as much the woman as women were five thousand years ago. Oh, I know all about you – you little girl whose hair tried so hard to be red. Your soul touched mine as we sat there writing words – words – words, the very words in which men try to tell things, and can't – and I know all about what you would do. But you shall not do it. Dear little copy-maker, would a man standing out on the end of a slippery plank have any right to cry to someone on the shore – "Come out here on this plank with me." If he loved the someone on the shore, would he not say instead – "Don't get on this plank." Me get off the plank – come with you to the shore – you are saying? But you see, dear, you only know slippery planks as viewed from the shore – God grant you may never know them any other way!

'It was you, was it not, who wrote our definition of happiness? Yes, I remember the day you did it. You were so interested; your cheeks grew so very red, and you pulled and pulled at your wavy hair. You said it was such an important definition. And so it is, Miss Noah, quite the most important of all. And on the page of life, Miss Noah, may happiness be written large and unblurred for you. It is because I cannot help you write it that I turn away. I want at least to leave the page unspoiled.

'I carry a picture of you. I shall carry it always. You are sitting before a fireplace, and I think of that fireplace as symbolising the warmth and care and tenderness and the safety that will surround you. And sometimes as you sit there let a thought of me come for just a minute, Miss Noah – not long enough nor deep enough to bring you any pain. But only think – I brought him happiness after he believed all happiness had gone. He was so grateful for that light which came after he thought the darkness had settled down. It will light his way to the end.

'We've come to Z, and it's goodbye. There is one thing I can give you without hurting you – the hope, the prayer, that life may be very, very good to you.'

The sheets of paper fell from her hands. She sat staring out into Dearborn Street. She began to see. After all, he had not understood her. Perhaps men never understood women; certainly he had not understood her. What he did not know was that she was willing to *pay* for her happiness – *pay* – pay any price that might be exacted. And anyway – she had no choice. Strange that he could not see that! Strange that he could not see the irony and cruelty of bidding her goodbye and then telling her to be happy!

It simplified itself to such an extent that she grew very calm. It would be easy to find him, easy to make him see – for it was so very simple – and then. . . .

She turned in her copy. She said goodbye quietly, naturally, rode down in the lumbering old elevator and started out into the now drenching rain towards the elevated trains which would take her to the West Side; it was so fortunate that she had heard him telling one day where he lived.

When she reached the station she saw that more people were coming down the stairs than were going up. They were saying things about the trains, but she did not heed them. But at the top of the stairs a man in uniform said: 'Blockade, Miss. You'll have to take the surface cars.'

She was sorry, for it would delay her, and there was not a minute to lose. She was dismayed, upon reaching the surface cars, to find she could not get near them; the rain, the blockade on the 'L', had caused a great crowd to congregate there. She waited a long time, getting more and more wet, but it was impossible to get near the cars. She thought of a cab, but could see none, they too having all been pressed into service.

She determined, desperately, to start to walk. Soon she would surely get either a cab or a car. And so she started, staunchly, though she was wet through now, and trembling with cold and nervousness.

As she hurried through the driving rain she faced things fearlessly. Oh yes, she understood – everything. But if he were not well – should he not have her with him? If he had that thing to fight, did he not need her help? What did men think women were like? Did he think she was one to sit down and reason out what would be advantageous? Better a little while with him on a slippery plank than forever safe and desolate upon the shore!

She never questioned her going; were not life and love too great to be lost through that which could be so easily put right?

The buildings were reeling, the streets moving up and down – that awful rain, she thought, was making her dizzy. Laboriously she walked on – more slowly, less steadily, a pain in her side, that awful reeling in her head.

Carriages returning to the city were passing her, but she had not strength to call to them, and it seemed if she walked to the kerb she would fall. She was not thinking so clearly now. The thing which took all her force was the lifting of her feet and the putting them down in the right place. Her throat seemed to be closing up – and her side – and her head. . . .

Someone had her by the arm. Then someone was speaking her name; speaking it in surprise – consternation – alarm.

It was Harold.

It was all vague then. She knew that she was in a carriage, and that Harold was talking to her kindly. 'You're taking me there?' she murmured.

'Yes – yes, Edna, everything's all right,' he replied soothingly.

'Everything's all right,' she repeated, in a whisper, and leaned her head back against the cushions.

They stopped after a while, and Harold was standing at the open door of the cab with something steaming hot which he told her to drink. 'You need it,' he said decisively, and thinking it would help her to tell it, she drank it down.

The world was a little more defined after that and she saw things which puzzled her. 'Why, it looks like the city,' she whispered, her throat too sore now to speak aloud.

'Why sure,' he replied banteringly, 'don't you know we have to go through the city to get out to the South Side?'

'Oh, but you see,' she cried, holding her throat, 'but you see, it's the *other* way!'

'Not tonight,' he insisted; 'the place for you tonight is home. I'm taking you where you belong.'

She reached over wildly, trying to open the door, but he held her back; she began to cry, and he talked to her, gently but unbendingly. 'But you don't *understand*!' she whispered, passionately. 'I've *got* to go!'

'Not tonight,' he said again, and something in the way he said it made her finally huddle back in the corner of the carriage.

Block after block, mile after mile, they rode on in silence. She felt overpowered. And with submission she knew that it was Z. For the whole city was piled inbetween. Great buildings were inbetween, and thousands of men running to and fro on the streets; man, and all man had built up, were inbetween. And then Harold – Harold who had always seemed to count for so little, had come and taken her away.

Dully, wretchedly – knowing that her heart would ache far worse tomorrow than it did tonight – she wondered about things. Did things like rain and streetcars and wet feet and a sore throat determine life? Was it that way with other people, too? Did other people have barriers – whole cities full of them – piled in between? And then did the Harolds come and take them where they said they belonged? Were there not *some* people strong enough to go where they wanted to go?

THE BLACK CAP

Katherine Mansfield

(1917)

(A lady and her husband are seated at breakfast. He is quite calm, reading the newspaper and eating; but she is strangely excited, dressed for travelling and only pretending to eat.)

She: Oh, if you should want your flannel shirts, they are on the right-hand bottom shelf of the linen press.

He: (at a board meeting of the Meat Export Company). No.

She: You didn't hear what I said. I said if you should want your flannel shirts, they are on the right-hand bottom shelf of the linen press.

He: (positively). I quite agree!

She: It does seem rather extraordinary that on the very morning that I am going away you cannot leave the newspaper alone for five minutes.

He: (mildly). My dear woman, I don't want you to go. In fact, I have asked you not to go. I can't for the life of me see . . .

She: You know perfectly well that I am only going because I absolutely must. I've been putting it off and putting it off, and the dentist said last time . . .

He: Good! Good! Don't let's go over the ground again. We've thrashed it out pretty thoroughly, haven't we?

Servant: Cab's here, m'm.

She: Please put my luggage in.

Servant: Very good, m'm.

(She gives a tremendous sigh.)

He: You haven't got too much time if you want to catch that train.

She: I know. I'm going. *(In a changed tone.)* Darling, don't let us part like this. It makes me feel so wretched. Why is it that you always seem to take a positive delight in spoiling my enjoyment?

He: I don't think going to the dentist is so positively enjoyable.

She: Oh, you know that's not what I mean. You're only saying that to hurt me. You know you are begging the question.

He: (laughing). And you are losing your train. You'll be back on Thursday evening, won't you?

She: (in a low, desperate voice). Yes, on Thursday evening. Good-bye, then. *(Comes over to him, and takes his head in her hands.)* Is there anything really the matter? Do at least look at me. Don't you – care – at – all?

He: My darling girl! This is like an exit on the cinema.

She: (letting her hands fall). Very well. Goodbye. *(Gives a quick tragic glance round the dining room and goes.)*

(On the way to the station.)

She: How strange life is! I didn't think I should feel like this at all. All the glamour seems to have gone, somehow. Oh, I'd give anything for the cab to turn round and go back. The most curious thing is that I feel if he really had made me believe he loved me it would have been much easier to have left him. But that's absurd. How strong the hay smells. It's going to be a very hot day. I shall never see these fields again. Never! never! But in another way I am glad that it happened like this; it puts me so finally, absolutely in the right forever! He doesn't want a woman at all. A woman has no meaning for him. He's not the type of man to care deeply for anybody except himself. I've become the person who remembers to take the links out of his shirts before they go to the wash – that is all! And that's not enough for me. I'm young – I'm too proud. I'm not the type of woman to vegetate in the country and rave over 'our' own lettuces . . .

What you have been trying to do, ever since you married me is to make me submit, to turn me into your shadow, to rely on me so utterly that you'd only to glance up to find the right time printed on me somehow, as if I were a clock. You have never been curious about me; you never wanted to explore my soul. No; you wanted me to settle down to your peaceful existence. Oh! how your blindness has outraged me – how I hate you for it! I am glad – thankful – thankful to have left you! I'm not a green girl; I am not conceited, but I do know my powers. It's not for nothing that I've always longed for riches and passion and freedom, and felt that they were mine by right. *(She leans against the buttoned back of the cab and murmurs.)* 'You are a Queen. Let mine be the joy of giving you your kingdom.' *(She smiles at her little royal hands.)* I wish my heart didn't beat so hard. It really hurts me. It tires me so and excites me so. It's like someone in a dreadful hurry beating against a door . . . This cab is only crawling along; we shall never be at the station at this rate. Hurry! Hurry! My love, I am coming as quickly as ever I can. Yes, I am suffering just like you. It's dreadful, isn't it unbearable – this last half-hour without each other . . . Oh, God! the horse has begun to walk again. Why doesn't he beat the great strong brute of a thing . . . Our wonderful life! We shall travel all over the world together. The whole world shall be ours because of our love. Oh, be patient! I am coming as fast as I possibly can . . . Ah, now it's downhill; now we really are going faster. *(An old man attempts to cross the road.)* Get out of my way, you old fool! He deserves to be run over . . . Dearest – dearest; I am nearly there. Only be patient!

(At the station.)

Put it in a first-class smoker . . . There's plenty of time after all. A full ten minutes before the train goes. No wonder he's not here. I mustn't appear to be looking for him. But I must say I'm disappointed. I never dreamed of being the first to arrive.

I thought he would have been here and engaged a carriage and bought papers and flowers . . . How curious! I absolutely saw in my mind a paper of pink carnations . . . He knows how fond I am of carnations. But pink ones are not my favourites. I prefer dark red or pale yellow. He really will be late if he doesn't come now. The guard has begun to shut the doors. Whatever can have happened? Something dreadful. Perhaps at the last moment he has shot himself . . . I could not bear the thought of ruining your life . . . But you are not ruining my life. Ah, where are you? I shall have to get into the carriage . . . Who is this? That's not him! It can't be – yes, it is. What on earth has he got on his head? A black cap. But how awful! He's utterly changed. What can he be wearing a black cap for? I wouldn't have known him. How absurd he looks coming towards me, smiling, in that appalling cap!

He: My darling, I shall never forgive myself. But the most absurd, tragic-comic thing happened. *(They get into the carriage.)* I lost my hat. It simply disappeared. I had half the hotel looking for it. Not a sign! So finally, in despair, I had to borrow this from another man who was staying there. *(The train moves off.)* You're not angry? *(Tries to take her in his arms.)*

She: Don't! We're not even out of the station yet.

He: (ardently). Great God! What do I care if the whole world were to see us? *(Tries to take her in his arms.)* My wonder! My joy!

She: Please don't! I hate being kissed in trains.

He: (profoundly hurt). Oh, very well. You are angry. It's serious. You can't get over the fact that I was late. But if you only knew the agony I suffered . . .

She: How can you think I could be so small-minded? I am not angry at all.

He: Then why won't you let me kiss you?

She: (laughing hysterically). You look so different somehow – almost a stranger.

He: (jumps up and looks at himself in the glass anxiously, and fatuously, she decides). But it's all right, isn't it?

She: Oh, quite all right; perfectly all right. Oh, oh, oh! *(She begins to laugh and cry with rage.)*

(They arrive.)

She: (while he gets a cab). I must get over this. It's an obsession. It's incredible that anything should change a man so. I must tell him. Surely it's quite simple to say: Don't you think now that you are in the city you had better buy yourself a hat? But that will make him realise how frightful the cap has been. And the extraordinary thing is that he doesn't realise it himself. I mean if he has looked at himself in the glass, and doesn't think that cap too ridiculous, how different our points of view must be . . . How deeply different! I mean, if I had seen him in the street I would have said I could not possibly love a man who wore a cap like that. I couldn't even have got to know him. He isn't my style at all. *(She looks round.)* Everybody is smiling at it. Well, I don't wonder! The way it makes his ears stick out, and the way it makes him have no back to his head at all.

He: The cab is ready, my darling. *(They get in.)*

He: (tries to take her hand). The miracle that we two should be driving together, so simply, like this.

(She arranges her veil.)

He: (tries to take her hand, very ardent). I'll engage one room, my love.

She: Oh, no! Of course you must take two.

He: But don't you think it would be wiser not to create suspicion?

She: I must have my own room. *(To herself.)* You can hang your cap *behind your own door*! *(She begins to laugh hysterically.)*

He: Ah! thank God! My Queen is her happy self again!

(At the hotel.)

Manager: Yes, Sir, I quite understand. I think I've got the very thing for you, Sir. Kindly step this way. *(He takes them into a small sitting room, with a bedroom leading out of it.)* This would suit you nicely, wouldn't it? And if you liked, we could make you up a bed on the sofa.

He: Oh, admirable! Admirable!

(The Manager goes.)

She: (furious). But I told you I wanted a room to myself. What a trick to play upon me! I told you I did not want to share a room. How dare you treat me like this? *(She mimics.)* Admirable! Admirable! I shall never forgive you for that!

He: (overcome). Oh, God, what is happening! I don't understand – I'm in the dark. Why have you suddenly, on this day of days, ceased to love me? What have I done? Tell me!

She: (sinks on the sofa). I'm very tired. If you do love me, please leave me alone. I – I only want to be alone for a little.

He: (tenderly). Very well. I shall try to understand. I do begin to understand. I'll go out for half an hour, and then, my love, you may feel calmer. *(He looks round, distracted.)*

She: What is it?

He: My heart – you are sitting on my cap. *(She gives a positive scream and moves into the bedroom. He goes. She waits a moment, and then puts down her veil, and takes up her suitcase.)*

(In the taxi.)

She: Yes, Waterloo. *(She leans back.)* Ah, I've escaped – I've escaped! I shall just be in time to catch the afternoon train home. Oh, it's like a dream – I'll be home before supper. I'll tell him that the city was too hot or the dentist away. What does it matter? I've a right to my own home . . . It will be wonderful driving up from the station: the fields will smell so delicious. There is cold fowl for supper left over from yesterday, and orange jelly . . . I have been mad, but now I am sane again. Oh, my husband!

THE PAIN

Pauline Smith

(1923)

All their married, childless life of nearly fifty years Juriaan van Royen and his wife Deltje had lived in the Aangenaam valley in lands that he hired from Mijnheer van der Wenter of Vergelegen.

His lands lay an hour by foot from the Vergelegen homestead, on a little plateau on the mountainside facing the north and the sun. The soil was poor and thin, and of all the poor men working hired lands in the Aangenaam valley Juriaan was one of the poorest. He was a tall, thin, loosely built man, slow and quiet in his speech, and slow and quiet in his movements. His lanky dust-coloured hair, fading with age instead of turning grey, and worn long like a Tak-Haar Boer's from the Transvaal, gave him a wild and unkempt look that seemed but to accentuate his gentleness of heart. For his wife Deltje his tenderness had increased with age, and, lately, with her pain. The little old woman, plump and round, with skin as soft and smooth as a child's, and a quiet, never-failing cheerfulness of spirit in spite of her pain, was dearer to him now than she had been as his bride. As his bride she had come to him up in the mountains from the harsh service of Mevrouw du Toit of Leeuw Kraal with but the clothes she wore and her Bible tied up in a red-and-white handkerchief. Mevrouw's eyes had been weak, and to save her mistress's eyes Deltje as a young girl had been taught to read. Juriaan could neither read nor write, and when on their marriage night Deltje had opened her Bible and read to him, it had seemed to him that no music in all the world could be so beautiful as this. In old age her voice had become thin as a bird's, but her reading was still beautiful to him. Their years of poverty, which might have embittered them, their childlessness, which might have driven them apart, had but drawn them closer together and it was together that they now faced Deltje's pain. And to them both, because all their lives they had been healthy, Deltje's pain was like a thing apart: a mysterious and powerful third person, who, for incomprehensible reasons, clutched at Deltje's side and forced her to lie helpless for hours on the low wooden bedstead in the little bedroom.

The three-roomed mud-walled house in which the old couple lived stood close to a small stream behind a row of peach trees. Every year from these trees they took a thanksoffering of dried fruit to the Thanksgiving at Harmonie, and year by year they had beaten the stones of the peaches into the earthen floor of the living-room. Every morning Deltje sprinkled this floor with clear water from the stream and swept it with a stiff besom. The floors of the kitchen and bedroom she smeared regularly with a mixture of cow-dung and ashes called mist. The little house smelt always of mist, of strong black coffee, the beans of which were ground with peas to make it go further, and of griddle cakes baked in the ashes of the open fire in the kitchen.

The living room, with its three chairs strung with thongs of leather, its table scrubbed a bright yellow with the yellow-bush that grew on the mountainside, and its gaily painted wagon-box, was a small square room with a half-door opening on to the yard behind the peach trees. This was the only door the house possessed, for the doorways between the living room and the kitchen and the living room and the bedroom were empty. The partition wall, built like the outer walls of mud, did not go up to the reed-and-thatch roof, but ended, within reach, in a flat ledge on which pumpkins, twisted rolls of tobacco, little bags of seed, bars of homemade soap and water-candles, and various odds and ends were stored. From the rafters hung cobs of dried mealies, and just outside the door was the worn mealie-stamper, cut out of a tree trunk and shaped like an hourglass, in which the mealies were pounded into meal. There was one window, in the wall opposite the half-door. It had no glass, and was closed by an unpainted wooden shutter. Built into the wall between the living room and the bedroom were three small shelves, and here Deltje kept their few treasures: her Bible, two cups and saucers, thick and heavy, with roses like red cabbages around them, a little pink mug, with 'A Present for a Good Girl' in letters of gold on one side of the handle and a golden Crystal Palace on the other, a green-and-red crocheted wool mat, a black-bordered funeral card in memory of Mijnheer van der

Wenter's mother, an ostrich egg, and a small box lined with blue satin and covered with rows of little shells round an inch-square mirror. This was the pride of their simple hearts, and these, after fifty years of life together, were their treasures.

It was on the uppermost of the three shelves that for over a year now Deltje had kept the little bottles of 'Grandmother's Drops' which, from time to time, Juriaan had got for her from the Jew-woman's store at Harmonie, for the pain in her side. At first the drops had seemed definitely to relieve Deltje's pain, to baffle the mysterious third person who caused it, and even when the attacks became more frequent and more violent the faith of both Deltje and Juriaan had persisted because of the printed word on the wrapper. But in the month of January Juriaan's faith at last was shaken. In that month of long hot days there came a succession of attacks which exhausted all the remaining drops and left Deltje weak and helpless as an infant on the low wooden bed. And leaving her there Juriaan went down in haste to the Jew-woman's store at Harmonie.

When Juriaan reached the little white-washed store with the sign 'Winkel' printed crookedly with a blue-bag over its door, he found there Piet Deiselmann, the transport-rider between Platkops dorp and Princestown village. Piet Deiselmann, eager, impetuous, a Platkops man who was full of pride for Dutch Platkops and contempt for English Princestown, was speaking to the old Jew-woman and her grandson of the new hospital which lately had been opened in Platkops dorp, and of which Juriaan up in the mountains had never heard before. The hospital was the first to be built in the Little Karoo, and it was Dutch Platkops that had built it. In Princestown, said Piet Deiselmann contemptuously, men might still die by hundreds for want of a hospital, but in Platkops there was now no need to suffer pain. One went to the Platkops hospital so ill that one had to be carried there, and one left it leaping and praising the Lord.

All that Piet Deiselmann said of the hospital filled Juriaan, with Deltje's damp twisted face always before him, with a strange agitation of hope, wonder, and fear. For long he dared not speak. But at last, in a voice that quavered and broke, he asked:

'And must a man then be rich to go to the hospital in Platkops dorp?'

'Rich!' cried Piet Deiselmann. 'Rich? Let a man be so poor as he can be to live and at the hospital they will take him in.'

'Our Father!' said Juriaan in wonder. 'Our Father!' And it was as if, staring at the transport-rider, he already saw Deltje, her round, soft, childish face alight with joy, leaping and praising the Lord on the hospital stoep.

Juriaan went back to the mountains and found Deltje as he had left her on the feather bed. He poured out some drops for her, made some strong black coffee and brought it to her with a little black bread, and then sitting down on a low stool by her side spoke of the hospital in Platkops dorp. All that Piet Deiselmann had said he repeated, and in his slow quiet speech everything Piet Deiselmann had said seemed to gain a greater significance. And holding Deltje's hand in his he told her how he would put the feather bed in the ox cart, and his reed and canvas tent over the cart, and his love, his heart, the joy of his life, would lie there like a bird in its nest; and so carefully as if it were the very Ark of the Lord that he were driving he would take her in to the hospital in Platkops dorp and her pain would be cured. . . . He spoke as Piet Deiselmann had done of men leaping and praising the Lord, and so great was now their faith in everything that Piet Deiselmann had said that it was as if within their old and worn bodies their hearts were already leaping and praising Him.

Early the next morning the old man began his preparations for the journey. He went first up to the kraal on the mountainside where Jafta Nicodemus, the Vergelegen shepherd, kept his master's flocks, and it was settled that for some rolls of tobacco Jafta would take charge of his goats and his hens. His lands he must leave to God. He went back to the house, and stretching an old sailcloth across a bamboo frame fixed this tent to his ox cart. Under the cart he tied the big black kettle and the three-legged pot which were their only cooking utensils. He filled a small water-cask from the stream and tied that also below the cart. He brought out the painted wagon-box and fixed it in front of the cart for a seat. In the box was their small store of provisions: biltong, a small bag of coffee, a kid-skin full of dried rusks, meal for griddle cakes, and the salted ribs of a goat recently killed. Behind the cart he tied some bundles of forage, and below the forage dangled a folding stool. On the floor of the cart he spread the feather bed, pillows and blankets for Deltje's nest.

When all was ready, and the two plough-oxen were inspanned, Deltje came out to the cart. She wore her black calico Sacrament gown and sunbonnet, and on her stockingless feet were veldschoen which Juriaan himself had made for her. She carried in her hand a red cotton handkerchief, sprinkled with white moons, in which were her Bible, the Present for a Good Girl, and the little satin-lined, shell-covered box. Excitement, or the drops, had eased for the time her pain, and her round, smooth, innocent face was alight with her faith in the Almighty, her faith in the hospital, and her faith in Juriaan. And as Juriaan helped her into the cart he called her again by those tender, beautiful, and endearing names which were the natural expression of his love.

The journey to Platkops dorp by ox cart from Vergelegen took three nights and the greater part of three days. They travelled slowly because of Deltje's pain, and with frequent outspans to rest their oxen. From Vergelegen to Harmonie all was familiar to them, but not for many years had they been further afield than Harmonie, and even in the blazing January heat the straight grey road through the brown parched veld, with far-lying homesteads in bare parched lands, was full of interest to them. At night, when the oxen moved steadily forward with a rhythm that the darkness accented, or when they outspanned and the flames of Juriaan's fire danced to the stars above them, their hearts were filled with a quiet content. And before them, day and night, they saw not the grey stone building which Piet Deiselmann had described, but a golden wonder like the Crystal Palace on Deltje's mug. And to this golden wonder, this haven of refuge for the sick and suffering, they clung with unwavering faith through those desperate hours when Deltje, like some gentle dumb animal, lay damp and twisted in the sweat and agony of her pain.

It was towards midday on the fourth day of their long journey that they reached Platkops dorp, a long straggling village on the east bank of the Ghamka river. Its low, white-washed thatched houses stood back from the wide Hoeg Straat in gardens or green lands sloping down to the river. The street was lined with poplars, willows, and giant eucalyptus trees, and one looked up this green avenue to the Zwartkops Mountains or down it to the Teniquotas. North, south, east, and west the Platkops plain was bounded by mountain ranges, and the village lay in the heart of the plain. The hospital was the only building on the west bank of the river, and was one of the few houses built of stone. It had as yet no trees, no garden, and no green lands around it, but stood, grey and new, with even its yard unenclosed, in the open veld. It did not look in the least like the Crystal Palace on Deltje's mug, but faith, hope, and the tears which dimmed their eyes as they came within sight of it made that bare building, surrounded by a wide stoep, beautiful to the old couple. They crossed the river by the nearest drift and drove slowly across the veld towards it.

When Juriaan and Deltje reached the hospital steps the building was already closed and shuttered for the midday heat, and beyond the creaking of the ox cart, and the slow 'Our Father! Our Father!' breathed by the old man as he gazed around him, all was silence. The closed doors and shutters, the empty stoep, upon which they had expected to see men and women, cured of their pain, leaping and praising God, did not shake their faith, as the faith of others might have been shaken, in Piet Deiselmann's report. That burning mid-day silence was for them but the Peace of God, and with the unquestioning patience of poverty and old age they awaited in it whatever was to befall them.

It was the matron who, half an hour later, found the ox cart at the stoep steps. The matron was a kindly, capable, middle-aged woman who spoke both English and Dutch. Juriaan, holding his soft, wide-brimmed hat in his hand, answered her questions humbly. He was Juriaan van Royen, seventy-five years old, working lands on Mijnheer van der Wenter's farm of Vergelegen in the Aangenaam valley, and in the cart there, in a nest that he had made for her of the feather bed and pillows, was his wife Deltje, seventy years, come to be cured of the pain in her side. . . .

The matron turned from the old man, so wild and unkempt, so humble and so gentle, to the patient suffering little old woman seated with her bundle on the feather bed. With Juriaan's help she lifted Deltje out of the cart, and together the old couple followed her up the steps to her office. Here she left them, and in that quiet darkened room they sat on a couch together like children, hand-in-hand. They did not speak, but now and then the old man, drawing his wife towards him, would whisper that she was his dove, his pearl, his rose of the mountains, and the light of his eyes.

When the matron returned she brought with her a young pleasant-faced nurse. Nurse Robert, she explained, would take Deltje to the women's ward, and here, on his afternoon round, the doctor would examine her. Juriaan, she said, must await the doctor's report, and had better drive his cart round to the side of the hospital and outspan. Afterwards he might go back to his lands in the Aangenaam valley, or across the river to his friends in Platkops dorp. . . . It was now that for the first time the old couple realised that the hospital was to part them, and that Deltje's cure was not to be immediate. God knows what the little old woman thought as, clinging to the red-and-white handkerchief which held her Bible, her mug, and her shell-covered box, she was led meekly away by the nurse; but for Juriaan it was as if the end of the world had come. Stunned and shaken, groping his way like a man suddenly blinded in paths that are strange to him, he went out into the dazzling sunshine and outspanned.

It was not until after coffee-time – but the old man had had no heart for coffee-making – that Juriaan was sent for to the matron's office, where the doctor was waiting for him. The doctor was an Englishman, and that he had settled in Dutch Platkops when he might have settled in English Princestown was a fact never forgotten by Platkops and never forgiven by Princestown. With the old man standing humbly before him he explained now, in slow careful Dutch, the nature of Deltje's pain. It was a bad pain. Such a pain in a younger woman might perhaps be cured, but for an old woman there was no cure, only a treatment that for a time might ease it. If Juriaan would leave his wife for some weeks in the hospital all that could be done for her the doctor would do, and it might be that after some weeks she would be well enough to go back again to the Aangenaam valley. It was for Juriaan himself to say whether she should stay, and it was for Juriaan to say whether, in the meantime, he would go back to his lands on the mountainside or to his friends in Platkops dorp.

The old man thanked the doctor, and in the quiet measured speech which gave weight and dignity to all he said, answered that if it was in the hospital that the doctor could ease Deltje's pain it was in the hospital that she must stay. As for himself, he could not go back to the Aangenaam valley without his love, his life, his dear one. Nor could he go to his friends in Platkops dorp, for he had none there. He was a stranger to Platkops dorp. All his life had he lived on the mountainside in the Aangenaam valley, and fifty years had his little dove lived with him. If it was not the will of the Lord that she should be cured of her pain, let the doctor do what he could to ease it, and let him, of his goodness and mercy, give Juriaan leave to camp out in the veld by the hospital to be near her until he could take her home. . . .

The doctor turned to the matron and said briefly: 'Let him stay. Take him to her.'

Juriaan followed the matron out of the office down a long, bare passage, which ended in a long, bare, bright room. In this room were six narrow white beds. By the side of each bed was a well-scrubbed locker, and above each bed hung a plain white card. The floor was as white as were the lockers, and this bright, bare cleanliness was all that at first the old man could grasp. Presently he saw that in three of the beds were women, wearing little white frilled caps that made them look like babies. And slowly it dawned upon him that one of these women, one of these babies, was Deltje.

At the sight of Deltje's smooth, round, innocent face set off so oddly by the little frilled cap, Juriaan forgot the strangeness of that strange room, forgot the white-capped heads in the other beds, forgot the matron standing by his side. He saw only his love, his joy, his treasure. And kneeling down by her side he drew her two brown hands into his and held them close against his breast.

That night, for the first time since their marriage, Juriaan and Deltje lay apart. For the old man there was neither rest nor sleep. For long he watched the lights in Platkops dorp twinkling across the river, and for long after those lights died out he watched the stars above him. He lay now on the feather bed in the cart, and now on the hard ground beneath it. He wandered like a ghost round the silent hospital buildings and came back to the ox cart with a pain that brought tears to his eyes, though he could trace it to no definite part of his body whatever. He did not now cry 'Our Father! Our Father!' for help. The silence of the night, the silence of the grey stone building which held his little dove, his pearl, was still for him the silence of the Peace of God. But it was of a God withdrawn as if forever from his reach.

For Deltje, too, the night was endless. For the first time in her life she lay, not in her shift and petticoats on a feather bed, but in a cotton nightgown on a narrow mattress. The unaccustomed freedom of her limbs made that narrow bed wide and empty as a desert to her. And when she slept, in short broken snatches between attacks of pain, it was to dream that Juriaan lay dead by her side and that she pressed against his cold body for comfort and warmth in vain. When morning came it was not the pain in Deltje's side that made life a mystery to the old couple. It was the pain in both their hearts.

Through the long, hot days, and the hot, still, moonlit nights that followed, the loneliness of the old people, and for Juriaan the sense of a God withdrawn, steadily increased. The ways of the hospital, the order and routine necessary for the running of it, remained to the end incomprehensible to them both. For fifty years on their mountainside in the Aangenaam valley life had been for them as simple as were their daily needs, as humble as were their hearts. In this new and bewildering world the kindness of the English doctor, of the matron, and of the nurse reached them only as the kindness of human beings reaches the suffering of dumb animals. On neither side was there, nor could there be, complete understanding. The doctor and the matron might know all that was to be known about the pain in Deltje's side. About the pain in her heart and in Juriaan's they knew nothing. And from the inquisitiveness of the other patients in the ward the little old woman shrank with a gentle timidity which increased her isolation.

Alone among strangers in that bright, bare room Deltje would lie, quiet and uncomplaining, thinking of her house on the mountainside: of the warmth and comfort of the feather bed in the little bedroom that smelled so pleasantly of mist: of the wooden shutter, held by a leather thong, which creaked with the lightest of mountain breezes: of the peach-stone floor, with patches of sunlight crossing it from the open half-door: of the peach trees by the little stream that never once in fifty years had failed them: of fruit-drying for the Thanksgiving: of the Thanksgiving service in front of the church door at Harmonie, when Juriaan, bareheaded among the men, would smile across to her among the women: of the journey home again and the first glimpse that came to one down in the valley road of the little brown-walled house perched high up on the mountainside by the peach trees and the stream. . . .

With his own hands had Juriaan built that house for her. For fifty years had the little stream quenched their thirst, and now they drank of a strange, lifeless water stored in tanks. For fifty years had they slept side by side in the little room with the friendly creaking shutter, and now they lay apart. . . . What was it that had brought them here? The pain in her side. . . . But she had now no pain in her side. All her pain was now in her heart. Every day she would insist to the nurse that she had now no pain in her side. And the nurse would laugh, jerk her head a little to one side, and say: 'Am I then a child? Wait a little, Tanta! Wait a little! It is for me to say when you have no pain in your side!' Of the pain in her heart she spoke only to Juriaan, when, in the evenings, he sat with her for half an hour. . . .

The old man had made his camp on that side of the hospital in which the women's ward lay, and from her bed Deltje could see the smoke of his fire as it rose into the still, hot, clear air. He seldom left the camp except to wander disconsolate round the hospital buildings, or out into the veld to attend to his oxen. Twice a day he sat for a little with Deltje in the ward, and in her thin, clear voice she would read to him from her Bible. But nothing that she read in that bright, bare room, smelling so strangely of disinfectants, brought comfort to his soul. His God was still withdrawn. Night and day the pain in his heart gave him no peace. He lived like a man in a trance. Once he was sent across the river to Platkops dorp. He saw there, in the windows of the shops in the Hoeg Straat, such things as he never before had seen and was never to see again, but they made no impression on his mind whatever. He passed down the Hoeg Straat as if in a dream of unbearable sadness and never revisited it.

It was the young, pleasant-faced Nurse Robert who had sent Juriaan in to Platkops dorp. To her there still remained the bright, hard self-confidence of youth, and in Juriaan and Deltje she saw only two aged innocents whose affairs it was her duty, and certainly her pleasure, to control. Her management of them, she was convinced, was for their good, and in all she did for them there was a certain brusque kindliness. It was she who answered for Deltje when the doctor made his daily round, and though even to the doctor Deltje would timidly protest that she had now no pain in her side, her protests were drowned in the brisk commonsense of the nurse. It was Nurse Robert, too, who timed Juriaan's visit to his wife, and who, on occasions, shooed him out of the ward like a hen. And, humble and gentle as they were, the aged innocents were unaccustomed to any control beyond that love of God and of each other which up on the mountainside had ruled their simple lives. This brisk, bright, personal interference bewildered them as nothing else in the hospital did. They came to resent it. They came to fear the pleasant-faced nurse as they had never before feared any other human being. She stood between them and the doctor: between them and the matron: and, by her refusal to allow that Deltje's pain was cured and her return to the Aangenaam valley possible, between them and everything that made life dear. With her brisk, bright contempt for the Aangenaam valley, and her praise for everything that Platkops, by contrast, produced, even to its rainwater, she drove them into a bewildered silence, and at last to flight.

It was the rainwater that, for the old couple, brought the pain in their hearts to its quiet and unnoticed crisis. In Platkops dorp the water in the furrows and rivers was so brackish that in marshy lands the ground had always a thin white coating of salt, and for drinking purposes rainwater was stored in iron tanks. For this water Deltje had what Nurse Robert considered an unreasonable distaste. It was in fact the gentle uncomplaining little old woman's one whimsy, and as the days passed and, though neither she nor Juriaan realised it, as her weakness increased, her mind dwelt more and more on the brown bubbling mountain stream which for fifty years had quenched her thirst. There came a day when in her weakness her talk wandered brokenly from the stream by the peach trees to the well of Bethlehem, and from David's cry for the water of that well, to the River of Water of Life. . . . Juriaan sitting helpless by her side felt that his heart must break with its sorrow, that his body must die of the dull heavy pain that possessed it. . . . And slowly, through his suffering, his mind came to its deliberate resolve.

When Nurse Robert ordered Juriaan out of the ward that evening the old man left by the French door close to Deltje's bed. In those hot January nights this door was left open, and only the outer shutters were closed. The catch of these, Juriaan knew, could be raised from the outside with a knife. He knew also that Deltje's clothes had been folded away into the locker that stood by her bed. There was now only one other patient in the ward, an old, old woman dozing her life away at the far end of the room. And because there were at present no serious cases in the hospital no one was on duty at night. On all these things his mind worked slowly, but clearly, as he went out into the veld to look for his oxen. He found them, drove them back to the cart, fed them, and tied them to it. He lit a fire and made himself some strong, black, bitter coffee. He ate nothing. His stock of provisions, in spite of his daily meal from the hospital kitchen, was now so low for what he had in hand that he dared not lessen it. Night had now fallen, and after arranging the feather bed and pillows into a little nest, the old man lay down on the hard ground beneath the cart. Above him the sky was sprinkled with stars and the Milky Way made a broad white path across the heavens. But Juriaan did not look at the stars, and if God walked in His starry heavens His servant Juriaan did not know it. His God was still withdrawn. Sorrow was all his company. . . .

When the last of the lights had twinkled into darkness across the river the old man took off his veldschoen and crept cautiously round the hospital buildings. Here, too, all was silence and darkness. He returned to the cart and inspanned the oxen, placing stones before the wheels. Then he went back to the hospital, mounted the stoep, raised the hasp of the shutters with his knife, and slipped into the silent ward, where Deltje on her narrow bed, that wide and empty desert, lay quietly awake. The old man went up to her and said, without haste, without fear, but with an infinite tenderness:

'Look now, my little one! Look now, my dove. Have I not made again a nest in the cart for you? And are not our oxen once more inspanned? Come now, in my arms will I carry you out to the cart, and back to the Aangenaam valley we will go.'

He stooped down, opened the locker, and drew out her clothes. With a strange, gentle deliberation he helped her into her petticoats, and tied up her Bible, her mug, and her shell-covered box. The bottle of medicine left standing on the locker he slipped into his pocket. Then he gathered the little old woman up into his arms and carried her out into the moonlit night.

In her little nest in the feather bed Deltje lay content. She had ceased now to tremble, and not for one moment did she question Juriaan's right to act as he was doing. Already her heart was filled with that sense of security which his mere presence brought her. Already the hospital was but a dream that only for a moment had parted them. The pain in her heart had gone. Of the pain in her side she would not think. Had she not learned in the hospital how to hide it? Up in the mountains sitting by the stream and drinking of its clear brown water she would have no pain. . . . Lying through the night by Juriaan's side she would have no pain. . . . She lay back among the pillows, a gentle, dying woman, her heart overflowing with its quiet content.

Seated on the wagon-box before her Juriaan drove steadily across the veld, through the drift, and out on to the Platkops-Princestown road. Slowly his numbed heart regained its warmth. Slowly he came to feel that his God was no longer withdrawn. Here, in the ox cart with his little love, was his God. Had He not eased her pain? If she was weak had He not given His servant Juriaan arms that were strong to carry her? Against his breast like a little child he would carry her, and so should she rest. . . .

They reached the top of the Groot Kop, the highest of the low, flat-topped hills that surrounded Platkops dorp, and here the old man wheeled round the cart and halted to rest his oxen. Below them, in the clear pale moonlight, lay the quiet village, but it was across the river that they looked, at the grey stone building standing there alone. A moment only they halted, then turned, and went on.

HOLIDAY GROUP

E M Delafield

(1926)

The Reverend Herbert Cliff-Hay's legacy had been paid at last. It seemed almost incredible, they had waited for it so long, talked about it so much, and alas! borrowed money upon it twice already. It reached them, indeed, in a terribly diminished form, what with death duties, and mysterious stamps, and fees of which they had had no previous cognisance.

The Reverend Herbert paid back all the borrowed money, and paid the premium on little Martin's Educational Annuity Policy a whole month before it was actually due, and took out a brand new Educational Annuity Policy for little Theodore, who had reached the age of nineteen months without his parents' having been able to afford this so necessary outlay on his behalf.

Their second child, Constance, being a girl, Herbert had not thought it necessary to do more than open a Post Office Savings Account for her. Constance, as a matter of fact, would have been his favourite child, if he had considered it right to have a favourite child – which he didn't – but with boys, one had to think about education. The legacy paid their debts, enabled him to put a tiny nest egg into the bank, and caused Herbert to make an announcement to his wife.

'We are going to have a holiday,' he said. 'A real holiday, Julia.'

Julia looked startled.

'A second honeymoon!' he cried.

'Except for the children . . .' hinted Julia, rather tactlessly, and almost indelicately.

'Naturally,' said the Reverend Herbert, frowning. He told her his plan . . .

'What about Ethel?'

Ethel was their general servant. It was very difficult for Mrs Cliff-Hay to find a servant, and still more difficult for her to keep one. Ethel had been with them six months, and Julia's great preoccupation in life, after the welfare of Herbert and the children, was how to make certain that Ethel would never leave.

'Ethel will look after the house, of course.'

'Dear, she won't sleep here alone, I'm perfectly certain. You know what girls are.'

'Well, well, we can settle about Ethel later, surely,' said the Reverend Herbert rather peevishly. 'Here am I, full of a surprise plan which I hope will be a joy and a pleasure to you, and all you can talk about is the wretched Ethel!'

It did indeed seem ungrateful looked at in that way.

'I didn't really mean it like that,' said Julia – although she had really meant it exactly like that. 'Of course it's a glorious idea, Herbert, and so kind of you to think of it all . . .'

When twelve o'clock on the 15th of July came, the packing was done, the suitcase and portmanteau belonging to Herbert, and a small tin trunk containing the effects of Julia and the three children, were locked and labelled, the basket, with sandwiches and bananas in it, stood ready. The village Ford that was to take them to the station was due in twenty minutes – and Herbert, Julia and their two elder children waited anxiously for the infant Theodore to wake from his morning sleep, so that the pram could be put into its sacking and get its label tied to the handle.

'You know how it'll upset him if we do wake him. I'd wake him in a minute, if it didn't mean that he'll be so cross all the way down,' said Julia for about the seventh time.

'That's all very well, dear, but I can't tie the covering on to the pram all in a minute, and we do not want to miss the train.'

'Miss the train!' echoed Martin, aged five, in great dismay.

'Shall I have a spade, Daddy?' said little Constance.

'If you're good, dear.'

'I can't think why he's sleeping so late this morning – it's always the way when one doesn't want them to –'

Julia made a hasty trip to the front door, outside which stood the pram. Theodore, inside it, still slept peacefully.

'Daddy, shall I have a spade?' Constance said, earnestly.

'Yes, darling.'

'A real spade, Daddy?'

'Yes, yes, certainly, when we get there. I say, Julia, you must really wake the child. This is nonsense.'

'I'd wake him in a minute, if it didn't mean that he'll be so cross all the way down. I can't think why he's sleeping like this – he never does as a rule, but it's always the way –'

Ethel appeared in the hall.

'The car is just coming up the lane, 'm. Didn't we ought to wake Baby?'

'He'll be so cross – there! Isn't he moving?'

'Mummie,' said Constance in a voice of passionate and uncontrollable anxiety, 'can't I have a spade?'

'Certainly, my pet, you shall have a spade. I promise you. Well, if that's the car, Ethel . . .'

Ethel darted towards the pram.

Theodore was awakened, and cried pitifully, and Julia hurried him into the house, and changed all the clothes he had on for other, similar clothes, that were clean instead of dirty, and Herbert tied up the pram and helped the driver to put the luggage on the car.

'Martin dear, run and tell Mother that we shall miss the train,' said Herbert, who had all his life suffered from train-fever.

Martin rushed in, shrieking: 'We shall miss the train, we shall miss the train!' And Julia said, 'Oh no, darling,' soothingly, and finished off Baby as quickly as she could, and ran out with him to the car.

'Can I sit in front?' said Martin.

'No, me,' said Constance.

'Daddy will sit in front.'

'With me on his lap – ?'

'No, me!'

'It's Martin's turn,' said Julia, who had to remember these

things. 'Constance darling, come and sit with Mother and Theodore in the back.'

'Tell me a story, Mother!' cried Constance.

Julia immediately said, 'Once upon a time there was a little pig who lived in a wood and – wave goodbye to Ethel, darling – Baby wave his little hand – ta-ta, Ethel! Are you all right Herbert?'

'Quite, thank you, dear. Have you any room for your feet?'

'Yes, thank you . . . lived in a wood and went out every day to look for acorns . . .'

The story lasted until they reached the station, when Julia said: 'Get out carefully, my pet, and wait for Mother.'

'Am I going to have a spade for the sands?'

'Yes, you shall all have spades.'

On these lines, the journey proceeded. Herbert was very kind, and took his turn in amusing the fractious Theodore, and Julia told stories, and reassured Constance about her spade, and from time to time smiled her pleasure at the holiday having really begun, and received Herbert's equally pleased and sympathetic smile in return. And it was a fine day, even if not a very warm one.

Everything was ready for them at 'Eventide', down to the six plain buns upon the tea table; and the moment tea was finished, they went out.

'To the shops, please, dear,' Julia said. 'I've got to order the things for our meals tomorrow. It's Sunday, you know, and she's got nothing in for us, except just the milk and the bread.'

'And shall we get my spade now, Mother?' said Constance in a trustful, uncomplaining voice.

'Yes, of course. Poor little thing, you have been patient!' cried Julia, really believing this, owing to the fabulous number of times that she had heard her daughter's request.

'Will you let me have some money, Herbert?'

'I'll come with you,' said the Reverend Herbert, and he took Martin's hand.

'Is the pram undone, darling? Because of Baby. It's too early to put him to bed, and besides, I couldn't leave him alone, in a strange room, anyway – but we ought to hurry, because the shops shut at six.'

They unwrapped the pram, and set out. Julia had a list, and they went – as fast as the pram, the narrow streets, the people, their unfamiliarity with the locality, and the short legs of Martin and Constance – would permit from the butcher to the grocer, and the grocer to the greengrocer, and the greengrocer to the baker. Everything seemed to be a little more expensive than the same things would have been at home, but one expected that, on a holiday.

When the shopping was done – and it included spades, buckets and sandshoes for all the children – it was time for Julia to go back and put Theodore to bed.

Herbert took the other two down to the sands. He was so good about the children, Julia reflected thankfully. Even at home, where he was busy, he often helped her with them on Ethel's afternoon out. Theodore was good, and went to sleep quickly, and Julia had done nearly all the unpacking before Herbert and the elder children came back and she had to put Martin and Constance to bed.

At half-past seven Reverend and Mrs Cliff-Hay had supper.

Mrs Parker had made it perfectly clear that when she said 'No cooking' in the evenings, she included things like potatoes, or even cocoa. But Julia had brought a spirit lamp, and boiled water herself, which made them independent.

After supper Herbert wanted to go for a walk, and Julia, who didn't like leaving the children, and was very tired besides, reluctantly went with him. She was but an abstracted companion, and Herbert, disappointed, was quite ready to come in again by nine o'clock. By ten, Julia, who could scarcely keep her eyes open, having seen that Martin and Constance and Theodore were all sleeping, went to bed herself.

'You won't be quite so tired, I hope, at nights, after a few days' holiday,' said the Reverend Herbert, when he in his turn got into the double bed.

He tried to make his voice sound only kind, and not resentful, but the effort was wasted upon Julia, who was sleeping like the dead.

The days sped by, only too quickly.

The order of them was always the same.

Between six and half-past six, Theodore woke, and was taken into his parents' bed so that he might not disturb the other two children, who seldom opened their eyes till seven o'clock. At half-past seven Mrs Parker brought the early-morning tea – without bread and butter – and Julia got up and washed and dressed and brushed the three children.

At half-past eight they had breakfast.

Then the sands – Julia doing the necessary shopping

on the way. There was always something to be ordered, or bought, for the children.

The weather wasn't too bad, for an English July. Julia thought it rather chilly, but then she had to adjust her pace to that of the baby, who could only toddle about, or sit on the sands scooping holes with his fingers.

While Theodore had his sleep in the pram, the others bathed.

Julia, years ago, had liked swimming, and Herbert was 'very good at it'. It brought home to her the fact that she was no longer very young, when she found herself secretly rather dreading the daily treat of the bathe. Perhaps it was the difference between being able to swim with Herbert, and having to remain close to the edge of the water, encouraging Martin, who was inclined to be nervous, and calling out, 'Yes, I see, darling,' to Constance, who was under the impression that she was swimming if she stuck her fat arms straight out in front of her, and kicked the water with her feet.

Herbert, as usual, was goodness itself.

He tried, although not successfully, to teach the two elder children to swim, and he squeezed out their wet bathing-dresses while Julia hurriedly dried and dressed them in the bathing-machine, and then he generally struck out to sea again, so as to give her time to dress herself before he sought the bathing machine. Still feeling damp and mottled, Julia would hasten out into the rather fitful sunshine, and distribute buns to the children, and try to warm her slightly discoloured hands by rubbing them in the sand. At least she kept her hair dry, for it was no longer the sort of hair that one rather enjoyed wetting, for the sake of letting it dry in the open air afterwards . . .

Her thoughts went back to other holiday times, which, strangely enough, seemed not at all remote, when she hadn't been 'Mother', but only Julia, and Mamma had been 'Mother' – the omniscient, all-powerful and ever-present universal provider.

Was it possible that Mamma, who had been dead ten years, had then felt exactly as Julia felt now?

She could certainly remember a reluctance, at the time incomprehensible, on the part of Mamma to join in delightful hill-climbing expeditions, or early-morning swims, at Weymouth.

Every year they had gone to Weymouth, Papa and Mamma and Julia.

One hadn't realised, in those days, that one was lucky to be taken to a nice hotel, where nobody bothered about 'extras', and there was a real meal at the end of the day as a matter of course – not just a slice of cold ham, and bread and cheese, and cocoa made over a spirit lamp.

('Oh, what a pig I am, to think about the food like that!' thought Julia. 'Though really it's on Herbert's account – except for the cocoa, which is such a comfort when one's cold or tired . . .')

Had Papa and Mamma really been well off? Julia, who had inherited their small savings, knew that they hadn't, although, of course, the value of money had altered altogether since the War. It had just been that, in the past, she hadn't had the responsibility of any of it – hadn't known or cared how the holiday was paid for, how the plans were made, how the meals were ordered, or anything else.

She had gone on being blissfully irresponsible until she was quite grown up. She could remember the last Weymouth holiday before Papa's death, when she had just left school, and she had wanted to go every night to the concert on the pier, with the schoolfriend who was staying with her. Papa had taken them, and Mamma, to their incredulous astonishment, evening after evening, had declared that she preferred to go to bed.

'But she was much older then, than I am now,' reflected Julia.

'Mother, look at me!' screamed Constance.

'I see, darling. Wonderful!'

'But did I turn head-over-heels?'

'Well – very nearly. Next time it'll be quite.'

'Mother, may I have the last bun?'

'No, Martin dear. It's really too near dinner time.'

'Then will you help me to build a castle exactly like the one we made yesterday?'

Julia got up, feeling stiff.

'Did I nearly turn head-over-heels?'

'Very nearly.'

Herbert emerged from the bathing-machine.

'Daddy, I turned head-over-heels.'

'Nearly,' Julia inserted automatically.

'I nearly turned head-over-heels.'

'Did you, dear? Well, Julia, did you enjoy the water? You look cold, my dear. If you didn't stay in the shallow water so much, but went right out of your depth at once, you wouldn't feel cold.'

'The walk up the hill will warm me.'

The steep ascent to York Terrace was not much liked by Martin and Constance with their short legs, and Julia always told them a story while they climbed.

Herbert pushed the pram.

After dinner, the two elder children were sent to rest for an hour on their beds, and Julia amused the baby downstairs, and Herbert read the paper.

Then they all went on the sands again, or once or twice for an excursion by charabanc, but the children were too young to enjoy these, and rendered the whole family unpopular with their fellow-passengers, except, indeed, with those who had with them children of the same age.

But Julia, unreasonably, didn't like being told that 'the little ones were all alike', and never let this opening lead to anything further.

Tea – the day fell naturally into the categorical division of time that separated one meal from another – was generally taken at their lodgings. The café in the High Street, where there was a small string band, was amusing, but it cost money, and little Theodore was really too young for that sort of place, and Constance, who was easily made bilious, was sure to eat something that would disagree with her later.

Very soon after tea Theodore was put to bed, and the other two children played in the sitting room, since it would be too much for them to walk down to the sea and back once more.

Julia came downstairs, read about *Little Black Sambo* or

The Tale of Peter Rabbit, and then took Constance and Martin upstairs. When she came down again it was usually nearly seven o'clock, and there was only time to do the mending that always seemed to be required on one garment or another.

At half-past seven, supper – that cold and skimpy meal that was disposed of in rather less than twenty minutes.

'How the time flies, doesn't it? I can't believe we've been here so long already. What about a little walk this evening?'

'Yes – only I don't much like leaving the children – if Baby did happen to wake – '

'Surely, with two women in the house –'

'Dear, I can't possibly ask Mrs Parker to go to him, and it wouldn't be any good if she did, either –'

'I suppose not. Well. You're not tired, are you, Julia?'

'Did I yawn? It must be the air. It's much stronger than the air at home.'

'It'll do us all good. The children look quite different.'

'Yes, don't they?' she said eagerly, and then immediately yawned again.

'Julia!' exclaimed the Reverend Herbert. The truth was, as they both knew too well, that Julia was intolerably sleepy. She was often sleepy at home, too, since she had never been without a baby in her room after the first year of her marriage, and was always awakened early in the morning – but at home she sat at her desk in the evenings, or sometimes played the piano, and kept herself awake that way.

At home, also, Herbert was busy, and took it for granted that she should go to bed before he did, but on a holiday – a second honeymoon – things should have been different.

He was kind, as ever – but he evidently didn't understand it.

Julia tried going to bed very early indeed, and getting some sleep before Herbert came up, on the understanding that he should wake her, when she would then be fresh and lively and ready for conversation.

But she wasn't fresh or lively, and indeed it proved to be almost impossible to wake her without the employment of real, physical violence.

'And yet,' said the Reverend Herbert, rather reproachfully, 'if one of the children so much as turns over in the night, you're awake directly.'

Julia wondered, but did not like to ask, if that was perhaps the reason she was so sleepy now. She said feebly that she thought there was an instinct which woke mothers on behalf of their children. 'When we get home,' she said hopefully, 'and I know that Martin and Constance are in their own nursery with Ethel next door, I shan't wake so early in the mornings, and then I shan't be so tired at night. Besides, it's this wonderful sea air. It's – doing – wonders.'

Julia's eyes grew fixed and watery, the muscles of her jaw became strangely set, and she tightly compressed her lips, in the suppression of an enormous yawn. 'Go to bed, my dear,' said her husband forbearingly. And she looked so miserable that he added, entirely to try and comfort her for her inadequacy, 'It's the sea air.'

Right up to the very last day of their fortnight at 'Eventide' the sea air continued to demonstrate its effects upon Julia.

The final evening was marred by the usual discrepancy

between the visitors' attitude towards their bill, and that of the landlady.

'Of course, I knew she'd stick it on at the end, as they always do,' said Julia, 'but really! When it comes to cruet, sixpence – and neither of us touches mustard or pepper, and I'm sure the poor children haven't eaten six-pennyworth of salt, the whole time they've been here.'

'Absurd! But still, if that's the only extra –'

'The only extra!' cried Julia. 'Why, the whole thing is extras. And she's put down that hideous glass vase that Baby smashed in our room as valued at three-and-eightpence.'

'Shall I have her in?' said the Reverend Herbert wearily. 'It's no use letting that sort of person think that one doesn't know one's being robbed.'

'No, of course it isn't.'

They both of them dreaded the interview with Mrs Parker, and knew that they had no possible chance of getting the better of her, but they felt, confusedly and miserably, that in some mysterious way they owed it to their caste to show Mrs Parker that her extortions were resented by them.

Julia, in a deprecating, apologetic voice, called Mrs Parker.

An interview on lines exceedingly familiar to Mrs Parker ensued.

At the end of thirty-seven minutes, the sum at the foot of Mrs Parker's bill, reduced by half-a-crown, had been paid by the Reverend Herbert, and the bill duly receipted by the landlady.

'Thank you, sir,' said Mrs Parker, her voice suddenly pitched in a more natural key.

‘I’m sure I hope you’ve all enjoyed your stay?’

‘Very much indeed, thank you. It’s done us all so much good.’

‘A thorough rest,’ said Herbert, not without a glance at Julia.

‘Perhaps we shall come again another year.’

‘I hope so, sir, I’m sure. Good night, sir, good night, ’m.’

‘Good night, Mrs Parker,’ they replied together with amiable smiles.

The door shut behind Mrs Parker.

‘I suppose they’re all alike,’ said Julia tolerantly. ‘After all, they’ve their living to get.’

‘It must be a dog’s life. And extortionate though she’s been, she’s let us down pretty lightly over the damage the children did. I saw that ink stain on the counterpane myself.’

‘And naughty little Constance’s hole in the wall, over the bed –’

‘It isn’t everywhere where they’ll take children at all.’

‘No, that’s true. One might do a great deal worse than come here another year. I mean, supposing we’re able to afford another holiday one year.’

‘Now that we’ve got this legacy, Julia dearest, and that our debts are all paid, I want to afford a holiday every year,’ said the Reverend Herbert, adding, with unwonted effusiveness, for he was a reserved man, ‘You and I, and little Martin and Constance and the baby – and perhaps other little ones, if we should be blessed with them. To get right away from home cares and worries and responsibilities, and have a thorough rest and change. I value it on your account even more than on my own.’

Julia laid her thin hand upon his plump one, and her eyes – her tired eyes – filled with the easy tears of utter contentment. She thought, as she had often thought before, that she was a very fortunate woman. Her heart swelled with gratitude at the thought of her kind husband, her splendid children, and the wonderful holiday that they had all had together.

THE MUSIC BOX

Malachi Whitaker

(1929)

A woman and a little boy were walking down the steep, cobbled street of a village. If they kept on walking for three miles they would come to a town, where there was a house which they wanted to find. They had seen the address in the advertisement column of the evening paper.

The woman was young. She was short, only about five feet in height, and she had small feet, of which she was very proud. The little boy had large, hazel eyes, both timid and thoughtful. He held his mother's hand. The two of them had the same expression of joyous solemnity; they were going to buy something.

The husband of the woman was called Theakstone Morphett. He was older than his wife, and worked in a stone quarry as a trimmer. He had sandy hair, and, as he shaved only once a week, on Saturdays, a growth of whisker and beard of the same glinting colour. His face was brick-red from exposure. He was a big-built man, without very much flesh, and he had a harsh, growling voice which frightened his son.

His wife had never been able to call him by his Christian name, Theakstone. It seemed to her silly, so she called him 'the father'. In the early days of her marriage she had referred to him as 'he', or, when driven into a corner, as 'the master', but she did not like to say this often, as it was too true. She seemed thankful when her child was born, as she could at last call her husband something definite.

As the little boy, whom she christened Henry, became able to talk, he, too, referred to this man as 't'father'. The family lived in the end house of the row, where the rough road wound up to the quarries and beyond that to the moors; and when the little boy, who was playing at some mysterious game of his, alone, saw the big man coming into sight, slowly swinging his yellow corduroy trousers with their funny, belted legs, he would run up the steps crying, 'Mother, 'ere's t'father!'

Henry could not quite make up his mind about t'father'. The house was certainly better and quieter without this man, who sprawled in the high-backed wooden chair that had the goatskin tied over the top of it, and looked discontentedly at his small son; who often let it be known that he would have preferred a big, fat, rollicking, sandy baby to this quiet creature with questioning eyes.

But there was no need to trouble much, there were too many interesting things in the world. Every Monday was washday. Even when he was a tiny baby Henry's mother would take him down into the cellar kitchen, underneath the living kitchen, where there was a brick-built copper for boiling the clothes in. She would light the fire with yellow-burning twigs, then a very little coal, and some coke, and soon there would be plenty of hot, soapy water. As soon as he was old enough she would give him a little water in a pail, and let him pretend to wash something – one of the red, spotted handkerchiefs which 't'father' took his dinner in, or even his own blue and red striped shirt. And he would kneel on the stone-flagged floor, rubbing away, sometimes looking out through the small window with the flat grating above it. When he got tired of that he would watch his mother bending over the great wooden tub, as she lifted out garments and rinsed them, and threw them with more or less accurate aim into the open mouth of the copper.

He could not bear to be far away from his mother; she was the only real part of his world. There were other children of the same age living near, but he did not feel the want of a playmate. Each Sunday his mother would take him to the tiny stone chapel, where they sat on plain, wooden forms, which had lengths of red baize upon them. The forms were slippery, and sometimes the baize would writhe noiselessly to the floor.

Everything at the chapel was delightful. There was a hanging chandelier filled with gas burners which had to be lighted, one by one, with a taper at the end of a pole, if ever the day grew too dark for the preacher to see. There was a pulpit with two lots of stairs running down from it, so that you could walk in at one side, and out of the other, if you were the preacher, and you wanted to. But the best thing of all was the music.

A harmonium was all they could afford at the chapel, and an elderly, very kind-faced woman played it. She sat with her back to the congregation, because she had no self-consciousness at all. She would slip on to the round stool in front of it, the gathers of her thick and proper skirt oozing gently over the edges; her feet would press firmly on the pedals, she would work them once or twice to fill the bellows with air, then the music would come.

The boy and his mother loved it. They sang the hymns loudly. There was one they often had. 'Toiling on,' they would sing, and the harmonium seemed to add, 'Ha, ha, ha! Toiling on! Ha, ha, ha!' It was worth coming to hear, however wet the day.

Once there had been a tea at the chapel, and they had both gone. The wooden forms were now arranged round long trestle tables. Plates of potted meat sandwiches, buns, biscuits and sweet cakes stood above the short or long, old or new tablecloths that had been lent. There was a huge copper tea-urn at the top, and great cups of tea were passed from hand to hand down the long expanse of table. Someone started singing, 'Be present at our table, Lord.' How they dragged it out! It seemed ages to the little boy, who had been so excited all day that he had hardly been able to cat his breakfast or dinner, and now wanted very much to begin. All the time they stood up, singing, he kept looking at the sandwich he had secretly chosen to start with; but directly grace was over, an old man with a long grey beard leaned over and almost snatched it. So the little boy sat sad and downcast, and it was a long time before he ate anything.

Although the tea had not been very pleasant, something happened afterwards which changed the whole evening.

There was a small cloakroom just inside the chapel, and on the day of the tea the precious harmonium had been moved into this place to give more room in the main hall. Here the boy found it. Furtively he tried the lid. It was open. His heart beat quickly as he put his hand on the soft-falling ivory keys. How pleasant they felt. He pulled up the chair without a back – the one used for reaching up to the cloakroom light – and sat down to play on the silent keys.

Soon he got tired of this and began to press the pedals. As he heard the rushing sound of the air, he touched a note. It sounded loud, but the piled hats and coats all around seemed to confine the noise to this one little room. Outside, there was a confused murmur of people talking together. The tall, clean women, with their stiff white aprons and curled fringes, were clearing the long tables. He became a little bolder, and suddenly a tune played under his hand – 'Toiling on! Ha, ha, ha!' He was frightened and happy, though however hard he tried he could not get past the first line.

'Music!' he whispered; then he jumped up and went to look for his mother.

She was helping to wash up. He stood beside her, tugging at her skirt, and a strange woman bent over him and said, 'No boys allowed in here; go out.' He did not answer her, but stood impatiently there until his mother noticed him.

He said, 'I want to whisper.'

She put down the dishcloth she had been holding, smiling apologetically at the strange woman.

'Henry wants to go somewhere,' she told her.

He waited until they were in the main hall with its

chattering crowd. Then he said, 'Come and listen to me play the harmonium!'

Guiltily they stole into the cloakroom and closed the door. The boy had a pink colour in his face, he was excited.

'Listen!' he cried.

He pressed down his feet and played his tune with confidence. Over and over again he played the first line of 'Toiling on!'

His mother leaned near him like a young girl.

'Wait a minute!' she cried, 'try this for the second line.'

Between them, miraculously, they found it. How happy they were. The noise grew louder, and their joy with it. When the door opened and Miss Altass – the playing lady – came in, there they froze into a picture of guilt, one sitting, the other half standing.

'You mustn't touch the harmonium,' said Miss Altass, not so gently as usual. She closed and locked it. They watched her, and did not say a word, only moved quietly away.

But afterwards, at home, they had something new to talk about. They could recall the scene a hundred times, and never tire. And one day the little boy said dreamily, 'I wish we had some music.'

His mother had just taken the last loaf from the oven and placed it on end on the baking board. She pushed the warm oven cloth under her chin and stood there thinking. The little boy looked up at her, and smiled because she was smiling. Gradually her face grew bleak; she said, 'T'father 'ud never let us 'ave any in the 'ouse. 'E doesn't like it.'

After that she had cheered up, and between them they

made a secret. She was going to save up for a harmonium, and then they would go and buy one. It would be hard to save, because there was never much money; but she could try. Penny by penny, a little hoard grew.

Twice 't'father' nearly discovered their secret. Once, the pot in which he kept his paper spills – spells, he called them – was empty, and he was looking everywhere for some more; and once he was looking for somewhere to hide something himself. But luckily he did not find the money. The little boy could hardly hold in his impatience. 'Can't we go now?' he would say, almost every day.

At last the mother got the greengrocer, who called every Thursday, to change her pennies into shillings for her. There were not many, but she thought, 'We might get an old one, that didn't cost much, and I would pay a bit every time I could save it.' She had often read notices in the brokers' windows, 'Weekly payments taken'.

It was a mild dull afternoon in early autumn when they walked down the street. As they passed Rumsden's Mill there was the sound of clattering machinery. Mrs Morphett had worked in a mill before she was married, and now a sudden yearning overcame her to be back among the racket of the machines. It was there she had dreamed her youthful dreams, which had not then included Theakstone Morphett. Fronting the road was a wooden door with a few holes in it, and she and the boy peered through them; they never passed without looking in. Nothing could be seen but wheels, whirling belts, and dust.

After they had looked as long as their excitement would let

them, they straightened themselves and walked on, down to the valley, over the bridge by the old Venture and up the other hillside. Mrs Morphett held in one hand a purse, containing her money, and the advertisement which she had cut out of the paper. It read, 'Musical instruments of all descriptions for sale. Unlimited choice. Apply 13 St Leonard's Terrace.'

At last they arrived at St Leonard's Terrace. For a long time the woman and her little boy did not dare to look for number thirteen, the road was so imposing. There were three-storeyed houses with big bay windows. Each had a small garden in front of it, with high, green-painted railings. Who would live in such houses but gentlemen, they thought, and were almost certain they had been directed to the wrong address. Even as they lingered, an old man came out of the gate of number thirteen, carrying a shabby violin case. He was muttering to himself as he passed them, and tremblingly buttoning up the top button of his coat. They watched him until he had turned the corner, then they opened the gate of thirteen and walked up to the house entrance and knocked.

In front of them was a large door, with a great amber-coloured knob on it. Henry stared at the knob, and thought it was so beautiful that for one moment he almost forgot the object of their visit. This door opened into a small, square hall, and beyond that was another door and a long passage. A tall, thin man with a black moustache answered their knock. Mrs Morphett looked first at his waistcoat, then at her own small feet, but she did not say anything. The little boy stiffened. 'Please have you got . . .' he began, but hearing his own voice, which sounded very loud, he fell silent.

'Come forward,' said the man, speaking in a deep, rich voice. They went forward only as far as the square hall, and stopped. 'Follow me,' he continued, still in the same deep tones, and they followed him down the passage into a large, uncarpeted room. There he left them, after saying, 'Pray excuse me, I will be back in a second.'

They stood in the dark back room, amid a profusion of fiddles, harps, pianos, and all shapes and sizes of musical instruments. They did not dare to move, and stood very quiet, almost holding their breath, until the man returned.

The little boy felt very proud of his mother as she looked up into the face of the dark gentleman and said, 'How much is the harmoniums?' She even managed to smile, a small, terrified smile. He thought she looked very pretty.

As soon as she heard the price she turned and made for the door, pulling the reluctant child with her; but before they could reach it, somehow the dark gentleman was in their way. He began to smile and talk to them, he did not want them to go without buying something. He showed them a square yellow box, covered with painted red flowers. 'This,' he said, 'might be something more in your line?'

As he spoke, he lifted the box onto an old packing case pushed into it a roll of perforated paper, and began to turn a handle. The boy and the woman stood as stiff as statues, but entranced. Beside this, a harmonium was nothing! The first tinkling tune it played was 'The Minstrel Boy', which Mrs Morphett had learned long ago at school. She nodded her head and began to hum, her eyes shining.

'What is it, mother?' whispered the little boy.

‘It’s a music box,’ said his mother, ‘and if it isn’t too dear, we’ll buy it.’

She imagined it playing for ever in the kitchen at home. They would put it on the end of the dresser, and treat it so carefully. When the grey, driving rain poured past the window, and the wind howled down from the moor, there it would be, ready to put heart into them; and afterwards, when Henry went to school – she could not bear to face that day, though it was already so near – it would always be a magnet to draw him safely back.

The man, who had been considering a price, smoothed down his moustache, and looked at them dubiously. He had intended to ask five shillings, but he put another shilling on for luck. In one corner of the room a violin string snapped, and they all started.

‘You can have it for six shillings,’ he said, ‘and the tunes alone are worth that.’

The mother and son looked at each other, he hopefully, she happily, then they both looked at the dark gentleman, who was stifling a yawn. And a few minutes afterwards they passed again the iron railings of numbers eleven, nine, seven, five, three, and one, the woman carrying a large box, inadequately wrapped, as if it were a holy thing.

They seemed to reach home in a moment. How well the box fitted its corner of the dresser, how the red flowers on its lid winked in the firelight! They played several tunes before they took off their outdoor things. His mother turned the handle while the little boy sat on his chair looking at her with solemn, ecstatic eyes. They were both serious, grave, and spoke little. Once, the mother said in a sharp, defiant voice, 'You sh'll 'ave an 'armonium next year,' although she knew it was next to impossible. The harmonium did not seem to matter so much now.

All at once they heard footsteps.

'It's t'father!' said the boy, in dismay. There was no meal ready for him.

They jumped up and ran to the door, looking like two children, flushed and happy. The little boy boldly took hold of one yellow trouser leg and cried, 'Father, father!' The man said, 'Wheer's my tea?'

'It won't be a minute.' His wife pushed the kettle into the heart of the fire and hurriedly put some things on the table.

The father seemed to be annoyed about something. He had lost a shilling that afternoon. It was not often that he put money on a horse, and, almost without exception, he lost. But he never gave up hoping that next time it would come off at a long price. All at once his glance fell on the music box.

'What's that contraption?' he growled.

Looking at him, the little boy began to whimper. It came over him that his father was possessed of power, and that he would use it cruelly. The mother seemed to feel that way too. Shading her face with the teapot, she stood waiting for the kettle to boil. She had the look of a child waiting to be whipped.

'Come on, let's be knowing. What's that contraption?' He was proud of the long word.

'It – it's a music box,' she said, almost inaudibly.

He looked at it dully.

The little boy watched his father's face. Then, still whimpering, he dragged a stool to the edge of the dresser, stood up on it, and began to turn the handle.

The man listened for a minute, then a heavy anger settled on his face. 'Shut that row!' he shouted, standing up and waving his arms. ''Oo brought that blasted thing into the 'ouse?'

The little boy stopped turning, and as he looked at the father, the bright colour ran out of his face, leaving only a sickly pallor around his two staring dark eyes. The lid of the kettle began to shake, but the mother did not pour the boiling water into the teapot.

'I brought it,' she said. She was as white as the little boy.

'Well, you can tek it back,' said the man. He kept looking at the box indignantly, as if it had done him some injury.

The water from the kettle began to splash onto the fire, and that was the only sound to be heard in the room.

As soon as the man had set off to his work the next morning, the woman slowly dressed to go out. She buttoned the boy into his overcoat, and opened the door. There was a fog, and they both coughed as they stepped out into the street. They had not been able to eat any breakfast, and they shivered in the chill morning air. The woman carried the music box, wrapped and ready to go back. She had cried until she was weary, and so had the little boy. They had asked again to be allowed to keep the music box, had promised that it shouldn't be played when 't'father' was in, but he simply said, 'Tek it back.' He could not see why his wife and son should want music when he did not.

The two walked very slowly, as the box seemed heavy. The mother was ashamed. She did not know how to approach the tall, dark gentleman; she was afraid he would not give her her money back. There was only one bright spot. She had not told her husband that the thing was paid for. Indeed, she had not had the chance, and the boy had clung to her dress, quietly, all the time her husband had shouted.

They stopped often to rest, but at last, once more, they were in St Leonard's Terrace. The tall houses were wrapped in fog, water dripped from the trees with their few twisted leaves, and the pavements were so greasy that many times they slipped and almost fell.

As his mother timidly knocked at the door, the little boy wiped the moisture from the amber-coloured knob, so that he could better see it. In doing so, he turned it, and the door opened softly beneath his hand. There was not a sound to be heard. He turned to his mother, looking up at her humbly, out of his swollen eyes. She seemed to understand him. Pushing open the door with her arm, she carefully lowered the parcel onto the floor of the little square hall, then she gently closed the door. Very soon the two figures had vanished in the fog.

HERE WE ARE

Dorothy Parker

(1931)

The young man in the new blue suit finished arranging the glistening luggage in tight corners of the Pullman compartment. The train had leaped at curves and bounced along straightaways, rendering balance a praiseworthy achievement and a sporadic one; and the young man had pushed and hoisted and tucked and shifted the bags with concentrated care.

Nevertheless, eight minutes for the settling of two suitcases and a hatbox is a long time.

He sat down, leaning back against bristled green plush, in the seat opposite the girl in beige. She looked as new as a peeled egg. Her hat, her fur, her frock, her gloves were glossy and stiff with novelty. On the arc of the thin, slippery sole of one beige shoe was gummed a tiny oblong of white paper, printed with the price set and paid for that slipper and its fellow, and the name of the shop that had dispensed them.

She had been staring raptly out of the window, drinking in the big weathered signboards that extolled the phenomena of codfish without bones and screens no rust could corrupt. As the young man sat down, she turned politely from the pane, met his eyes, started a smile and got it about half done, and rested her gaze just above his right shoulder.

'Well!' the young man said.

'Well!' she said.

'Well, here we are,' he said.

'Here we are,' she said. 'Aren't we?'

'I should say we were,' he said. 'Eeyop. Here we are.'

'Well!' she said.

'Well!' he said. 'Well. How does it feel to be an old married lady?'

'Oh, it's too soon to ask me that,' she said. 'At least – I mean. Well, I mean, goodness, we've only been married about three hours, haven't we?'

The young man studied his wristwatch as if he were just acquiring the knack of reading time.

'We have been married,' he said, 'exactly two hours and twenty-six minutes.'

'My,' she said. 'It seems like longer.'

'No,' he said. 'It isn't hardly half-past six yet.'

'It seems like later,' she said. 'I guess it's because it starts getting dark so early.'

'It does, at that,' he said. 'The nights are going to be pretty long from now on. I mean. I mean – well, it starts getting dark early.'

'I didn't have any idea what time it was,' she said. 'Everything was so mixed up, I sort of don't know where I am, or what it's all about. Getting back from the church, and then all those people, and then changing all my clothes, and then everybody throwing things, and all. Goodness, I don't see how people do it every day.'

'Do what?' he said.

'Get married,' she said. 'When you think of all the people, all over the world, getting married just as if it was nothing. Chinese people and everybody. Just as if it wasn't anything.'

'Well, let's not worry about people all over the world,' he said. 'Let's don't think about a lot of Chinese. We've got something better to think about. I mean. I mean – well, what do we care about them?'

'I know,' she said. 'But I just sort of got to thinking of them, all of them, all over everywhere, doing it all the time. At least, I mean – getting married, you know. And it's – well, it's sort of such a big thing to do, it makes you feel queer. You think of them, all of them, all doing it just like it wasn't anything. And how does anybody know what's going to happen next?'

'Let them worry,' he said. 'We don't have to. We know darn well what's going to happen next. I mean. I mean – well, we know it's going to be great. Well, we know we're going to be happy. Don't we?'

'Oh, of course,' she said. 'Only you think of all the people, and you have to sort of keep thinking. It makes you feel funny. An awful lot of people that get married, it doesn't turn out so well. And I guess they all must have thought it was going to be great.'

'Come on, now,' he said. 'This is no way to start a honeymoon, with all this thinking going on. Look at us – all married and everything done. I mean. The wedding all done and all.'

'Ah, it was nice, wasn't it?' she said. 'Did you really like my veil?'

'You looked great,' he said. 'Just great.'

'Oh, I'm terribly glad,' she said. 'Ellie and Louise looked lovely, didn't they? I'm terribly glad they did finally decide on pink. They looked perfectly lovely.'

'Listen,' he said. 'I want to tell you something. When I was standing up there in that old church waiting for you to come up, and I saw those two bridesmaids, I thought to myself, I thought, "Well, I never knew Louise could look like that!" Why, she'd have knocked anybody's eye out.'

'Oh, really?' she said. 'Funny. Of course, everybody thought her dress and hat were lovely, but a lot of people seemed to think she looked sort of tired. People have been saying that a lot, lately. I tell them I think it's awfully mean of them to go around saying that about her. I tell them they've got to remember that Louise isn't so terribly young any more, and they've got to expect her to look like that. Louise can say she's twenty-three all she wants to, but she's a good deal nearer twenty-seven.'

'Well, she was certainly a knock-out at the wedding,' he said. 'Boy!'

'I'm terribly glad you thought so,' she said. 'I'm glad someone did. How did you think Ellie looked?'

'Why, I honestly didn't get a look at her,' he said.

'Oh, really?' she said. 'Well, I certainly think that's too bad. I don't suppose I ought to say it about my own sister, but I never saw anybody look as beautiful as Ellie looked today. And always so sweet and unselfish, too. And you didn't even notice her. But you never pay attention to Ellie, anyway. Don't think

I haven't noticed it. It makes me feel just terrible. It makes me feel just awful, that you don't like my own sister.'

'I do like her!' he said. 'I'm crazy for Ellie. I think she's a great kid.'

'Don't think it makes any difference to Ellie!' she said. 'Ellie's got enough people crazy about her. It isn't anything to her whether you like her or not. Don't flatter yourself she cares! Only, the only thing is, it makes it awfully hard for me you don't like her, that's the only thing. I keep thinking, when we come back and get in that apartment and everything, it's going to be awfully hard for me that you won't want my own sister to come and see me. It's going to make it awfully hard for me that you won't ever want my family around. I know how you feel about my family. Don't think I haven't seen it. Only, if you don't ever want to see them, that's your loss. Not theirs. Don't flatter yourself!'

'Oh, now, come on!' he said. 'What's all this talk about not wanting your family around? Why, you know how I feel about your family. I think your old lady – I think your mother's swell. And Ellie. And your father. What's all this talk?'

'Well, I've seen it,' she said. 'Don't think I haven't. Lots of people they get married, and they think it's going to be great and everything, and then it all goes to pieces because people don't like people's families, or something like that. Don't tell me! I've seen it happen.'

'Honey,' he said, 'what is all this? What are you getting all angry about? Hey, look, this is our honeymoon. What are you trying to start a fight for? Ah, I guess you're just feeling sort of nervous.'

'Me?' she said. 'What have I got to be nervous about? I mean. I mean, goodness, I'm not nervous.'

'You know, lots of times,' he said, 'they say that girls get kind of nervous and yippy on account of thinking about – I mean. I mean – well, it's like you said, things are all so sort of mixed up and everything, right now. But afterwards, it'll be all right. I mean. I mean – well, look, honey, you don't look any too comfortable. Don't you want to take your hat off? And let's don't ever fight, ever. Will we?'

'Ah, I'm sorry I was cross,' she said. 'I guess I did feel a little bit funny. All mixed up, and then thinking of all those people all over everywhere, and then being sort of way off here, all alone with you. It's so sort of different. It's sort of such a big thing. You can't blame a person for thinking, can you? Yes, don't let's ever, ever fight. We won't be like a whole lot of them. We won't fight or be nasty or anything. Will we?'

'You bet your life we won't,' he said.

'I guess I will take this darned old hat off,' she said. 'It kind of presses. Just put it up on the rack, will you, dear? Do you like it, sweetheart?'

'Looks good on you,' he said.

'No, but I mean,' she said, 'do you really like it?'

'Well, I'll tell you,' he said. 'I know this is the new style and everything like that, and it's probably great. I don't know anything about things like that. Only I like the kind of a hat like that blue hat you had. Gee, I liked that hat.'

'Oh, really?' she said. 'Well, that's nice. That's lovely. The first thing you say to me, as soon as you get me off on a train away from my family and everything, is that you don't like my hat. The first thing you say to your wife is you think she has terrible taste in hats. That's nice, isn't it?'

'Now, honey,' he said, 'I never said anything like that. I only said –'

'What you don't seem to realise,' she said, 'is this hat cost twenty-two dollars. Twenty-two dollars. And that horrible old blue thing you think you're so crazy about, that cost three ninety-five.'

'I don't give a darn what they cost,' he said. 'I only said – I said I liked that blue hat. I don't know anything about hats. I'll be crazy about this one as soon as I get used to it. Only it's kind of not like your other hats. I don't know about the new styles. What do I know about women's hats?'

'It's too bad,' she said, 'you didn't marry somebody that would get the kind of hats you'd like. Hats that cost three ninety-five. Why didn't you marry Louise? You always think she looks so beautiful. You'd love her taste in hats. Why didn't you marry her?'

'Ah, now, honey,' he said. 'For heaven's sake!'

'Why didn't you marry her?' she said. 'All you've done, ever since we got on this train, is talk about her. Here I've sat and sat, and just listened to you saying how wonderful Louise is. I suppose that's nice, getting me all off here alone with you, and then raving about Louise right in front of my face. Why didn't you ask her to marry you? I'm sure she would have jumped at the chance. There aren't so many people asking her to marry them. It's too bad you didn't marry her. I'm sure you'd have been much happier.'

'Listen, baby,' he said, 'while you're talking about things like that, why didn't you marry Joe Brooks? I suppose he could have given you all the twenty-two-dollar hats you wanted, I suppose!'

'Well, I'm not so sure I'm not sorry I didn't,' she said. 'There! Joe Brooks wouldn't have waited until he got me all off alone and then sneered at my taste in clothes. Joe Brooks wouldn't ever hurt my feelings. Joe Brooks has always been fond of me. There!'

'Yeah,' he said. 'He's fond of you. He was so fond of you he didn't even send a wedding present. That's how fond of you he was.'

'I happen to know for a fact,' she said, 'that he was away on business, and as soon as he comes back he's going to give me anything I want, for the apartment.'

'Listen,' he said. 'I don't want anything he gives you in our apartment. Anything he gives you, I'll throw right out the window. That's what I think of your friend Joe Brooks. And how do you know where he is and what he's going to do, anyway? Has he been writing to you?'

'I suppose my friends can correspond with me,' she said. 'I didn't hear there was any law against that.'

'Well, I suppose they can't!' he said. 'And what do you think of that? I'm not going to have my wife getting a lot of letters from cheap travelling salesmen!'

'Joe Brooks is not a cheap travelling salesman!' she said. 'He is not! He gets a wonderful salary.'

'Oh yeah?' he said. 'Where did you hear that?'

'He told me so himself,' she said.

'Oh, he told you so himself,' he said. 'I see. He told you so himself.'

'You've got a lot of right to talk about Joe Brooks,' she said. 'You and your friend Louise. All you ever talk about is Louise.'

'Oh, for heaven's sake!' he said. 'What do I care about Louise? I just thought she was a friend of yours, that's all. That's why I ever even noticed her.'

'Well, you certainly took an awful lot of notice of her today,' she said. 'On our wedding day! You said yourself when you were standing there in the church you just kept thinking of her. Right up at the altar. Oh, right in the presence of God! And all you thought about was Louise.'

'Listen, honey,' he said, 'I never should have said that. How does anybody know what kind of crazy things come into their heads when they're standing there waiting to get married? I was just telling you that because it was so kind of crazy. I thought it would make you laugh.'

'I know,' she said. 'I've been all sort of mixed up today, too. I told you that. Everything so strange and everything. And me all the time thinking about all those people all over the world, and now us here all alone, and everything. I know you get all mixed up. Only I did think, when you kept talking about how beautiful Louise looked, you did it with malice and forethought.'

'I never did anything with malice and forethought!' he said. 'I just told you that about Louise because I thought it would make you laugh.'

'Well, it didn't,' she said.

'No, I know it didn't,' he said. 'It certainly did not. Ah, baby, and we ought to be laughing, too. Hell, honey lamb, this is our honeymoon. What's the matter?'

'I don't know,' she said. 'We used to squabble a lot when we were going together and then engaged and everything, but I thought everything would be so different as soon as you were married. And now I feel so sort of strange and everything. I feel so sort of alone.'

'Well, you see, sweetheart,' he said, 'we're not really married yet. I mean. I mean – well, things will be different afterwards. Oh, hell. I mean, we haven't been married very long.'

'No,' she said.

'Well, we haven't got much longer to wait now,' he said. 'I mean – well, we'll be in New York in about twenty minutes. Then we can have dinner, and sort of see what we feel like doing. Or I mean. Is there anything special you want to do tonight?'

'What?' she said.

'What I mean to say,' he said, 'would you like to go to a show or something?'

'Why, whatever you like,' she said. 'I sort of didn't think people went to theatres and things on their – I mean, I've got a couple of letters I simply must write. Don't let me forget.'

'Oh,' he said. 'You're going to write letters tonight?'

'Well, you see,' she said, 'I've been perfectly terrible. What with all the excitement and everything. I never did thank poor old Mrs Sprague for her berry spoon, and I never did a thing about those bookends the McMasters sent. It's just too awful of me. I've got to write them this very night.'

'And when you've finished writing your letters,' he said, 'maybe I could get you a magazine or a bag of peanuts.'

'What?' she said.

'I mean,' he said, 'I wouldn't want you to be bored.'

'As if I could be bored with you!' she said. 'Silly! Aren't we married? Bored!'

'What I thought,' he said, 'I thought when we got in, we could go right up to the Biltmore and anyway leave our bags, and maybe have a little dinner in the room, kind of quiet, and then do whatever we wanted. I mean. I mean – well, let's go right up there from the station.'

'Oh, yes, let's,' she said. 'I'm so glad we're going to the Biltmore. I just love it. The twice I've stayed in New York we've always stayed there, Papa and Mamma and Ellie and I, and I was crazy about it. I always sleep so well there. I go right off to sleep the minute I put my head on the pillow.'

'Oh, you do?' he said.

'At least, I mean,' she said. 'Way up high it's so quiet.'

'We might go to some show or other tomorrow night instead of tonight,' he said. 'Don't you think that would be better?'

'Yes, I think it might,' she said.

He rose, balanced a moment, crossed over and sat down beside her.

'Do you really have to write those letters tonight?' he said.

'Well,' she said, 'I don't suppose they'd get there any quicker than if I wrote them tomorrow.'

There was a silence with things going on in it.

'And we won't ever fight any more, will we?' he said.

'Oh, no,' she said. 'Not ever! I don't know what made me do like that. It all got so sort of funny, sort of like a nightmare, the way I got thinking of all those people getting married all the time; and so many of them, everything spoils on account of fighting and everything. I got all mixed up thinking about them. Oh, I don't want to be like them. But we won't be, will we?'

'Sure we won't,' he said.

'We won't go all to pieces,' she said. 'We won't fight. It'll all be different, now we're married. It'll all be lovely. Reach me down my hat, will you, sweetheart? It's time I was putting it on. Thanks. Ah, I'm so sorry you don't like it.'

'I do so like it!' he said.

'You said you didn't,' she said. 'You said you thought it was perfectly terrible.'

'I never said any such thing,' he said. 'You're crazy.'

'All right, I may be crazy,' she said. 'Thank you very much. But that's what you said. Not that it matters – it's just a little thing. But it makes you feel pretty funny to think you've gone and married somebody that says you have perfectly terrible taste in hats. And then goes and says you're crazy, besides.'

'Now, listen here,' he said. 'Nobody said any such thing. Why, I love that hat. The more I look at it the better I like it. I think it's great.'

'That isn't what you said before,' she said.

'Honey,' he said. 'Stop it, will you? What do you want to start all this for? I love the damned hat. I mean, I love your hat. I love anything you wear. What more do you want me to say?'

'Well, I don't want you to say it like that,' she said.

'I said I think it's great,' he said. 'That's all I said.'

'Do you really?' she said. 'Do you honestly? Ah, I'm so glad. I'd hate you not to like my hat. It would be – I don't know, it would be sort of such a bad start.'

'Well, I'm crazy for it,' he said. 'Now we've got that settled, for heaven's sake. Ah, baby. Baby lamb. We're not going to have any bad starts. Look at us – we're on our honeymoon. Pretty soon we'll be regular old married people. I mean. I mean, in a few minutes we'll be getting in to New York, and then we'll be going to the hotel, and then everything will be all right. I mean – well, look at us! Here we are married! Here we are!'

'Yes, here we are,' she said. 'Aren't we?'

A LOVELY TIME

Dorothy Whipple

(1933)

She got in from the office earlier than usual because she had been lucky with buses. She thought she would write to Lucy to keep her mind off the cold. There were gas fires in the bedrooms at Vale House, but she was determined not to light hers until she was undressing for bed; the meter was a glutton for shillings and ate a great hole in her money every week.

Only one light was allowed in the bedroom, but by means of a long flex from the ceiling she had made it into a bed lamp, which bloomed now like an orange in the dusk it created. She sat down under it to write to Lucy, who had remained at home in Ilkeston.

'I have just come in from the office. It is a cold night, but my little lamp makes a glow, and my little room feels very peaceful after the busy day. Oh, Lucy, it is wonderful living in London.'

Yes, it was wonderful, especially when she wrote about it to Lucy, but her feet were very cold. She took off her damp shoes and put on her bedroom slippers. She settled herself again with pen and pad, but before she could write another word, there was a knock on the door, and in came Sheila Spence, with her hair in lead curlers under a pink shingle cap.

'Oh, you're in at last, Barnesy darling,' she cried. 'I've been umpteen times before. You must help me out tonight. You must come out to dinner with me and Geoff Potter and Perry Gifford. Rosamund's just telephoned to say she's too seedy to come, and I can't let them down. We must be four. Do say you'll come. We're going to Barteolozzi's and then on to a night club sort of place. You'll like the chaps, and Gifford writes or something. Do say you'll come, darling!'

Alice – since she had come to London she spelt it 'Alys' and pronounced it to rhyme with 'knees'; she would have liked to do something with 'Barnes' too, only it was difficult on account of letters from home and that kind of thing – Alice stared at Sheila while her poised pen deposited a large blot on the letter to Lucy.

'Oh, Miss Spence . . .' she breathed at last. No one had asked her out since she came to London, and now here was an invitation to dinner and a night club! Dinner and a night-club . . . !

'You'll come then?' said Sheila. 'Cheers. Have you got an evening dress? Without sleeves, I mean? Good. Well, get a move on, darling. I've had my hair in Queen Besses since I got in from the office. What are you going to do with yours?' she eyed Alice's lank locks with some anxiety.

'I don't know. What can I do? I'll do anything,' promised Alice.

Sheila considered her.

'Well, I think an Eton Crop's your style,' she said. 'What about borrowing Shandon's "Stickit", or whatever it is she uses for hers, and then you can plaster it behind your ears. Make it sleek and smart, see?'

'D'you think she'd lend me some? I could pay her back tomorrow,' said Alice hopefully.

'Oh, don't you bother about that. I'll go and get it from her. She's in.' Sheila knew she was in because she had first given her the invitation she now gave to Alice. But Shandon couldn't go, and Alice was Hobson's Choice and must be made the best of.

Alice hurriedly put away the letter to Lucy and fled to the bathroom for hot water. Then she recklessly lit the gas fire. The first time you went out with young men to dinner and a night club, you didn't stop to cavil about a shilling in the meter.

She sang as she took off her work-a-day clothes. Fancy Miss Spence asking *her*! It was most kind, because she hardly knew her really and yet she called her darling and asked her out to dinner and a night club. Oh, London life had begun! She had been lonely, she had been dull, she had been cold and felt the food at Vale House inadequate, but now the lights had gone up, the fun, the excitement, the experience she had come for were going to begin!

'I say,' said Sheila, putting her head in again. 'Dutch treats, you know. We're all paying for ourselves. That's all right, isn't it?'

'Oh, of *course*,' said Alice, snatching at her cotton kimono.

'It won't be much at Barteolozzi's,' said Sheila consolingly. 'But it's jolly good food all the same. Got any cigarettes?'

'Oh, I'm afraid I haven't,' said Alice. She didn't really like the taste of cigarettes, and only smoked when she wished to be smart.

'Well, you can get some on the way. I'll take some too. And matches.'

'I haven't a fancy box for the matches,' faltered Alice.

'Oh, don't bother about that. Nobody has.'

Alice smiled happily once more and went on with her dressing. She was so glad she had the artificial satin cloak. It was strawberry pink and had a ruched collar. Lucy had made it for her to come to London with, but although she had been in London more than four months, she had never had it out of its box. Now she was going to wear it at last.

She recklessly cut a piece out of the top of her winter vest so that it should not show above her black frock. She knew she was being thriftless and in every way awful, but she was going to have a lovely time, and nothing, nothing must spoil it. The brand-new woollen vest must be sacrificed.

She put on the black dress. It hung from her shoulders as it had hung from its coat-hanger; in fact, there was little difference between the two means of support, for although Alice was twenty, she was as small and bony as a child. She put on a string of pink beads so pale as to be almost invisible, and draped a white ninon scarf round her neck, finishing it with an elegant knot on one shoulder.

Then she moved the bed lamp to the dressing table to do her face. No rouge, she decided, but plenty of powder, lipstick and eyeblack. When she had finished, she hung over the reflection in the glass, looking for herself. She was almost unrecognisable, but rather modern and highbrow-looking all the same, she thought, with a little thrill.

'Ready?' enquired Sheila, coming in to look her over. She herself was highly coloured, with dark curls, wet lips, green earrings, and a full bosom. She wore a green gown and her black coat with the civet cat collar.

'Oh, Miss Spence, you do look lovely!' cried Alice.

Sheila didn't know what to say about Alice.

'Have you got the hair stuff on?' she enquired, to give herself time.

'No, I'm just going to put it on,' said Alice, sprinkling vigorously from Miss Shandon's bottle. 'Oh, isn't it funny? It's like boiled starch.'

'I expect that's what it is,' said Sheila. 'Here, give me the comb! I'll do the back. Brush it very smooth. There! Well, I must say it's made a difference to you. Are you ready now?'

'Yes,' said Alice, snatching up the artificial satin cloak and her handbag, and casting one more look at her unaccustomed self in the mirror.

'Come on then. We've got to meet them there.'

Alice put out the light and followed in the wake of Sheila's scent. The night was cold and murky, but although the satin cloak was thin, excitement kept Alice warm. They stopped at the corner for Alice to buy cigarettes, and then they caught the bus in the Euston Road.

'See,' said Alice to herself, sitting happily beside Sheila on the high seat by the door. 'Nobody stares in London when you go out in evening dress.'

She smiled to think what a commotion she would make

in a tram at home in a pink satin cloak and no hat at seven-thirty in the evening.

She wondered what she could talk about to Mr Gifford. She gathered that he would be allotted to her, because Miss Spence was evidently keen on the other one. Alice wished she had read the latest works of the Sitwell family, or been able to understand what she had seen of the verse of Mr T S Eliot. At any rate, she had read *The Good Companions*.

She smoothed her hair nervously. The ends pricked her, it even rattled a little when she touched it. But it was smart. She thought she would buy a bottle of that stuff when she could afford to. It wouldn't be this week, after those cigarettes. When you went out with men in London, they treated you as if you were a man too. Horace, at home, always paid for Lucy. She thought of Horace with some scorn. He wasn't really modern. He didn't quite know what was what.

They got out at Goodge Street and made their way to Barteolozzi's restaurant. It was ordinary enough outside, being merely two steamy plate-glass windows, but when they opened the door, it was like stepping into another world to Alice. Her eyes fell straight away on an enormous man shovelling spaghetti into a mouth like a stoke-hole, and as she followed Sheila to the stairs, a waitress called down the lift into the kitchen for *pane*.

Pane! How thrilling! That must be Italian for bread.

Pane! *Pane*! whispered Alice ecstatically. Oh, this was the wide wide world! This was even more than London; it was the cosmos. She would be able to ask for *pane* when she went home to Ilkeston for her holiday.

‘We’ll bag that table near the window,’ said Sheila. ‘They don’t seem to be here yet.’

Alice followed Sheila to a table for four, and laid the pink satin cloak over the back of her chair. She got out the cigarettes and the matches to be ready, and they sat down to wait for the young men.

Sheila took a mirror from her handbag and began to fluff up her curls, powder her nose, run a moistened finger along her eyelashes and redden her already red lips.

Alice took a look at herself in her mirror too, but as her face was still satisfactorily as white as chalk, and her brows and lashes as black as coal, there was no need to do any more. Her mirror was so small she could not see that her hair had risen at the back of her head in a stiff hackle, which caused amusement to people at other tables. She sat in bliss and ignorance, looking very small, young and a little peculiar.

This restaurant was a funny, hot place, she thought, but exciting. That notice on the wall: ‘*Bianco Appasito* – 6d.’ Was it a wine, she wondered, with that lovely name?

‘*Bianco Appasito*,’ she said that over too.

‘Gifford’s always late,’ said Sheila. ‘And Geoff’s almost as bad.’

Alice looked out of the window into a room across the street where they hadn’t pulled down the blind. A little boy was standing on a chair to be undressed. His enormous mother played with him, and his father stood by in his shirt sleeves. Alice felt as if she had looked right into Life.

Girls in black frocks and minute white aprons bustled past their table with bowls of minestrone and folded omelettes and unrecognisable but savoury dishes. Alice was very hungry, having lunched on salad and a new kind of milk, and had no tea at all. At home, she used to have a large high tea as soon as she got in, but now she had to wait until half-past seven for dinner every night. She did it gladly because it was part of London life, but it often made her feel very queer. She did wish now that the young men would come and let her begin to eat.

Still, she must wait, she must bear her hunger, she told herself, because they were the means, the cause of this lovely evening. They would come, dinner would follow them, and then they would lead the way to a Night Club. Fancy going to a Night Club! It had been one of her dreams, and now it was coming true!

'Oh, there they are!' cried Sheila, jumping up and starting in pursuit of two young men who had turned down the room in the opposite direction.

Alice took another hurried look into her mirror, and as hurriedly put it away again. Her heart beat fast. The young men were here; London young men, and one a writer.

Sheila brought them triumphantly to the table. One had fair hair and the other was dark and dishevelled.

'Barnesy, Geoff Potter and Perry Gifford,' said Sheila. 'And chaps, meet Barnesy. She's a dear and she comes from Ilkeston.'

Alice wished Miss Spence hadn't mentioned Ilkeston, but she smiled widely on the young men. Indeed, from now on, she smiled widely at everything. She was so happily excited that when anyone spoke, it was as if a string was pulled and Alice smiled.

Now that the young men had come, things began to happen.

'Hi, Maddelena!' called Perry Gifford, making Alice jump.

A girl came to the table and held Gifford's hand benevolently while they discussed the menu.

'*Tournedos aux champignons* is the best for tonight,' she counselled, her kind dark eyes beaming on Alice whose thinness roused her compassion. 'You all have *tournedos* and *sauté* potatoes. Yes?'

Alice agreed with the others, although she did not know what *tournedos* meant. She hoped it was abundant and eatable.

'And four cocktails Barteolozzi?' asked Maddelena. 'Two lagers, one glass white wine ordinaire, and for you, Mademoiselle?'

Alice said water, please, and Maddelena went to the top of the stairs to shout down the order, beginning with '*quatro* cocktails' and ending with '*aqua*'. Alice thought she would enjoy water as never before, since it had been called by the name the Romans used for it.

The dinner ordered, the young men turned their attention to their companions. Mr Potter stroked Sheila's arm with one hand, while with the fingers of the other, he pressed in the waves of his fair hair, or sought the spots on the back of his neck.

Alice was conscious of the gaze of Mr Gifford and was thrilled. Perhaps he would put her in a book. She began to tear the waxed paper from the new packet of cigarettes to give herself countenance while under the observation of a writer.

She did not see the look he transferred to Sheila before he turned away, a look that said as plainly as any words: 'How you had the *nerve* to bring me this . . .'

'Will you smoke?' asked Alice, with a smile.

He looked over his shoulder consideringly at the packet.

'Perhaps I will,' he said.

Alice put a cigarette between her own lips, and striking a match lit first his and then her own. She was very gallant. She felt she had copied Sheila very successfully. Men used to do these things for women, but now it was the other way round. Much newer and smarter, she reflected, and was glad she had not betrayed her provincialism by waiting for him to light up for her.

She smoked very slowly, because she had read once that novices gave themselves away by smoking too fast. Once she managed to blow down her nose, but it was a great effort to suppress a cough afterwards. She decided to practise inhalation in the privacy of her room at Vale House.

'You write, don't you?' she said in a respectful tone to Gifford.

'Sometimes,' he answered indifferently. He did not encourage enquiries about his literary activities, which were as yet unsuccessful.

'What are you working at now?' asked Alice softly, in what she hoped was the right phraseology.

'I never discuss my work,' said Mr Gifford shortly.

Alice shrank, and looked out of the window again, but the little boy had gone to bed. Mr Gifford glared balefully at the stiff poke of hair at the back of her head, and again at Sheila, who giggled and went on eating the middle out of Mr Potter's bread.

Something like a panic was going on in Alice's small breast, as she kept her head turned away to the window. Whatever could she talk about next to Mr Gifford? He was so Byronic and difficult, and the other two across the table were so engrossed with each other. Topics ran through her mind like mice, but she couldn't catch any of them. Aeroplanes, or had you to say airplanes now? Music, but she didn't know anything about it. Theatres, but she hadn't been able to afford to go to any yet.

'Oh, dear . . . oh, dear . . .' she cried silently. 'What shall I talk about? What will he think of me?'

The eternal anxiety of youth! 'What will he think of me?' not 'What do I think of him?' Poor Alice!

'*Ecco*,' said the maternal voice of Maddelena, placing a cocktail before her.

Alice smiled again. The dreadful moment was past. She leaned her sharp little elbows on the table and drank her cocktail with the others.

'Here's how!' said Gifford.

'Happy Days!' said Sheila and Geoff.

'Thank you,' said Alice.

It didn't sound right, somehow. She was faintly worried again, and wondered if there was a little book to be bought on the subject of what to say when drinking cocktails. But the worry was soon dispelled by the mounting influence of a cocktail on an empty stomach. Alice began to feel queer, but happy. She thought her legs had left her, but when she felt for her knees under the table they were surprisingly still there.

Reassured, Alice leant impulsively towards Perry Gifford.

'Won't it be lovely at the Night Club?' she said, beaming into his face.

'That is hardly the term I should use,' he said without warmth. 'I should say it will be . . .'

He looked at her and left it at that.

Alice felt rebuked for using such a word as 'lovely' to a writer who must, of course, be particular about the choice of words. 'Lovely' was a slack sort of word; you used it for everything whether you meant it or not. She must be more careful in future.

She smiled apologetically at Mr Gifford.

The ninon scarf and the black dress slipped a little and revealed one small bony shoulder. She left it like that, and felt elegant and rather fast. She did not know her winter vest showed, but Perry Gifford did, and that, as he put it to himself, settled it.

Maddelena arrived with a steaming copper dish and proceeded to serve out the contents. Alice was immensely relieved to find that *tournedos* were comfortable steaks with rich dark sauce and potatoes in rosettes. She smiled happily and began at last to appease her hunger. Mr Gifford became engrossed in his dinner and did not need to be talked to. Sheila and Geoff across the table were very gay together and held hands between mouthfuls.

It was only by the exercise of great self-control that Alice managed to leave a little of the steak for manners, and the caramel cream she chose afterwards because it was the cheapest, disappeared almost before she had properly looked at it.

'We'll have coffee at the club,' said Sheila, collecting the sums due for the dinner to hand over to Mr Potter. 'Come along, Barnesy, we'll go and do our faces. Find out what Perry keeps mouthing to me about,' she said in an aside to Geoff. 'I can't make out what he wants. Come along, Barnesy.'

Alice caught up the strawberry satin cloak and what remained of the cigarettes, and followed Sheila to the tiny cloakroom, where the paint was labelled wet and they had to keep their elbows into their sides as they powdered their noses.

'Wasn't the dinner good?' said Alice. 'It was excellent.'

'Your hair's come unstuck at the back,' said Sheila.

'Oh, has it?' Alice was alarmed. 'Oh, what can I do to it?'

'I think you'd better wet your comb and plaster it down again,' said Sheila. Alice thought she detected a faint coldness in her voice. But perhaps it was her fancy, because when she spoke again Sheila was quite friendly.

'I say, darling,' she said suddenly. 'Could you possibly lend me five bob for tonight? I'm getting short. You know how it is when you go out. And Geoff never has any money. I'll give it you back on Friday, I swear I will.'

'Oh, yes, Miss Spence, I'll lend it you with pleasure,' said Alice, blushing under her white powder at the embarrassment the other must feel at having to ask a comparative stranger for a loan.

‘It’s awfully decent of you,’ said Sheila.

‘Don’t mention it,’ begged Alice, handing her two half-crowns, and looking surreptitiously to see that there was still some money left. Lending money had not entered into her calculations for the week.

‘Now for the club,’ said Sheila gaily.

‘Oh, won’t it be lovely?’ said Alice, squeezing her friend’s arm as they went down the stairs to where the young men stood. As they approached, Perry Gifford walked off to the door. He even went through it.

‘These writers are very queer,’ admitted Alice to herself.

‘Sheila, one moment,’ said Mr Potter, drawing her apart.

Alice stood at the foot of the stairs, holding the satin cloak round her and humming to herself. The Night Club, the Night Club . . . this is London, this is Life . . .!

She looked at Sheila listening to Geoff. When Sheila looked at anyone, she looked from eye to eye, from one eye to the other very fast. Alice tried to do it to an imaginary face, and felt dizzy. She hummed again. The Night Club, the Night Club . . . What a lot she would have to write to Lucy!

Sheila was coming towards her.

‘Now are we ready?’ called Alice gaily, advancing.

‘I say, Miss Barnes,’ said Sheila, drawing her back to the foot of the stairs. ‘I’m ever so sorry, but Perry Gifford finds he can’t go on to the club after all. He says he’s got to go home and do some writing. You know how it is. If he feels in the mood, he has to go, hasn’t he?’

‘Oh, yes,’ said Alice, her face relaxing with relief. If this was all . . .

'Well, you see,' said Sheila, fiddling with her green earrings and looking from one eye to the other in Alice's face, which was stiffening again with apprehension. 'Well, you see, that makes us three, doesn't it? And three's not much use at a dance club, is it? I mean to say, it wouldn't be much fun for you if you went, would it? You see what I mean.'

Alice saw at last, and blushed to have been so long about it.

'Oh,' she said hurriedly,' I quite understand. Don't worry about me. I can go home.'

Home did not seem to be the right word.

'I can go back,' she amended.

'I'm ever so sorry, Miss Barnes,' said Sheila, retreating towards Geoff.

'Oh, it's quite all right,' said Alice. 'Goodnight, Mr Potter. Goodnight, Miss Spence.'

'*Good* night,' said Sheila, with a gushing smile, taking Mr Potter's arm.

Mr Potter raised his hat a little way, and with a wide, aching smile of her own, Alice left them.

She got a bus at the corner and went back to Endsleigh Street. She opened the door of Vale House with the key attached by string and a safety-pin to her bag, and tiptoed into the hall. She hoped to reach her room without being seen, but before she had passed the great mirror in the tarnished gilt frame, Miss Taylor came out of the dining-room.

'Hello, Miss Barnes, you're back early,' she said.

Alice smiled once more and murmured 'Yes' as if admitting to a crime.

'I thought you and Sheila were going to make a night of it,' cried jolly Miss Taylor.

'Oh, no,' murmured Alice, slipping past her to the stairs.

'Well, it'll do you more good to go to bed early,' called Miss Taylor.

Alice murmured again, and reached the haven of her room.

She took off the satin cloak, the black dress, the powder and the eyeblack. Her head ached, her heart ached and she was cold. She couldn't light the gas-fire now, or for a long time to come. She realised with bitterness that Sheila would not pay back the five shillings. She had protested too much. She said: 'I swear I will.' That meant she wouldn't. Besides, she looked from eye to eye.

Alice hurried into bed to get warm, but before she turned out the lamp she finished the letter to Lucy.

'I went out to dinner tonight,' she wrote, and then paused.

What could she say? She thought a long time, staring into the shadows of her narrow room. She would never be able to be gay and smart like other people, she thought; never know what to say, what to wear, what to do; never be happy and at ease. It was terrible, terrible to be so lonely, so outside . . .

But because no one, not even Lucy, must know that she had been thus weighed in London scales and found wanting, she wrote at last: 'I had a lovely time.'

ROMAN FEVER

Edith Wharton

(1934)

From the table at which they had been lunching two American ladies of ripe but well-cared-for middle age moved across the lofty terrace of the Roman restaurant and, leaning on its parapet, looked first at each other, and then down on the outspread glories of the Palatine and the Forum, with the same expression of vague but benevolent approval.

As they leaned there a girlish voice echoed up gaily from the stairs leading to the court below. 'Well, come along, then,' it cried, not to them but to an invisible companion, 'and let's leave the young things to their knitting,' and a voice as fresh laughed back: 'Oh, look here, Babs, not actually knitting –' 'Well, I mean figuratively,' rejoined the first. 'After all, we haven't left our poor parents much else to do . . .' and at that point the turn of the stairs engulfed the dialogue.

The two ladies looked at each other again, this time with a tinge of smiling embarrassment, and the smaller and paler one shook her head and coloured slightly.

'Barbara!' she murmured, sending an unheard rebuke after the mocking voice in the stairway.

The other lady, who was fuller, and higher in colour, with a small determined nose supported by vigorous black eyebrows, gave a good-humoured laugh. 'That's what our daughters think of us.'

Her companion replied by a deprecating gesture. 'Not of us individually. We must remember that. It's just the collective modern idea of Mothers. And you see –' Half guiltily she drew from her handsomely mounted black handbag a twist of crimson silk run through by two fine knitting needles. 'One never knows,' she murmured. 'The new system has certainly given us a good deal of time to kill; and sometimes I get tired just looking – even at this.' Her gesture was now addressed to the stupendous scene at their feet.

The dark lady laughed again, and they both relapsed upon the view, contemplating it in silence, with a sort of diffused serenity which might have been borrowed from the spring effulgence of the Roman skies. The luncheon hour was long past, and the two had their end of the vast terrace to themselves. At its opposite extremity a few groups, detained by a lingering look at the outspread city, were gathering up guidebooks and fumbling for tips. The last of them scattered, and the two ladies were alone on the air-washed height.

'Well, I don't see why we shouldn't just stay here,' said Mrs Slade, the lady of the high colour and energetic brows. Two derelict basket chairs stood near, and she pushed them into the angle of the parapet, and settled herself in one, her gaze upon the Palatine. 'After all, it's still the most beautiful view in the world.'

'It always will be, to me,' assented her friend Mrs Ansley,

with so slight a stress on the 'me' that Mrs Slade, though she noticed it, wondered if it were not merely accidental, like the random underlinings of old-fashioned letter writers.

'Grace Ansley was always old-fashioned,' she thought; and added aloud, with a retrospective smile: 'It's a view we've both been familiar with for a good many years. When we first met here we were younger than our girls are now. You remember?'

'Oh, yes, I remember,' murmured Mrs Ansley, with the same undefinable stress. 'There's that head waiter wondering,' she interpolated.

She was evidently far less sure than her companion of herself and of her rights in the world.

'I'll cure him of wondering,' said Mrs Slade, stretching her hand toward a bag as discreetly opulent-looking as Mrs Ansley's. Signing to the head waiter, she explained that she and her friend were old lovers of Rome, and would like to spend the end of the afternoon looking down on the view – that is, if it did not disturb the service? The headwaiter, bowing over her gratuity, assured her that the ladies were most welcome, and would be still more so if they would condescend to remain for dinner. A full moon night, they would remember. . . .

Mrs Slade's black brows drew together, as though references to the moon were out of place and even unwelcome. But she smiled away her frown as the headwaiter retreated. 'Well, why not? We might do worse. There's no knowing, I suppose, when the girls will be back. Do you even know back from *where*? I don't!'

Mrs Ansley again coloured slightly. 'I think those young Italian aviators we met at the Embassy invited them to fly to Tarquinia for tea. I suppose they'll want to wait and fly back by moonlight.'

'Moonlight – moonlight! What a part it still plays. Do you suppose they're as sentimental as we were?'

'I've come to the conclusion that I don't in the least know what they are,' said Mrs Ansley. 'And perhaps we didn't know much more about each other.'

'No, perhaps we didn't.'

Her friend gave her a shy glance. 'I never should have supposed you were sentimental, Alida.'

'Well, perhaps I wasn't.' Mrs Slade drew her lids together in retrospect; and for a few moments the two ladies, who had been intimate since childhood, reflected how little they knew each other. Each one, of course, had a label ready to attach to the other's name; Mrs Delphin Slade, for instance, would have told herself, or anyone who asked her, that Mrs Horace Ansley, twenty-five years ago, had been exquisitely lovely – no, you wouldn't believe it, would you, though, of course, still charming, distinguished. . . . Well, as a girl she had been exquisite; far more beautiful than her daughter, Barbara, though certainly Babs, according to the new standards at any rate, was more effective – had more *edge*, as they say. Funny where she got it, with those two nullities as parents. Yes; Horace Ansley was – well, just the duplicate of his wife. Museum specimens of old New York. Good-looking, irreproachable, exemplary. Mrs Slade and Mrs Ansley had lived opposite each other – actually as well as figuratively –

for years. When the drawing room curtains in No. 20 East 73rd Street were renewed, No. 23, across the way, was always aware of it. And of all the movings, buyings, travels, anniversaries, illnesses – the tame chronicle of an estimable pair. Little of it escaped Mrs Slade. But she had grown bored with it by the time her husband made his big *coup* in Wall Street, and when they bought in upper Park Avenue had already begun to think: 'I'd rather live opposite a speakeasy for a change; at least one might see it raided.' The idea of seeing Grace raided was so amusing that (before the move) she launched it at a woman's lunch. It made a hit, and went the rounds – she sometimes wondered if it had crossed the street, and reached Mrs Ansley. She hoped not, but didn't much mind. Those were the days when respectability was at a discount, and it did the irreproachable no harm to laugh at them a little.

A few years later, and not many months apart, both ladies lost their husbands. There was an appropriate exchange of wreaths and condolences, and a brief renewal of intimacy in the half-shadow of their mourning; and now, after another interval, they had run across each other in Rome, at the same hotel, each of them the modest appendage of a salient daughter. The similarity of their lot had again drawn them together, lending itself to mild jokes, and the mutual confession that, if in old days it must have been tiring to 'keep up' with daughters, it was now, at times, a little dull not to.

No doubt, Mrs Slade reflected, she felt her unemployment more than poor Grace ever would. It was a big drop from being the wife of Delphin Slade to being his widow. She had always regarded herself (with a certain conjugal pride) as his equal in social gifts, as contributing her full share to the making of the exceptional couple they were: but the difference after his death was irremediable. As the wife of the famous corporation lawyer, always with an international case or two on hand, every day brought its exciting and unexpected obligation: the impromptu entertaining of eminent colleagues from abroad, the hurried dashes on legal business to London, Paris or Rome, where the entertaining was so handsomely reciprocated; the amusement of hearing in her wakes: 'What, that handsome woman with the good clothes and the eyes is Mrs Slade – *the* Slade's wife? Really? Generally the wives of celebrities are such frumps.'

Yes; being *the* Slade's widow was a dullish business after that. In living up to such a husband all her faculties had been engaged; now she had only her daughter to live up to, for the son who seemed to have inherited his father's gifts had died suddenly in boyhood. She had fought through that agony because her husband was there, to be helped and to help; now, after the father's death, the thought of the boy had become unbearable. There was nothing left but to mother her daughter; and dear Jenny was such a perfect daughter that she needed no excessive mothering. 'Now with Babs Ansley I don't know that I *should* be so quiet,' Mrs Slade sometimes half-enviously reflected; but Jenny, who was younger than her brilliant friend, was that rare accident, an extremely pretty girl who somehow made youth and prettiness seem as safe as their absence. It was all perplexing – and to Mrs Slade a little boring. She wished that Jenny would fall in love –

with the wrong man, even; that she might have to be watched, out-manoeuvred, rescued. And instead, it was Jenny who watched her mother, kept her out of draughts, made sure that she had taken her tonic . . .

Mrs Ansley was much less articulate than her friend, and her mental portrait of Mrs Slade was slighter, and drawn with fainter touches. 'Alida Slade's awfully brilliant; but not as brilliant as she thinks,' would have summed it up; though she would have added, for the enlightenment of strangers, that Mrs Slade had been an extremely dashing girl; much more so than her daughter, who was pretty, of course, and clever in a way, but had none of her mother's – well, 'vividness', someone had once called it. Mrs Ansley would take up current words like this, and cite them in quotation marks, as unheard-of audacities. No; Jenny was not like her mother. Sometimes Mrs Ansley thought Alida Slade was disappointed; on the whole she had had a sad life. Full of failures and mistakes; Mrs Ansley had always been rather sorry for her. . . .

So these two ladies visualised each other, each through the wrong end of her little telescope.

For a long time they continued to sit side by side without speaking. It seemed as though, to both, there was a relief in laying down their somewhat futile activities in the presence of the vast Memento Mori which faced them. Mrs Slade sat quite still, her eyes fixed on the golden slope of the Palace of the Caesars, and after a while Mrs Ansley ceased to fidget with her bag, and she too sank into meditation. Like many intimate friends, the two ladies had never before had occasion to be silent together, and Mrs Ansley was slightly embarrassed by what seemed, after so many years, a new stage in their intimacy, and one with which she did not yet know how to deal.

Suddenly the air was full of that deep clangour of bells which periodically covers Rome with a roof of silver. Mrs Slade glanced at her wristwatch. 'Five o'clock already,' she said, as though surprised.

Mrs Ansley suggested interrogatively: 'There's bridge at the Embassy at five.' For a long time Mrs Slade did not answer. She appeared to be lost in contemplation, and Mrs Ansley thought the remark had escaped her. But after a while she said, as if speaking out of a dream: 'Bridge, did you say? Not unless you want to. . . . But I don't think I will, you know.'

'Oh, no,' Mrs Ansley hastened to assure her. 'I don't care to at all. It's so lovely here; and so full of old memories, as you say.' She settled herself in her chair, and almost furtively drew forth her knitting. Mrs Slade took sideways note of this activity, but her own beautifully cared-for hands remained motionless on her knee.

'I was just thinking,' she said slowly, 'what different things Rome stands for to each generation of travellers. To our grandmothers, Roman fever; to our mothers, sentimental dangers – how we used to be guarded! – to our daughters, no more dangers than the middle of Main Street. They don't know it – but how much they're missing!'

The long golden light was beginning to pale, and Mrs Ansley lifted her knitting a little closer to her eyes. 'Yes, how we were guarded.'

'I always used to think,' Mrs Slade continued, 'that our mothers had a much more difficult job than our grandmothers. When Roman fever stalked the streets it must have been comparatively easy to gather in the girls at the danger hour; but when you and I were young, with such beauty calling us, and the spice of disobedience thrown in, and no worse risk than catching cold during the cool hour after sunset, the mothers used to be put to it to keep us in – didn't they?'

She turned again toward Mrs Ansley, but the latter had reached a delicate point in her knitting. 'One, two, three – slip two; yes, they must have been,' she assented, without looking up.

Mrs Slade's eyes rested on her with a deepened attention. 'She can knit – in the face of *this*! How like her. . . .'

Mrs Slade leaned back, brooding, her eyes ranging from the ruins which faced her to the long green hollow of the Forum, the fading glow of the church fronts beyond it, and the outlying immensity of the Colosseum. Suddenly she thought: 'It's all very well to say that our girls have done away with sentiment and moonlight. But if Babs Ansley isn't out to catch that young aviator – the one who's a Marchese – then I don't know anything. And Jenny has no chance beside her. I know that too. I wonder if that's why Grace Ansley likes the two girls to go everywhere together! My poor Jenny as a foil – !' Mrs Slade gave a hardly audible laugh, and at the sound Mrs Ansley dropped her knitting.

'Yes – ?'

'I – oh, nothing. I was only thinking how your Babs carries everything before her. That Campolieri boy is one of the best matches in Rome. Don't look so innocent, my dear – you know he is. And I was wondering, ever so respectfully, you understand . . . wondering how two such exemplary characters as you and Horace had managed to produce anything quite so dynamic.' Mrs Slade laughed again, with a touch of asperity.

Mrs Ansley's hands lay inert across her needles. She looked straight out at the great accumulated wreckage of passion and splendour at her feet. But her small profile was almost expressionless. At length she said, 'I think you overrate Babs, my dear.'

Mrs Slade's tone grew easier. 'No; I don't. I appreciate her. And perhaps envy you. Oh, my girl's perfect; if I were a chronic invalid I'd – well, I think I'd rather be in Jenny's hands. There must be times . . . but there! I always wanted a brilliant daughter . . . and never quite understood why I got an angel instead.'

Mrs Ansley echoed her laugh in a faint murmur. 'Babs is an angel too.'

'Of course – of course! But she's got rainbow wings. Well, they're wandering by the sea with their young men; and here we sit . . . and it all brings back the past a little too acutely.'

Mrs Ansley had resumed her knitting. One might almost have imagined (if one had known her less well, Mrs Slade reflected) that, for her also, too many memories rose from the lengthening shadows of those august ruins. But no; she was simply absorbed in her work. What was there for her to worry about? She knew that Babs would almost certainly come back engaged to the extremely eligible Campolieri. 'And she'll sell the New York house, and settle down near them in Rome, and never be in their way . . . she's much too tactful. But she'll have an excellent cook, and just the right people in for bridge and cocktails . . . and a perfectly peaceful old age among her grandchildren.'

Mrs Slade broke off this prophetic flight with a recoil of self-disgust. There was no one of whom she had less right to think unkindly than of Grace Ansley. Would she never cure herself of envying her! Perhaps she had begun too long ago.

She stood up and leaned against the parapet, filling her troubled eyes with the tranquilising magic of the hour. But instead of tranquilising her the sight seemed to increase her exasperation. Her gaze turned toward the Colosseum. Already its golden flank was drowned in purple shadow, and above it the sky curved crystal clear, without light or colour. It was the moment when afternoon and evening hang balanced in midheaven.

Mrs Slade turned back and laid her hand on her friend's arm. The gesture was so abrupt that Mrs Ansley looked up, startled.

'The sun's set. You're not afraid, my dear?'

'Afraid – ?'

'Of Roman fever or pneumonia? I remember how ill you were that winter. As a girl you had a very delicate throat, hadn't you?'

'Oh, we're all right up here. Down below, in the Forum, it does get deathly cold, all of a sudden . . . but not here.'

'Ah, of course you know because you had to be so careful.' Mrs Slade turned back to the parapet. She thought: 'I must make one more effort not to hate her.' Aloud she said: 'Whenever I look at the Forum from up here, I remember that story about a great-aunt of yours, wasn't she? A dreadfully wicked great-aunt?'

'Oh, yes; Great-aunt Harriet. The one who was supposed to have sent her young sister out to the Forum after sunset to gather a night-blooming flower for her album. All our great-aunts and grandmothers used to have albums of dried flowers.'

Mrs Slade nodded. 'But she really sent her because they were in love with the same man –'

'Well, that was the family tradition. They said Aunt Harriet confessed it years afterward. At any rate, the poor little sister caught the fever and died. Mother used to frighten us with the story when we were children.'

'And you frightened *me* with it, that winter when you and I were here as girls. The winter I was engaged to Delphin.'

Mrs Ansley gave a faint laugh. 'Oh, did I? Really frightened you? I don't believe you're easily frightened.'

'Not often; but I was then. I was easily frightened because I was too happy. I wonder if you know what that means?'

'I – yes . . .' Mrs Ansley faltered.

'Well, I suppose that was why the story of your wicked aunt made such an impression on me. And I thought: "There's no more Roman fever, but the Forum is deathly cold after sunset – especially after a hot day. And the Colosseum's even colder and damper."'

‘The Colosseum – ?’

‘Yes. It wasn’t easy to get in, after the gates were locked for the night. Far from easy. Still, in those days it could be managed; it was managed, often. Lovers met there who couldn’t meet elsewhere. You knew that?’

‘I – I dare say. I don’t remember.’

‘You don’t remember? You don’t remember going to visit some ruins or other one evening, just after dark, and catching a bad chill? You were supposed to have gone to see the moon-rise. People always said that expedition was what caused your illness.’

There was a moment’s silence; then Mrs Ansley rejoined: ‘Did they? It was all so long ago.’

‘Yes. And you got well again – so it didn’t matter. But I suppose it struck your friends – the reason given for your illness, I mean – because everybody knew you were so prudent on account of your throat, and your mother took such care of you. . . . You *had* been out late sightseeing, hadn’t you, that night?’

‘Perhaps I had. The most prudent girls aren’t always prudent. What made you think of it now?’

Mrs Slade seemed to have no answer ready. But after a moment she broke out: ‘Because I simply can’t bear it any longer –’

Mrs Ansley lifted her head quickly. Her eyes were wide and very pale. ‘Can’t bear what?’

‘Why – your not knowing that I’ve always known why you went.’

‘Why I went – ?’

'Yes. You think I'm bluffing, don't you? Well, you went to meet the man I was engaged to – and I can repeat every word of the letter that took you there.'

While Mrs Slade spoke Mrs Ansley had risen unsteadily to her feet. Her bag, her knitting and gloves, slid in a panic-stricken heap to the ground. She looked at Mrs Slade as though she were looking at a ghost.

'No, no – don't,' she faltered out.

'Why not? Listen, if you don't believe me. "My one darling, things can't go on like this. I must see you alone. Come to the Colosseum immediately after dark tomorrow. There will be somebody to let you in. No one whom you need fear will suspect" – but perhaps you've forgotten what the letter said?'

Mrs Ansley met the challenge with an unexpected composure. Steadying herself against the chair she looked at her friend, and replied: 'No; I know it by heart too.'

'And the signature? "Only *your* DS." Was that it? I'm right, am I? That was the letter that took you out that evening after dark?'

Mrs Ansley was still looking at her. It seemed to Mrs Slade that a slow struggle was going on behind the voluntarily controlled mask of her small quiet face. 'I shouldn't have thought she had herself so well in hand,' Mrs Slade reflected, almost resentfully. But at this moment Mrs Ansley spoke. 'I don't know how you knew. I burned that letter at once.'

'Yes; you would, naturally – you're so prudent!' The sneer was open now. 'And if you burned the letter you're wondering how on earth I know what was in it. That's it, isn't it?'

Mrs Slade waited, but Mrs Ansley did not speak.

'Well, my dear, I know what was in that letter because I wrote it!'

'You wrote it?'

'Yes.'

The two women stood for a minute staring at each other in the last golden light. Then Mrs Ansley dropped back into her chair. 'Oh,' she murmured, and covered her face with her hands.

Mrs Slade waited nervously for another word or movement. None came, and at length she broke out: 'I horrify you.'

Mrs Ansley's hands dropped to her knees. The face they uncovered was streaked with tears. 'I wasn't thinking of you. I was thinking – it was the only letter I ever had from him!'

'And I wrote it. Yes; I wrote it! But I was the girl he was engaged to. Did you happen to remember that?'

Mrs Ansley's head drooped again. 'I'm not trying to excuse myself . . . I remembered . . .'

'And still you went?'

'Still I went.'

Mrs Slade stood looking down on the small bowed figure at her side. The flame of her wrath had already sunk, and she wondered why she had ever thought there would be any satisfaction in inflicting so purposeless a wound on her friend. But she had to justify herself.

'You do understand? I'd found out – and I hated you, hated you. I knew you were in love with Delphin – and I was afraid; afraid of you, of your quiet ways, your sweetness . . . your . . .

well, I wanted you out of the way, that's all. Just for a few weeks; just till I was sure of him. So in a blind fury I wrote that letter . . . I don't know why I'm telling you now.'

'I suppose,' said Mrs Ansley slowly, 'it's because you've always gone on hating me.'

'Perhaps. Or because I wanted to get the whole thing off my mind.' She paused. 'I'm glad you destroyed the letter. Of course I never thought you'd die.'

Mrs Ansley relapsed into silence, and Mrs Slade, leaning above her, was conscious of a strange sense of isolation, of being cut off from the warm current of human communion. 'You think me a monster!'

'I don't know . . . It was the only letter I had, and you say he didn't write it.'

'Ah, how you care for him still!'

'I cared for that memory,' said Mrs Ansley.

Mrs Slade continued to look down on her. She seemed physically reduced by the blow – as if, when she got up, the wind might scatter her like a puff of dust. Mrs Slade's jealousy suddenly leaped up again at the sight. All these years the woman had been living on that letter. How she must have loved him, to treasure the mere memory of its ashes! The letter of the man her friend was engaged to. Wasn't it she who was the monster?

'You tried your best to get him away from me, didn't you? But you failed; and I kept him. That's all.'

'Yes. That's all.'

'I wish now I hadn't told you. I'd no idea you'd feel about it as you do; I thought you'd be amused. It all happened so long ago, as you say; and you must do me the justice to remember that I had no reason to think you'd ever taken it seriously. How could I, when you were married to Horace Ansley two months afterward? As soon as you could get out of bed your mother rushed you off to Florence and married you. People were rather surprised – they wondered at its being done so quickly; but I thought I knew. I had an idea you did it out of *pique* – to be able to say you'd got ahead of Delphin and me. Kids have such silly reasons for doing the most serious things. And your marrying so soon convinced me that you'd never really cared.'

'Yes. I suppose it would,' Mrs Ansley assented.

The clear heaven overhead was emptied of all its gold. Dusk spread over it, abruptly darkening the Seven Hills. Here and there lights began to twinkle through the foliage at their feet. Steps were coming and going on the deserted terrace – waiters looking out of the doorway at the head of the stairs, then reappearing with trays and napkins and flasks of wine. Tables were moved, chairs straightened. A feeble string of electric lights flickered out. A stout lady in a dustcoat suddenly appeared, asking in broken Italian if anyone had seen the elastic band which held together her tattered Baedeker. She poked with her stick under the table at which she had lunched, the waiters assisting.

The corner where Mrs Slade and Mrs Ansley sat was still shadowy and deserted. For a long time neither of them spoke. At length Mrs Slade began again: 'I suppose I did it as a sort of joke –'

'A joke?'

‘Well, girls are ferocious sometimes, you know. Girls in love especially. And I remember laughing to myself all that evening at the idea that you were waiting around there in the dark, dodging out of sight, listening for every sound, trying to get in – of course I was upset when I heard you were so ill afterward.’

Mrs Ansley had not moved for a long time. But now she turned slowly toward her companion. ‘But I didn’t wait. He’d arranged everything. He was there. We were let in at once,’ she said.

Mrs Slade sprang up from her leaning position. ‘Delphin there? They let you in? Ah, now you’re lying!’ she burst out with violence.

Mrs Ansley’s voice grew clearer, and full of surprise. ‘But of course he was there. Naturally he came –’

‘Came? How did he know he’d find you there? You must be raving!’

Mrs Ansley hesitated, as though reflecting. ‘But I answered the letter. I told him I’d be there. So he came.’

Mrs Slade flung her hands up to her face. ‘Oh, God – you answered! I never thought of your answering. . . .’

‘It’s odd you never thought of it, if you wrote the letter.’

‘Yes. I was blind with rage.’

Mrs Ansley rose, and drew her fur scarf about her. ‘It is cold here. We’d better go. . . . I’m sorry for you,’ she said, as she clasped the fur about her throat.

The unexpected words sent a pang through Mrs Slade. ‘Yes; we’d better go.’ She gathered up her bag and cloak. ‘I don’t know why you should be sorry for me,’ she muttered.

Mrs Ansley stood looking away from her toward the dusky

mass of the Colosseum. 'Well – because I didn't have to wait that night.'

Mrs Slade gave an unquiet laugh. 'Yes, I was beaten there. But I oughtn't to begrudge it to you, I suppose. At the end of all these years. After all, I had everything; I had him for twenty-five years. And you had nothing but that one letter that he didn't write.'

Mrs Ansley was again silent. At length she took a step toward the door of the terrace, and turned back, facing her companion.

'I had Barbara,' she said, and began to move ahead of Mrs Slade toward the stairway.

DIMANCHE

Irène Némirovsky

(1934)

In Rue Las Cases it was as quiet as during the height of summer, and every open window was screened by a yellow blind. The fine weather had returned: it was the first Sunday of spring, a warm and restless day that took people out of their houses and out of the city. The sky glowed with a gentle radiance. The birds in Place Sainte-Clotilde chirped lazily, while the raucous screeching of cars leaving for the country echoed in the peaceful streets. The only cloud in the sky was a delicately curled white shell that floated upwards for a moment, then melted into the ether. People raised their heads with surprise and anticipation; they sniffed the air and smiled.

Agnès half closed the shutters: the sun was hot and the roses would open too quickly and die. Nanette ran in and stood hopping from one foot to the other.

'May I go out, Mother? It's such nice weather.'

Mass was almost over. The children were already coming down the street in their bright sleeveless dresses, holding their prayer books in their white-gloved hands and clustering round a little girl who had just taken her first communion. Her round cheeks were pink and shining under her veil. A procession of bare legs, all pink and gold, as downy as the skin of a peach, sparkled in the sunshine. The bells were still ringing, slowly and sadly as if to say: 'Off you go, good people, we are sorry not to be able to keep you any longer. We have sheltered you for as long as we could, but now we have to give you back to the world and to your everyday life. Time to go. Mass is over.'

The bells fell silent. The smell of hot bread filled the street, wafting up from the open bakery; you could see the freshly washed floor gleaming, and the narrow mirrors on the walls glinting faintly in the shadows. Then everyone had gone home.

Agnès said: 'Nanette, go and see if Papa is ready, and tell Nadine that lunch is on the table.'

Guillaume came in, radiating the scent of lavender water and good cigars which always made her feel slightly nauseated. He seemed even more high-spirited, healthy and plump than usual.

As soon as they had sat down, he announced: 'I'll be going out after lunch. When you've been suffocating in Paris all week, it's the least . . . Are you really not tempted?'

'I don't want to leave the little one.'

Nanette was sitting opposite him and Guillaume smiled at her and tweaked her hair. The previous night she had had a temperature, but so slight that her fresh complexion showed no sign of pallor.

'She's not really ill. She has a good appetite.'

'Oh, I'm not worried, thank God,' said Agnès. 'I'll let her go out until four o'clock. Where are you going?'

Guillaume's face visibly clouded over. 'I . . . oh, I don't know yet . . . you always want to organise things in advance . . . somewhere around Fontainebleau or Chartres, I'll see, wherever I end up. So? Will you come with me?'

'I'd love to see the look on his face if I agreed,' thought Agnès. The set smile on her lips annoyed her husband. But she answered, as she always did: 'I've got things to do at home.'

She thought, 'Who is it this time?'

Guillaume's mistresses: her jealousy, her anxiety, the sleepless nights, were now in the long distant past. He was tall and overweight, going bald, his whole body solidly balanced, his head firmly planted on a thick, strong neck. He was forty-five, the age at which men are at their most powerful, dominant and self-confident, the blood coursing thickly through their veins. When he laughed he thrust his jaw forward, to reveal a row of nearly perfect white teeth.

'Which one of them told him, "You look like a wolf or a wild animal when you smile"?' wondered Agnès. 'He must have been incredibly flattered. He never used to laugh like that.'

She remembered how he used to weep in her arms every time a love affair ended, gulping as if he was trying to inhale his tears. Poor Guillaume . . .

'Well, I . . .' said Nadine.

She started each sentence like that. It was impossible to detect a single word or a single idea in anything she thought or said that did not relate to herself, her clothes, her friends, the ladders in her stockings, her pocket money, her own pleasure. She was . . . triumphant. Her skin had the pale, velvety brightness of jasmine and of camellias, and you could see the blood beating just beneath the surface: it rose girlishly in her cheeks, swelling her lips so that it looked as though a pink, heady wine was about to gush from them. Her green eyes sparkled.

'She's twenty,' thought Agnès, trying, as so often, to keep her eyes closed and not to be wounded by her daughter's almost overwhelming beauty, the peals of laughter, the egoism, the fervour, the diamond-like hardness. 'She's twenty years old, it's not her fault . . . Life will tame her, soften her, make her grow up.'

'Mother, may I take your red scarf? I won't lose it. And, Mother, may I come back late?'

'And where are you going?'

'Mother, you know perfectly well! To Chantal Aumont's house in Saint-Cloud. Arlette is coming to fetch me. May I come home late? After eight o'clock, anyway? You won't be angry? Then I won't have to go through Saint-Cloud at seven o'clock on a Sunday evening.'

'She's quite right,' said Guillaume.

Lunch was nearly over. Mariette was serving the meal quickly. Sunday . . . As soon as the washing-up was done, she too would be going out.

They ate orange-flavoured crêpes; Agnès had helped Mariette make the batter.

'Delicious,' said Guillaume appreciatively.

The clattering of dishes could be heard through the open windows: it was only a faint sound from the dark ground-floor flat where two spinsters lived in the gloom, but was louder and livelier in the house across the way where there was a table laid for twelve with the place settings gleaming on the neat folds of the damask tablecloth, and a basket of white roses for a first communion decorating the centre.

'I'm going to get ready, Mother. I don't want any coffee.'

Guillaume swallowed his quickly and silently. Mariette began to clear the table.

'What a hurry they're in,' thought Agnès, as her thin, skilful hands deftly folded Nanette's napkin. 'Only I . . .'

She was the only one for whom this wonderful Sunday held no attraction.

'I never imagined she'd become so stay-at-home and dull,' thought Guillaume as he looked at her. He took a deep inward breath and, proudly conscious of the sense of vigour that surged through his body, felt his chest expand with the fine weather. 'I'm in rather good shape, holding up surprisingly well,' he thought, as his mind turned to all the reasons (the political crisis, money worries, the taxes he owed, Germaine – who cramped his style, devil take her) why he could justifiably feel as miserable and depressed as anyone else. But on the contrary! 'I've always been the same. A ray of sunshine, the prospect of a Sunday away from Paris, a nice bottle of wine, freedom, a pretty woman at my side – and I'm twenty again! I'm alive,' he congratulated himself, looking at his wife with veiled hostility; her cold beauty and the tense, mocking line of her lips irritated him. He said aloud: 'Of course, I'll telephone you if I spend the night in Chartres. In any case, I'll be back tomorrow morning, and I'll drop in at home before I go to the office.'

Agnès thought, with a strange, weary detachment, 'One day, after a lavish lunch, just as he's kissing the woman he's with, the car he's driving will crash into a tree. I'll get a phone call from Senlis or Auxerre.' Will you suffer? she demanded curiously of the mute, invisible image of herself waiting in the shadows. But the image, silent and indifferent, did not reply, and the powerful silhouette of Guillaume came between it and her.

'See you soon, darling.'

'See you soon, dear.'

Then Guillaume was gone.

'Shall I lay tea in the drawing-room, madame?' asked Mariette.

'No, I'll do it. You may go as soon as you've tidied the kitchen.'

'Thank you, madame,' said the girl, blushing fiercely as if she was near a blazing fire. 'Thank you, madame,' she repeated, with a dreamy expression that made Agnès shrug sardonically.

Agnès stroked Nanette's smooth, black hair, as the little girl first hid in the folds of her dress and then poked her head out giggling.

'We'll be perfectly happy, just the two of us, sweetheart.'

Meanwhile, in her room, Nadine was quickly changing her clothes, powdering her neck, her bare arms, and the curve of her breast where, unseen in the car, Rémi had placed his dry, passionate lips, caressing her with quick, burning kisses.

Half-past two . . . Arlette had still not arrived. 'With Arlette here, Mother won't suspect anything.' The rendezvous was at three. 'To think that Mother doesn't notice anything. And she was young once . . .' she thought, trying in vain to imagine her mother's youth, her engagement and her early married life.

'She must always have been like this. Everything calm, orderly, wearing those white lawn collars . . . "Guillaume, don't spoil my roses." Whereas, I . . .'

She shivered, gently biting her lips as she looked at herself in the mirror. Nothing gave her more pleasure than her body, her eyes, her face, and the shape of her young, white neck as straight as a column. 'It's wonderful to be twenty,' she thought fervently. 'Do all young women feel like me, do they relish their happiness, their energy, the fire in their blood? Do they feel these things as fiercely and deeply as I do? For a woman, being twenty in 1934 is . . . is incredible,' she told herself. She summoned up disjointed memories of nights on a campsite, coming back at dawn in Rémi's car (and there were her parents thinking she was on an innocent trip with her friends on the Île Saint-Louis, watching the sun rise over the Seine), skiing, swimming, the pure air and cold water on her body, Rémi digging his nails into her neck, gently pulling back her short hair . . . 'And my parents are blind to it all! I suppose in their day . . . I can imagine my mother at my age, at her first ball, her eyes modestly lowered. Rémi . . . I'm in love,' she told her reflection, smiling into the mirror. 'But I must be careful of him – he's so good-looking and so sure of himself, he's been spoilt by women, by flattery. He must like making people suffer.'

‘But then, we’ll see who’ll be the strongest,’ she muttered, as she nervously clenched her fists, feeling her love pounding in her heart, making her long to take part in this game of cruelty and passion.

She laughed out loud. And her laugh rang out so clearly and arrogantly in the silence that she stopped to listen, as if enchanted by the beauty of a rare and perfect musical instrument.

‘There are times when I think I’m in love with myself more than anything else,’ she thought, as she put on her green necklace, every bead of which gleamed and reflected the sun. Her smooth, firm skin had the brilliant glow of young animals, flowers, or blossom in May, a glossiness that is fleeting but completely perfect. ‘I shall never be as beautiful again.’

She sprayed perfume on her face and shoulders, deliberately wasting it; today anything sparkling and extravagant suited her! ‘I’d love a bright red dress and gypsy jewellery.’ She thought of her mother’s tender, weary voice: ‘Moderation in all things, Nadine!’

‘The old!’ she thought contemptuously.

In the street Arlette’s car had stopped outside the house. Nadine grabbed her bag and, cramming her beret on her head as she ran, shouted ‘Goodbye, Mother’ and disappeared.

‘I want you to have a little rest on the sofa, Nanette. You slept so badly last night. I’ll sit next to you and do some work,’ said Agnès. ‘Then you may go out with mademoiselle.’

Nanette rolled her pink smock in her fingers for a while, rubbed her face against the cushions as she turned over and over, yawned, and went to sleep. She was five and, like Agnès, had the pale, fresh complexion of someone fair-haired, yet had black hair and dark eyes.

Agnès sat down quietly next to her. The house was sleeping silently. Outside, the smell of coffee hung in the air. The room was flooded with a soft, warm, yellow light. Agnès heard Mariette carefully close the kitchen door and walk through the flat; she listened to her footsteps fading away down the back stairs. She sighed: a strange, melancholy happiness and a delicious feeling of peace overcame her. Silence fell over the empty rooms and she knew that nobody would disturb her until evening; not a single footstep, nor any unknown voice would find its way into the house, her refuge . . . The street was empty and quiet. There was only an invisible woman playing the piano, hidden behind her closed shutters. Then all was quiet. At that very moment Mariette, clutching her Sunday imitation pigskin bag in her large, bare hands, was hurrying to the station where her lover was waiting for her, and Guillaume, in the woods at Compiègne, was saying to the fat, blonde woman sitting next to him: 'It's easy to blame me, I'm not really a bad husband, but my wife . . .' Nadine was in Arlette's little green car, driving past the gates of the Luxembourg Gardens. The chestnut trees were in flower. Children ran about in little sleeveless knitted tops. Arlette was thinking bitterly that nobody was waiting for her; nobody loved her. Her friends put up with her because of her precious green car and, behind their horn-rimmed glasses, her round eyes made mothers trust her. Lucky Nadine!

A sharp wind was blowing; the water from the fountains splashed sideways, covering passers-by with spray. The saplings in Place Sainte-Clotilde swayed gently.

'It's so peaceful,' thought Agnès.

She smiled; neither her husband nor her elder daughter had ever seen this rare, slow, confident smile on her lips.

She got up and quietly went to change the water for the roses; carefully she cut their stems; they were gradually coming into flower although their petals seemed to be opening reluctantly, fearfully, as if with some kind of divine modesty.

'How lovely it is here,' she thought.

Her house was a refuge, a warm enclosed shell sealed against the noise outside. When, in the wintry dusk, she walked along the Rue Las Cases, an island of shadows, and saw the stone sculpture of the smiling woman above the door, that sweet, familiar face decorated with narrow, carved ribbons, she felt oddly relaxed and peaceful, floating in waves of happiness and calm. Her house . . . how she loved the delicious silence, the slight, furtive creaking of the furniture, the delicate inlaid tables shining palely in the gloom. She sat down; although she normally held herself so erect, now she curled up in an armchair.

'Guillaume says I like objects more than human beings . . . That may be true.'

Objects enfolded her in a gentle, wordless spell. The copper and tortoiseshell clock ticked slowly and peacefully in the silence.

The familiar musical clinking of a silver cup gleaming in

the shadows responded to her every movement, her every sigh, as if it were her friend.

Where do we find happiness? 'We pursue it, search for it, kill ourselves trying to find it, and all the time it's just here,' she said to herself. 'It comes just when we've stopped expecting anything, stopped hoping, stopped being afraid. Of course there is the children's health . . .' and she bent automatically to kiss Nanette's forehead. 'Fresh as a flower, thank God. It would be such a relief not to hope for anything any more. How I've changed,' she thought, remembering the past, her insane love for Guillaume, that little hidden square in Passy where she used to wait for him on spring evenings. She thought of his family, her hateful mother-in-law, the noise his sisters made in their miserable, gloomy drawing-room. 'Ah, I can never have enough silence!' She smiled, whispering as if the Agnès of an earlier time were sitting next to her, listening incredulously, her dark plaits framing her pale young face:

'Yes, aren't you surprised? I've changed, haven't I?'

She shook her head. In her memory every day in the past was rainy and sad, every effort was in vain, and every word that was uttered was either cruel or full of lies.

'Ah, how can one regret being in love? But, luckily, Nadine is not like me. Today's young girls are so cold, so unemotional. Nadine is a child, but even later on she'll never love or suffer as I did. So much the better, thank God, so much the better. And by the look of things Nanette will be like her sister.'

She smiled: it was strange to think that these smooth, chubby, pink cheeks and unformed features would turn into a woman's face. She put out a hand to stroke the fine black hair. 'These are the only moments when my soul is at peace,' she thought, remembering a childhood friend who used to say, 'my soul is at peace' as she half-closed her eyes and lit a cigarette. But Agnès did not smoke. And it was not that she liked to dream, more that she preferred to sit and occupy herself with some humdrum but specific task: she would sew or knit, stifle her thoughts, and force herself to stay calm and silent as she tidied books away or, one at a time, carefully washed and dried the Bohemian glassware, the tall, thin antique glasses with gold rims that they used for champagne. 'Yes, at twenty happiness seemed different to me, rather terrible and overwhelming; yet one's desires become easier to achieve once they have largely run their course,' she thought, as she picked up her sewing basket, with its piece of needlework, some silk thread, her thimble and her little gold scissors. 'What more does a woman need who is not in love with love?'

'Let me out here, Arlette, will you?' Nadine asked. It was three o'clock. 'I'll walk for a bit,' she said to herself, 'I don't want to get there first.'

Arlette did as she asked. Nadine jumped out of the car.

'Thank you, *chérie*.'

Arlette drove off. Nadine walked up the Rue de l'Odéon, forcing herself to slow down and suppress the excitement spreading through her body. 'I like being out in the street,' she thought, happily looking round at everything. 'I'm stifled at home. They can't understand that I'm young, I'm twenty years old, I can't stop myself singing, dancing, laughing, shouting.

It's because I'm full of joy.' The breeze, fanning her legs through the thin material of her dress, was delicious. She felt light, ethereal, floating: and just then it seemed to her that nothing could tether her to the ground. 'There are times when I could easily fly away,' she thought, buoyed up with hope. The world was so beautiful, so kind! The glare of the midday sun had softened and was turning into a pale, gentle glow; on every street corner women were holding out bunches of daffodils, offering them for sale to passers-by. Families were happily sitting outside the cafés, drinking fruit juice as they clustered round a little girl fresh from communion, her cheeks flushed, her eyes shining. Soldiers strolled slowly along, blocking the pavement, walking beside women dressed in black with large, red, bare hands. 'Nice,' said a boy walking past, blowing a kiss to Nadine as he eyed her. She laughed.

Sometimes love itself, even the image of Rémi, disappeared. There remained simply a feeling of exultation, and a feverish, piercing happiness, both of which were almost agonisingly unbearable.

'Love? Does Rémi love me?' she asked herself suddenly, as she reached the little bistro where he was due to meet her. 'What do I feel? We're mostly just friends, but what good is that? Friendship and trust are all right for old people. Even tenderness is not for us. Love, well that's something else.' She remembered the sharp pain that tender words and kisses sometimes seemed to conceal. She went inside.

The café was empty. The sun was shining. A clock on the wall ticked. The small inside room where she sat down smelt of wine and the dank air from the cellar.

He was not there. She felt her heart tighten slowly in her chest. 'I know it's quarter past three, but surely he would have waited for me?'

She ordered a drink.

Each time the door opened, each time a man's shadow appeared, her heart beat faster and she was filled with happiness; each time it was a stranger who came in, gave her a distracted look and went to sit down in the shadows. She clasped and unclasped her hands nervously under the table.

'But where can he be? Why doesn't he come?'

Then she lowered her head and continued to wait.

Inexorably, the clock struck every quarter of an hour. Staring at its hands, she waited without moving a muscle, as if complete silence, complete stillness, would somehow slow the passing of time. Three thirty. Three forty-five. That was nothing, one side or the other of the half hour made little difference, even when it was three forty, but if you said 'twenty to four, quarter to four', then you were lost, everything was ruined, gone for ever. He wasn't coming, he was laughing at her! Who was he with at that very moment? To whom was he saying: 'That Nadine Padouan? I've really taken her for a ride!' She felt sharp, bitter little tears prick her eyes. No, no, not that! Four o'clock. Her lips were trembling. She opened her bag and blew on her powder puff, the powder enveloping her in a stifling, perfumed cloud; as she looked in the little mirror she noticed that her face was quivering and distorted as if under water. 'No, I'm not going to cry,' she thought, savagely clenching her teeth together. With shaking hands she took out her lipstick and outlined her lips, then powdered the satin-smooth, bluish hollow under her eyes where, one day, the first wrinkle would appear. 'Why has he done this? Did he just want a kiss one evening, is that all?' For a moment she felt despairing and worthless. All the painful memories that are part of even a happy and secure childhood flooded into her mind: the undeserved slap her father had given her when she was twelve; the unfair teacher; those little English girls who, so long in the past, so long ago, had laughed at her and said, 'We won't play with you. We don't play with kids.'

'It hurts. I never knew it could hurt so much.'

She gave up watching the clock but stayed where she was, quite still. Where could she go? She felt safe here and comfortable. How many other women had waited like her, swallowing their tears like her, unthinkingly stroking the old imitation-leather banquette, warm and soft as an animal's coat? Then, all at once, she felt proud and strong again. What did any of it matter? 'I'm in agony, I'm unhappy.' Oh, what fine new words these were: love, unhappiness, desire. She rolled them silently on her lips.

'I want him to love me. I'm young and beautiful. He will love me, and if he doesn't, others will,' she muttered as she nervously clenched her hands, her nails as shining and sharp as claws.

Five o'clock . . . The dim little room suddenly shone like a furnace. The sun had moved round. It lit up the golden liqueur in her glass and the telephone booth opposite her.

'A phone call?' she thought feverishly. 'Maybe he's ill?'

'Oh, come on,' she said, with a furious shrug. She had spoken out loud; she shivered. 'What's the matter with me?'

She imagined him lying bleeding, dead in the road; he drives like a madman . . .

'Supposing I telephoned? No!' she murmured, acknowledging for the first time how weak and downcast she felt.

At the same time, deep down, a mysterious voice seemed to be whispering: 'Look. Listen. Remember. You'll never forget today. You'll grow old. But at the instant of your death you'll see that door opening, banging in the sunshine. You'll hear the clock chiming the quarters and the noise in the street.'

She stood up and went into the telephone booth, which smelt of dust and chalk; the walls were covered with scribbles. She looked for a long time at a drawing of a woman in the corner. At last she dialled Jasmin 10-32.

'Hello,' said a woman's voice, a voice she did not recognise.

'Is that Monsieur Rémi Alquier's apartment?' she asked, and she was struck by the sound of her words: her voice shook.

'Yes, who is it?'

Nadine said nothing; she could clearly hear a soft, lazy laugh and a voice calling out:

'Rémi, there's a young girl asking for you . . . What? Monsieur Alquier isn't in, mademoiselle.'

Slowly, Nadine hung up and went outside. It was six o'clock and the brightness of the May sunshine had faded; a sad, pale dusk had taken over. The smell of plants and freshly watered flowers rose from the Luxembourg Gardens. Nadine walked aimlessly down one street, then down another. She whistled quietly as she walked. The first lights were coming on in the houses, and although the streets were not yet dark, the first gas lamps were being lit: their flickering light shone through her tears.

In Rue Las Cases Agnès had put Nanette to bed; half-asleep, she was still talking quietly to herself, shyly confiding in her toys and the shadows in the room. As soon as she heard Agnès, however, she cautiously stopped.

'Already,' Agnès thought.

She went into the drawing-room. She walked across it without turning on the lights, and leant by the window. It was getting dark. She sighed. The spring day concealed a latent bitterness which seemed to emerge as evening came, just as sweet-smelling peaches can leave a sour taste in the mouth. Where was Guillaume? 'He probably won't come back tonight. So much the better,' she said to herself, as she thought of her cool, empty bed. She touched the cold window. How many times had she waited like this for Guillaume? Evening after evening, listening to the clock ticking in the silence and the creaking of the lift as it slowly went up, up, past her door, and then back down. Evening after evening, at first in despair, then with resignation, then with a heavy and deadly indifference. And now? Sadly, she shrugged her shoulders.

The street was empty and a bluish mist seemed to float over everything, as if a fine shower of ash had begun to fall gently from the overcast sky. The golden star of a street lamp lit up the shadows, and the towers of Sainte-Clotilde looked as if they were retreating and melting into the distance. A little car full of flowers, returning from the country, went past; there was just enough light to see bunches of daffodils tied onto the headlights. Concierges sat outside on their wicker chairs, hands folded loosely in their laps, not talking. Shutters were being closed at every window and only the faint pink light of a lamp could be glimpsed through the slats.

'In the old days,' remembered Agnès, 'when I was Nadine's age, I was already spending long hours waiting in vain for Guillaume.' She shut her eyes, trying to see him as he was then, or at least how he had seemed to her then. Had he been so handsome? So charming? My God, he had certainly been thinner than he was now, his face leaner and more expressive, with a beautiful mouth. His kisses . . . she let out a sad, bitter little laugh.

'How I loved him . . . the idiot I was . . . stupid idiot . . . He didn't say anything loving to me. He just used to kiss me, kiss me until my heart melted with sweetness and pain. For eighteen months he never once said "I love you", or "I want to marry you" . . . I always had to be there, at his feet. "At my disposal," he would say. And, fool that I was, I found pleasure in it. I was at that age when even defeat is intoxicating. And I would think: "He will love me. I will be his wife. If I give him enough devotion and love, he will love me."'

All of a sudden she had an extraordinarily precise vision of a spring evening long ago. But not a fine, mild one like this evening; it was one of those rainy, cold Parisian springs when heavy, icy showers start at dawn, streaming through the leafy trees. The chestnut trees in blossom, the long day and the warm air seem like a cruel joke. She was sitting on a bench in an empty square, waiting for him; the soaking box hedges gave off a bitter smell; the raindrops falling on the pond slowly, sadly marked the minutes drifting inexorably by. Cold tears ran down her cheeks. He wasn't coming. A woman had sat down next to her, looked at her without speaking, hunching her back against the rain and tightly pinching her lips together, as if thinking, 'Here's another one.'

She bowed her head a little, resting it on her arms as she used to do in the old days. A deep sadness overcame her.

'What is the matter with me? I am happy really; I feel very calm and peaceful. What's the good of remembering things? For heaven's sake, it will only make me resentful, and so pointlessly angry!'

And a picture came into her mind of her sitting in a taxi driving along the dark, wet avenues of the Bois de Boulogne; it was as if she could once again taste and smell the pure, cold air coming in through the open window, as Guillaume gently and cruelly felt her naked breast, as if he were squeezing the juice from a fruit. All those quarrels, reconciliations, bitter tears, lies, bad behaviour, and then that rush of sweet happiness when he touched her hand, laughing, as he said: 'Are you angry? I like making you suffer a bit.'

'That's all gone, it will never happen again,' she said aloud despairingly. And all at once, she was aware of tears pouring down her face. 'I want to suffer again.'

'To suffer, to despair, to long for someone! I have no one in the world left to wait for! I'm old. I hate this house,' she thought feverishly, 'and this peace and calm! But what about the children? Oh yes, the illusion of motherhood is the strongest and yet the most futile. Of course I love them, they're all I have in the world. But that's not enough. I want to rediscover those lost years, the suffering of the past. But at my age love would be unpleasant. I'd like to be twenty! Lucky Nadine! She's in Saint-Cloud, probably playing golf! She doesn't have to worry about love! Lucky Nadine!'

She started. She had not heard the door open, nor Nadine's footsteps on the carpet. Wiping her eyes, she said abruptly: 'Don't put the light on.'

Without replying, Nadine came to sit next to her. It was dark now. They did not look at each other.

After a while Agnès asked:

'Did you have a nice time, sweetheart?'

'Yes, thank you, Mother,' said Nadine.

'What time is it?'

'Almost seven, I think.'

'You've come back earlier than you thought,' Agnès said absent-mindedly.

Nadine did not answer, wordlessly tinkling the thin gold bracelets on her bare arms.

'How quiet she is,' Agnès thought, slightly surprised. She said aloud: 'What is it, sweetheart? Are you tired?'

'A bit.'

'You must go to bed early. Now go and wash, we're going to eat in five minutes. Don't make a noise in the hall, Nanette is asleep.'

As she spoke the telephone started ringing. Nadine suddenly looked up. Mariette appeared:

'It's for Miss Nadine.'

Nadine left the room, her heart pounding, conscious of her mother's eyes on her. She silently closed the door of the little office where the telephone was kept.

'Nadine? . . . It's me, Rémi . . . Oh, we are angry, are we? Look, forgive me . . . Don't be horrid . . . Well I'm saying sorry! There, there,' he said, as if coaxing a restive animal. 'Be kind to me, my sweet . . . What could I do? She was an old flame, I was being charitable. Ah, Nadine, you can't think the sweet nothings you give me are enough? Do you? Well, do you?' he repeated, as she heard the sweet, voluptuous sound of his laugh through his tightly closed lips. 'You must forgive me. It's true I don't dislike kissing you when you're cross, when your green eyes are blazing. I can see them now. They're smouldering, aren't they? How about tomorrow? Do you want to meet tomorrow at the same time? What? I swear I won't stand you up . . . What? You're not free? What a joke! Tomorrow? Same place, same time. I've said, I swear . . . Tomorrow?' he said again.

Nadine said:

'Tomorrow.'

He laughed:

'There's a good girl,' he said in English. 'Good little girlie. Bye bye.'

Nadine ran into the drawing-room. Her mother had not moved.

'What are you doing, Mother?' she cried, and her voice, her burst of laughter, made Agnès feel bitter and troubled, almost envious. 'It's dark in here!'

She put all the lights on. Her eyes, still wet with tears, were sparkling; a dark flush had spread over her cheeks. Humming to herself, she went up to the mirror and tidied her hair, smiling at her face, which was now alight with happiness, and at her quivering, parted lips.

'Well, you're happy all of a sudden,' Agnès said. She tried to laugh, but only a sad, grating little sound escaped her. She thought: 'I've been blind! The girl's in love! Ah, she has too much freedom, I'm too weak, that's what worries me.' But she recognised the bitterness, the suffering in her heart. She greeted it like an old friend: 'My God, I'm jealous!'

'Who was that on the telephone? You know perfectly well that your father doesn't like telephone calls from people we don't know, or these mysterious meetings.'

'I don't understand what you mean, Mother,' Nadine said, as she looked at her mother with bright, innocent eyes that made it impossible to read the secret thoughts within them: mother, the eternal enemy, pathetic in her old age, understanding nothing, seeing nothing, withdrawing into her shell, her only aim to stop youth from being alive! 'I really don't understand. It was only that the tennis match which should have happened on Saturday has been postponed until tomorrow. That's all.'

'That's all, is it!' Agnès said, and she was struck by how dry and harsh her own voice sounded.

She looked at Nadine. 'I'm mad. It must have been my remembering the past. She's still only a child.' For a moment she had a vision of a young girl with long black hair sitting in a desolate square in the mist and rain; she looked at her sadly and then banished her for ever from her mind.

Gently she touched Nadine's arm.

'Come along,' she said.

Nadine stifled a sardonic laugh. 'Will I be as . . . gullible, when I'm her age? And as placid? Lucky Mother,' she thought with gentle scorn. 'It must be wonderful to be so naïve and to have such an untroubled heart.'

THE PHOTOGRAPH

Phyllis Bentley

(1935)

'I shall say I'm twenty-nine,' said Miss Timperley recklessly. 'And I shall have my photograph specially taken.'

The slip before her read: 'Mrs Geoffrey Nash, Les Fougères, Olny-sur-Mer, wants by beginning of next month governess for two children, one eight, one six. Elder child rather backward. Applicants must know French. As personal interview impossible, send photograph. Excellent references *essential*.' 'Dear Miss Timperley,' said the Knowall Teachers' Agency, in a covering note: 'We think your French and your references may secure this post for you. Please apply direct to Mrs Nash.'

'My references,' said Miss Timperley proudly, 'are certainly what Mrs Nash requires. There is *no* difficulty about *them*.'

And, indeed, there was not; masses and masses of grateful letters from parents lay locked away in Miss Timperley's jewel-box. Jane improved so much in your care; Tommy has now quite caught up with other boys of his own age; Mary never has those tempers now; we shall always be grateful for your handling of John – oh, there was no difficulty about references, or about Miss Timperley's ability. It was other things which made difficulties: one other thing, to be exact. Miss Timperley sighed as she remembered what that other thing was.

She had been out of a job for three months now, since her last backward pupil had come triumphantly up to the mark and passed into a large girls' school; her bank balance was getting low, and somehow the outlook did not seem very bright. Usually Miss Timperley passed from one family to another, recommended as the person who had worked wonders with my sister-in-law's youngest, but this, quite by chance, did not happen this time, and Miss Timperley had been obliged to make the round of the agencies.

It was her reception there which had chilled her to the bone, lowered the hitherto dauntless flag of her courage. Her age? asked the agencies. Ah. Qualifications? Ah. Nobody wanted governesses nowadays, said the agencies, when these preliminaries were over; everybody sent their children to properly organised schools. And quite right too, agreed Miss Timperley; oh, they need not think she did not know all the advantages of work and play in common, she recommended school *always* for normal, healthy children; but there were some children, unluckier than the rest, who, by reason of some illness, perhaps, some misfortune, some accident of heredity or environment, were not suited to the hearty rough and tumble of school life, some children who needed special care. Those were the children, said Miss Timperley proudly, to whom she could be useful. 'M'yes,' said the agencies doubtfully, and made a note. Most people who wanted governessess nowadays, they continued, wanted *nursery* governesses, bright, jolly young things to nurse the baby and play with the children to keep them quiet. And even those, added the agencies, in a desponding tone, were usually specially trained nowadays.

'I am not a nursery governess,' said Miss Timperley, sitting very erect, with two spots of colour on her faded cheeks. 'The profession is an excellent one, no doubt, and has important duties; but it is not mine.'

'No – no,' agreed the agencies, even more doubtfully, and made another note. 'Still, that is the position, Miss Timperley. However,' said the agencies, rising, 'we have your name, Miss Timperley, and will let you know immediately if anything turns up. Are you on the telephone?'

No, Miss Timperley's modest bed-sitting room was not on the telephone; indeed, there was no telephone in all good Mrs Ladstone's house. But Miss Timperley would call at the agency every morning about eleven, and then, if anything had turned up . . .

But nothing ever had. And by and by Miss Timperley began to perceive that the agencies thought her rather old for her job. They talked so much about young nursery governesses who, or young qualified schoolteachers just out of the training college who, that some of the feeling they were too polite to put into words filtered through into Miss Timperley's by no means dull brain. At first she was indignant: the very idea! Then she began to wonder. She had already noticed how young most of the applicants she saw in the agencies were – really too young for any serious responsibility, she had thought, conscious of superior fitness. But were they really too young, or was she too old? She began to wonder. . . . And then one day the climax came. Something 'turned up' at one of the agencies, a post which would really suit her, they thought, said the agency with a bright, relieved air. Off went Miss Timperley joyously to an address in the suburbs, and had the door of a smallish house opened to her by a harassed, pretty girl – quite a child, thought Miss Timperley, far too young for so many household cares – with a baby in her arms and two other children clinging to her skirts. This young mother listened to Miss Timperley with a rather perplexed air, and then suddenly exclaimed:

'Oh, I see! You've come after the post. I didn't understand at first. You see, I wanted someone young.'

The shock was rather severe. After a moment Miss Timperley managed to writhe her lips into a trembling smile; she stooped and caressed the eldest child's cheek with one finger and murmured: 'I see. A mistake, of course. I see.' The girl must have been struck by the expression on her face, for she added, hastily: 'I need someone who will help me in the house as well. It's not at *all* the kind of post the agency should have offered *you*,' she said, with a great deal of scorn for the agency and compliment to Miss Timperley. She also said: 'Would you care to come in for a moment, and rest?' But Miss Timperley declined; she was not at all tired, she said. (And she wanted to be alone.) After that she wondered no longer. She knew. And she did not go every day to the agencies.

And now, all of a sudden, this beautiful, this glorious chance! (Just in time, too. Of course, Mrs Ladstone would readily permit one to fall into arrears for a week or two, Mrs

Ladstone was so good and kind, and particularly devoted to Miss Timperley because she came from her native Yorkshire; but then, that was just why one did not want to ask her.) Yes, here was this utterly delightful opportunity. Miss Timperley was *sure* she was just the woman for the situation at Olny-sur-Mer, the very one. Her French. Her references. The backward child. Yes! the post *must* be hers. But Miss Timperley thought she knew why the agency sounded so doubtful. Well! She would say she was twenty-nine, and she would have a new, modern, young, almost coquettish – Miss Timperley smiled and bridled at the word – photograph taken. She could not afford it of course; but the thing had to be done. She put on her clothes with quite a rakish air, and betook herself to an expensive West End photographer.

At first everything was very disheartening. The beautiful young woman who received Miss Timperley in a room hung with blue velvet assured her that it was an unheard-of thing for Mr Angelo to take anybody's photograph without appointment. People made appointments *weeks* ahead. It was *most* improbable that he would even *see* her that morning. Young Mr Arnold Angelo perhaps might. . . No, Miss Timperley did not want young Mr Arnold Angelo, or anybody else except the head of the firm. It was important, she insisted, most urgent and important. She was so very emphatic and determined about this – for was not Olny-sur-Mer at stake? – that the beautiful reception clerk relented, and conceded that Miss Timperley might wait for a few minutes while she, the clerk, saw what she could do. She left the room on this errand, and Miss Timperley wandered about, admiring the glossy visages displayed in elaborate showcases and on the walls. None of them, she noticed, seemed to wear a frown.

'Does Mr Angelo re-touch a good deal?' she demanded of a younger (and not quite so beautiful, though very nearly) assistant clerk who was addressing envelopes at a resplendent desk.

'A certain amount of re-touching is always necessary, madam,' replied the young thing haughtily.

'Ah!' said Miss Timperley in a superior tone, as if shocked by this practice. (But somehow she felt relieved.)

After ten minutes' agonising suspense Miss Timperley learned that she had had a great, an enormous, a quite colossal slice of luck. The reception clerk, her beautiful eyes quite beaming, came back to say that Lady-Something-or-other had telephoned to cancel her appointment, so that if Miss Timperley cared to wait a few minutes, Mr Angelo would be free, and would take her at once. Miss Timperley was delighted by this condescension on Mr Angelo's part; here was a piece of luck indeed! It showed that the stars were on her side; Olny grew perceptibly nearer.

'While you are waiting, madam, perhaps you would care to choose a style?' said the beauty, flipping over the pages of a large album.

'I don't like those green ones,' said Miss Timperley boldly. 'Nor the mauve.'

'No, madam,' acquiesced the beauty. 'Madam prefers sepia, perhaps?'

'Yes – yes,' said Miss Timperley doubtfully, not quite sure what sepia was. 'Oh! Yes! Sepia,' she decided. 'Like that.'

'What size would madam prefer?' inquired the beauty.

‘What are the prices?’ demanded Miss Timperley timidly.

The prices were enormous.

‘I require only quite a small one,’ ventured Miss Timperley. ‘Quite a small one, you understand.’

‘Certainly, madam,’ replied the beauty – so that Miss Timperley felt quite drawn to the girl. How wrong it was to think people unkind and cold because they were not very gushing just at first! This girl was charming. ‘Like this, perhaps?’ suggested charming girl.

The price was still very large, but what could one do? Think of Olny! This detail being settled, the beauty suggested that Miss Timperley should repair to one of the dressing rooms and make herself ready to be photographed. Miss Timperley, disconcerted, looked questioningly at the girl.

‘If madam wishes to change her dress?’ suggested the beauty. ‘Or tidy her hair?’ she pursued, reading Miss Timperley’s horrified denial of dress-changing in her eyes.

Miss Timperley agreed to tidy her hair, and the girl led her upstairs and along corridors to a small room, very elegantly equipped and full of mirrors. ‘This is very different from the practice in my young days,’ thought Miss Timperley, glancing round. ‘How wonderfully arranged everything is now! Don’t go!’ she cried in a sudden panic to the clerk. The girl waited with an expectant air. ‘Tell me,’ said Miss Timperley, in a voice which shyness muffled. ‘Would you advise me to keep my hat on, or no?’

The girl’s calm eyes took in Miss Timperley’s hat. ‘Without it would be best, I think, madam,’ she said quietly. ‘Madam’s hair is so charming.’

Miss Timperley, soothed and flattered, turned to the glass; when she turned to the clerk again she was gone. Miss Timperley bolted the door with a little bolt she found and began to rearrange her hair. She combed it this way, she combed it that, she looked at it from the right, she looked at it from the left; finally she powdered her nose. Then, feeling quite ready to face Mr Angelo, she sat down on the luxurious settee and picked up a copy of the *Prattler*. She read it through from end to end, started up in alarm to find herself still alone, combed her hair, powdered her nose, and looked at herself from all angles in the mirror. The she read the *Prattler* again, then she combed her hair again, then she read the *Prattler*. . . . Had they forgotten her altogether? Timidly Miss Timperley drew back the bolt and opened the door; she peered along the passage, but there was no one there. With a sigh, she bolted the door again and read the *Prattler*. Suddenly there came a loud thundering knock; Miss Timperley, terrified, fumbled hurriedly with the bolt; in half a minute, trembling like a fawn, she found herself in the presence of Mr Angelo.

He was an elderly man with white hair and a kind face; he asked Miss Timperley to sit down, and looked at her shrewdly. She for her part was busy gazing at the studio and its paraphernalia; such a high-up room, my dear, with a sloping glass roof, an enormous camera like a clothes-horse shrouded in black, and all sorts of the oddest wheeled screens – some white, some black, some possibly sepia. There did not seem to be anything to screw your head up with, as there used to be in Miss Timperley's younger days, but various antique tables and stools stood about, all very correct and handsome. Miss Timperley heard herself explaining the urgency of the photograph, and how important it was that it should be a good one. 'I should like it,' she said, 'to look' – somehow she could not bring herself to say 'young' – 'I should like it to look rather lively.' The photographer bowed his head in understanding and posed Miss Timperley, seated coyly upon an antique stool. An assistant – another beautiful girl – now appeared abruptly, stuck her head beneath the black cloth, and murmured something to Mr Angelo. He, too, put his head beneath the cloth, then stood up and gazed with an uncomplimentary air at Miss Timperley.

'I hope I'm not a bad subject,' said she, uncomfortable.

'Oh, not at all, not at all,' said Mr Angelo without conviction. He advanced to her with mincing footsteps, delicately moved her head sideways about a millimetre, and stepped back to look at the result. Then he took a little rubber bulb in one hand, and was just about to fire, as Miss Timperley mentally expressed it, when there came another murmur from beneath the cloth. 'Ah, yes! Just so!' said Mr Angelo. He snatched a large green curtain from a table and spread it on the floor before Miss Timperley. ('Quite Sir Walter Raleigh-ish' thought Miss Timperley.) 'To prevent the reflection from the floor,' explained Mr Angelo kindly.

Well! He took her like that, he took her like this, he brought up a purple light which sizzled, and placed it on a level with Miss Timperley's ear; he tilted the head, he adjusted the shoulders, he crossed and uncrossed the hands, he moved the stool about, he pushed the screens vigorously up and down the room – this part reminded Miss Timperley of a cricket match she had witnessed with her last employers. He was very competent *indeed*, reflected Miss Timperley gratefully, *no* one could have taken more trouble, really. Of course, that was the difference between these really good photographers and the poor ones; and the photographs – for he took several – were sure to be splendid. Miss Timperley, harassed at the beginning of the sitting, felt tired to death before the end, but she continued to simper valiantly; it was *so* important, and the photographs were sure to be superb. As a special favour, a very special favour, Mr Angelo promised she should have the proofs the next day but one; and then, flushed and exhausted but triumphant, Miss Timperley found herself in the street.

The next day would have been rather dreary if Miss Timperley had not had the resource of telling Mrs Ladstone all about Messrs Angelo. But Mrs Ladstone's marvel at the wonders of the studio satisfied even Miss Timperley's longing for appreciation, and the day soon passed, and the morrow came, and the second post came, and the proofs came – Mrs Ladstone brought them up specially, though she was busy making a pie when they arrived, panting up the four flights of stairs with cheerful zeal. Miss Timperley, excited, tore open the envelope and took out the four reddish-looking proofs.

Oh God! Was she really like that? Was it she, that haggard, old, worn woman who looked out at her? Had she really that timid, nervous, incompetent air? Did her hair really look so thin? Her mouth so fallen? Her eyes so weak? Oh, no! Oh, no! The photographs were bad, bad, bad! Yet Messrs

Angelo . . . No, they were bad! Yet Mr Angelo had taken such pains. . . . No, they were bad!

'They're not a bit like me!' cried Miss Timperley, in a high anguished tone. 'Not a bit!'

'Nay, lovey,' expostulated Mrs Ladstone cheerfully: 'They're as like as life. Just your pleasant look, they have. They're right down good. It just shows,' said Mrs Ladstone: 'I've allus said it paid to get the best, and it just shows.'

When she had gone, lumbering cheerfully down the stairs to resume the pie, Miss Timperley looked at the photographs again. Then she looked in the mirror, bending forward, scrutinising every feature, every line of her face, with merciless keenness. Yes! The photographs were good ones. The agency was right. The young mother was right. Miss Timperley was old.

'I shan't send the photograph,' panted Miss Timperley: 'I shall say I'm in my early thirties. I shan't send the photograph. I shan't.'

But suddenly Miss Timperley seized upon pen and paper, sat down at the table, selected the least repulsive of the four proofs. Her expression was not weak now, but high and resolved; for Miss Timperley had taken a decision. Was she, *she*, Captain Timperley's daughter, to tell a lie, suppress the photographic truth? Was she to gain a position by deception? Was she so far beaten by life as that? No! A thousand times no! She might lose the post, she might never get a post again, she might starve, she might (which Miss Timperley thought worse) become a burden to her relations; but better that than a lie, a deception; better to starve than to cheat. 'Let us accept what life brings us and face it out,' said Miss Timperley, taking up her pen: 'Let us at any rate go down with our flag flying.' And in her beautiful, clear, upright hand, she wrote:

Dear Madam, I wish to apply for the post of governess to your two children. I must tell you frankly that I am fifty-eight years of age. . . . I enclose an unfinished photograph. . . . As regards French . . . With backward children I have had considerable experience . . . my references . . .

Yours sincerely, Letitia Timperley.

And suddenly she wept, pressing her thin fingers against her anguished face.

A week later Mrs Ladstone again panted up the staircase, a letter between her floury fingers. 'It's from France, lovey,' she said.

Miss Timperley winced. There was no hope from France, she knew. She opened it wretchedly, and unfolded the sheet with spiritless fingers.

Dear Miss Timperley [she read], I think I had better explain my needs a little further. I am obliged to go to Marseilles at the end of July to meet my husband, who is returning from India on sick leave. He will have to stay at Marseilles some time to rest after the journey. You will understand that, though the children's *bonne* is good, I do not care to leave them alone in a seaside resort with her. I must have someone English, someone who speaks French well, and someone I can trust, to leave in charge of the whole household while I am away. In the circumstances I could not employ anyone young, and I think you are just the woman I require. Your references are excellent . . . your French . . . Doreen, born in India, a little backward . . . probably remain with me after my husband's return, as I shall be much occupied with him . . . four months at least . . . tickets . . . passports . . . boat . . . train . . . salary . . .

The salary was enormous.

Miss Timperley flung herself on Mrs Ladstone's neck. 'It was the photograph,' she babbled between her happy tears, 'the photograph which did it! I should never have got the place but for the photograph!'

'I always said it were a good one,' said Mrs Ladstone with conviction.

THE EXILE

Betty Miller

(1935)

They waited uneasily for her first appearance. It was already five o'clock, and a rich autumnal dusk hung in the air. Edmund Moore was restless, more so than his wife, for if it merely worried her from the domestic point of view that they were effecting this change in their staff, embarking on a very new venture with goodness knows what consequences to the interior life of the household, to him there was a more fundamental sense of disturbance in this imminent event. His old conservative desire to retain the present unaltered was alarmed at the prospect of change, of having to assimilate an entirely new person. He dreaded the adjustments, physical and practical, that had to be made to accommodate her. Lois had said: 'We can't put her in Jenny's old room – it's so small and poky.' To which he answered: 'It was all right for Jenny, wasn't it?' thinking with regret of their late 'general', who, five months advanced along the road to maternity, had departed – somewhat tardily – to seek matrimonial justification for her state. Lois sighed with tolerant impatience: 'Edmund, dear,' she said, kindly and a little firmly, implying that she had held this argument with him before and in precisely the same terms, 'Irina is not the *ordinary* type of servant. Mrs Clark told me on the 'phone that she was really a very cultured person.'

'Then why's she doing this sort of work?'

'She's an *émigré*, dear. The revolution in Russia, you know. Why, in Paris there are grand-duchesses who are waitresses and chambermaids.'

'Oh, well.' He paused; wandered to the window. No sign yet. 'Anyway, if she's as good as all that, why did Mrs Clark want to get rid of her?'

Lois serenely picked out a thread from her skein: she was mending a pair of gun-metal silk stockings. She was herself, as a matter of fact, a little vague on that point, as Mrs Clark had indubitably hedged. But being free, therefore, to construct her own explanation, she answered with assurance: 'They haven't got room to keep a proper servant any more. They're going to get a daily.' She drew the fine mesh of the stocking on to her leg, and contemplated it, head askew. Her husband watched her: she had beautiful limbs, full and shapely: these mist-fine stockings transparently, alluringly clouded the flesh.

'Wonder if Arthur's had another smash with the car?' he said presently. Arthur Moore, his young brother who lived with them (they were childless), had gone in his small rackety second-hand Ford to fetch her and her trunk at the station.

'Shouldn't be surprised,' Lois said, unperturbed. 'He was in a hurry to get back, because he wanted to take one of his flappers to a dance or something.' She lifted her fair, shingled head: 'I believe I can hear them now,' she said.

There was a soft splutter of rubber tyres, then the screech of brakes biting to. And there was Arthur coming up the path, swaying, with a large suitcase in either hand, while behind him walked a pale, slender woman in black, who did not glance about her as she came, but followed carefully, soberly in his wake. Lois put down her work-bag: she walked out into the hall, the sandals she lately affected tapping on the parquet as she went and revealing her toes (which were round and plump like button mushrooms) between their golden strapping. Her perfume, imperceptible when she sat still, unfurled with her movement and came to his nostrils, sombre, expensive.

'Here you are, Lois. On the nail.' Arthur plonked down the suitcases, and stood opening and closing his fists to sense the muscular relaxation. Lois (who, having known him since early boyhood, had no feeling for him that was not really quasi-maternal) glanced with familiar pleasure at his face: strong-set of bone, but with an elongated shapeliness, lips full, the colour sweetly ruddy above young male bristle. His copper-red hair was tangled over his brow. He stood swaying above them, taller than either by a head and shoulders. The Russian woman waited, head slightly bent, a faint, grave smile on her features. Lois, after an examining glance (she had the knack of absorbing all the external details of another woman in the swift shoot of an eye), took the situation in hand: 'Good evening, Irina. I'm glad you managed to come today, after all. I hope it wasn't too inconvenient for you. No? That's good. Now, Arthur, would you mind just taking Irina's cases up to her room: then when you've taken your things off, Irina, you must have a cup of tea, and then I'll show you the workings of the house a bit.'

The woman smiled. 'Thank you, Mrs Moore,' she said. Her voice, for such a pale, effacing person, was surprisingly deep and vibrant. Arthur said 'Oke' (his vocabulary increasingly belonged to a sort of new Esperanto generated in America and broadcast to the world through innumerable sound-recording machines. His sister-in-law, fifteen years older than he, often found it difficult to understand what he was talking about) and bumped up the carpeted oak stairs with the suitcases. Arthur was faintly disappointed in the new arrival: his imagination, Hollywood-stimulated, had promised him some lovely refugee wearing an embroidered blouse, with painted eyes and dark, endearing mouth. He was nonplussed in front of this pale, reserved woman. And yet, as she passed him on the threshold of her room where he had dumped her cases (with a last look at a place which was now to become unfamiliar, private to another's personality) and she thanked him for his pains, something in her glance, which, upraised to his tallness, she suddenly revealed as peculiarly intense and pallid, remained with him, lightly disturbing.

He did not see her again until the evening meal. Lois, however, was closeted with her in the kitchen, and the sound of their voices, the clink of china, came occasionally to the two men idling in the lounge with the evening papers. They looked up as Lois entered: she was flushed, and appeared pleased with herself. Her husband raised his eyebrows: 'Well?' he said. Arthur abandoned the Amusements column and listened casually. Lois came closer, conspiratorial. 'Well,' she said in a lowered voice, 'I think it's going to work out very nicely.'

'Um.' Edmund looked sceptical. He had not been married to Lois for eight years without having learnt to distrust her premature enthusiasms: during that time a long series of domestics had passed through the household, each in turn acclaimed and lauded at the outset, upbraided and maligned at their abruptly hastened departure. Edmund, long accustomed, bowed to this régime: his digestion was already destroyed by these spasmodic and variegated cookings, his hope of better things (meals suavely served and well seasoned, rooms unobtrusively kept clean, socks regularly darned) to all intents and purposes well extinct. He listened, therefore, with some politeness to his wife's whispered accounts: the tilt of his disillusioned, slanting eyebrows did not alter.

But Lois, undeterred, full of her muted enthusiasm: 'And, my dear, she seems to know the most *wonderful* dishes – things you only get in restaurants. You know that cold chicken we had left over from Tuesday?' (Her husband nodded, a trifle emphatically.) 'Well, she suggested making creamed chicken and celery.'

'Sounds good,' Arthur supplied from his corner.

'Wait till you taste it first,' Edmund said.

And they filed into the dining room; waited in self-conscious silence for her first appearance. She came in, pushing the rattling little dinner trolley over the parquet and the sham Persian rugs. She was wearing a white overall. Her hair was a nondescript brownish colour, parted in the middle, and severely drawn away from her face. As she put the covered dishes down, they elaborately bandied about some innocuous topic of conversation. Edmund, glancing at her face, saw for the first time how startlingly pale she was, and wondered if she were, perhaps, very tired. She went out noiselessly.

Lois served: the dish was very expertly garnished with parsley, with golden slips of lemon. They took up their forks: with an air of portentousness, they tasted. The blonde and delicate meat was perfectly flavoured, exquisitely creamed. They glanced at each other. Edmund was the first to break the silence.

'Golly!' he said. He spoke with emotion.

* * *

'A treasure, my dear, a real treasure.' Lois was busy on the 'phone in her bedroom. Ladies of this semi-suburban, semi-countrified village were to hear it all: to burn with envy. Dressed in a camellia-pink satin negligée, she was having one of her usual afternoon séances, which meant that she reclined for twenty minutes with pads over her eyes (according to the latest beauty book) and then spent the rest of the hour casually 'phoning, or sitting at her mirror-angled dressing table, re-manicuring her nails (a glossy scarlet), patting skin-food into her face, trying on new make-up, plucking her eyebrows. Utterly happy. A vain child with its toys. It did not worry Lois that she was fast approaching forty – she had the inestimably valuable knack of complete adaptability to any circumstance which the years might bring – indeed, she seemed thoroughly to enjoy a stage in her life which many other women would have found trying, to say the least. If she had lost the fine ardour of early youth, she had gained a rich tranquillity, an emotional leisure – and the increasing complexity of the beauty treatments necessary at this stage afforded her, instead of mortification, the greatest entertainment, occupation, and satisfaction.

'A real treasure,' she emphatically told the mouthpiece, smiling into its listening cavity. For there was no doubt about it this time. Irina was not only an exquisite cook, but she was clean in her kitchen, adept and thorough at the housework, incredibly willing, a very hard worker. Mrs Moore could not congratulate herself sufficiently. She dialled again.

There was a knock, and Irina herself discreetly entered. Lois hung up. It was on some household point. They discussed, Lois still sitting idly at her dressing table. Irina, standing, looked down on her. Her pale face was expressionless, she answered quietly in that deep, contained voice. Her hands, clasped before her, were bare, muscular, well-boned. Lois, sitting there among her crystal bottles, her milk-of-roses lotions, satin negligée draping her soft, ample body, felt suddenly strange about herself. In a new uncomfortable moment, she saw in the glass a picture of unthinking fleshly profligacy. Startled, she wondered to herself: 'Does the woman despise me?' But there was no condemnation in the pale blue eyes, no judgment or resentment. Nevertheless, some very sharp and fundamental contrast had emerged between the two women; something new to Lois and which disturbed her curiously.

Abruptly, the reserve of the Russian seemed intolerable to her. She felt that she must effect some contact, get an avowal of human emotion which might perhaps even faintly condone her own attitude towards life. She said, lifting a polishing pad to her rounded nails and affecting the usual woman-to-woman tone: 'Well, Irina, tell me something about yourself. Have you got a young man?'

Irina showed no surprise. She shook her head. 'No,' she said. She remained waiting, hands still clasped; her nails were short-cut, pale, ribbed as though from hard, practical work. (Yet it was by no means the ill-adjustment of social distinctions that made Lois so subtly, newly uncomfortable; there was here some psychic difference that accused her.)

'Mrs Clark told me you had been married in Russia. I suppose your husband was killed in the revolution?' Sympathetic and yet insistent. Lois could be like that. She enjoyed confidential interchange, and was prepared to do a little soft bullying to get it.

The woman said quietly: 'I was married. My husband was murdered.'

Oh, dear. But this had to be elucidated. Lois felt it imperative that she should know what lay behind that pale reserve, that enigmatic face. (As a child, she could never resist opening a parcel, whoever it might be addressed to.) Her anxious expression was an entreaty for further confidence. But she was slightly taken aback when the other proffered the tale without hesitation and without emotion, as though relating some event read in a book (as Lois afterwards described it to Edmund). Irina had apparently married a few months before the revolution; she was nineteen at the time. They were poor, and after the marriage they took in boarders. There was a young engineer. He was a friend of Irina's husband; yet he and Irina fell desperately in love and, united in this guilt, seemed to draw a bitter ardour from their very treachery. For some time they lived thus: the woman in a state of tense perverse exaltation between two men whom (she calmly avowed) she equally loved. One day the husband returned unexpectedly. The inevitable happened; her lover, tension at last released, stabbed him to death. The revolution had already broken out. She had no one else in the world but her lover. They tried to flee the country. Starving, they made their way to the port, and there, while they were waiting for a ship, the man got typhus and died.

'But,' said Lois, secretly appalled by the starkness of the narrative, the curiously indifferent attitude of the woman telling it, 'that was a long time ago, now. Have you never loved anyone else, since?'

Irina smiled. 'Oh, no,' she said. She sounded almost amused at the suggestion.

Lois gave it up. But she took the tale to Edmund (not noticing that Arthur, who had seemed to her lately a little out of sorts, was intently listening). 'What I *can't* understand,' she said, 'is her extraordinary indifference about the whole affair. She didn't seem to care two pins.'

Edmund said tolerantly, 'Well, it's her own business,' and returned to the study of a bulb catalogue – gardening was his pleasant passion. But Arthur sat, staring fixedly into the grate.

When, a moment later, Irina herself came softly into the room to draw the curtains, his eyes followed her movements with hypnotic obedience. There was something about the

Russian that disturbed him deeply, without rousing either his admiration or his masculine feeling. Lois saw his attentiveness: struck, she began to wonder. She was not to know that the tale she had unfolded Arthur had already heard the previous evening. Lois and Edmund were out bridge-playing. Feeling lonely in the empty house, he had suddenly, on some strong impulse (directed unconsciously by his gradually-forming preoccupation), gone into the kitchen with the pretext of wanting a cup of tea. While the kettle was boiling, he lounged against the table, drawing her into conversation. Presently, she told him the tale quite simply, as she had told it to Lois. He listened, feeling, to his surprise, how it seemed to enter into him coldly, dolorously. For, with sudden unmistakable clarity, he perceived that she looked back to that period of her life as to the time when all the real events and emotions had taken place for her, and that nothing now, in the bare, bleak present, could ever again compare with the meaning, the intensity of those days.

As she spoke, her pallid eyes fixed, drawn inwards, it became startlingly obvious that what remained of her life after that time had been blighted: consumed by the past, by those strange, tragic months. She was bound in that past situation: it claimed her, used her up. So that her life in the present was meaningless: she existed, imprisoned in our day-to-day sequence, imprisoned in Time. She was an exile, not only from a country (a geographical area can after all be reclaimed), but from her own real life. As a personality she was dead. The attributes, the mechanics that composed that former personality, were still there, capable of being brought into momentary play, but without any focus-point of direction, without present appreciation and forward-looking purpose, unrelated to anything in the present, animated at all only because the body that bound them together was still resolutely functioning, the spirit of its organic life not yet unwound.

The young man was silent suddenly: a ghostliness had skirted his spirit. He stood abashed in the midst of his own fleshly, enjoyable, well-established life: ashamed of his plenitude, made uneasy. The bare light of the kitchen illumined both their faces: a momentary silence bound them as in some intense searching communion. The two faces thus seen together – his, full, warm, ruddy, staring downwards with unwilling obsession at the other, lean-boned, devoured by pallor, remote – looked like the vivid picture drawn by some mediæval artist to symbolise Life's deep hidden pre-occupation with Death.

* * *

Arthur had discovered her secret. Lois – without understanding – somehow divined. Only Edmund seemed to remain indifferent. He did, however, occasionally notice that although she performed her duties very efficiently, it was with a peculiar manner which at first he was at a loss to explain to himself, until, still saying nothing, as was his habit, he began to watch her more closely; from which observation crystallised the impression (unpleasant to him) that she was clinging on to these daily-recurring tasks as on to a lifebelt: that without their external form to support her spirit, she would go under, completely vanish.

Gradually, this small childless household of average sensual beings grew to new uneasy awareness. They did not at first avow as much. But each were conscious in themselves and finally in the others of a sudden heightening of tension whenever Irina came into the room with her trays, or passed them silently in the passage. The deadly negativeness of this being in their midst seemed to draw the spirit uneasily, as towards a void: there was a centre of annihilation there that perilously sucked. Materially, the household had never been so well, so smoothly and so pleasantly run. At the same time, all these benefits came to them subtly blighted. There was in their midst someone to whom life meant really nothing: measuring themselves, their joys, pleasures, ambitions against that awoke in each of them something curiously restive, something that undermined with alarming ease all their ordinary standard of values.

* * *

Lois, sitting among her crystal bottles, found herself staring unwillingly at the soft pouted face that watched her from the mirror. She saw herself: mature, sterile. Her hand, which had been raised to rouge her mouth, remained suspended, drooped. A new derision in her snapped the action; rendered it useless. She sat vacant.

Her eyes went to the window, and she stared out. Down in the garden she saw Arthur moodily strolling, hands in his pockets, shoulders hunched. On ordinary days, he was never to be seen at this hour: he was up to town in his car, or off with some slim, smart girl to a roadhouse, to a swimming pool.

The kitchen door opened: Lois stiffened (as she found herself doing, lately, whenever Irina might appear). Sure enough, she saw her come out: she had a basket and a knife; she was going to cut vegetables for the evening meal. How stealthily, neatly she walks, thought Lois: like a cat. She saw Arthur swing round; saw him hesitate; then follow her across the grass to the small kitchen garden.

Irina looked up as the young man approached. He stood staring down at her; his face surly, ravaged. He said, abruptly: 'You avoid me all the time.'

This was untrue: she glanced in surprise. He stood biting his lips. He did not know what to say – how to say it. He could not explain to her that she roused in him an obscure obsession by comparison with which all his little lusts of the flesh were pale, transitory, weakling. She drew him, and he knew that she could only offer him annihilation: but dangerously, he craved to that experience as if a blind impulse had gained control and were pushing him to the edge.

Edmund, coming along just then with his old straw gardening hat on his head and watering can in one hand, saw them. He stopped; looked keenly out of his level grey eyes. 'Morbid,' he pronounced aloud. Ignoring their surprise, he turned and went away.

That evening he made up his mind that they must get rid of Irina. She must go. He had no regrets for the succulent dishes that must vanish with her. After all, he thought, there was more real comfort in the old days. The cooking was bad, but nothing disturbed the spiritual comfort of the household, which comfort is after all the real basis of life.

He said so, tentatively, to Arthur. The young man looked at him, sombrely, under the flame of coppery hair that coiled always on his brows. 'All right,' he said. 'If that's all you want. To stew comfortably in your own juice and pretend that things are going to last for ever.'

Said Edmund, his elder brother (prosperous of paunch beneath his waistcoat): 'Which is exactly how one *has* to live, my dear Arthur – in the present, in the permanent to achieve anything at all – if only a happy normal life – and believe me, as your Americans say, that's some achievement.'

They were both slightly surprised at themselves: they had never held this type of conversation before.

'What sort of life are we living,' Arthur began, passionately; 'what meaning, what spiritual value –?' He broke off, ashamed of these large words. For a moment he looked very young, sheepish. But his brow darkened again. 'Just suffocating in day-to-day material things – doping ourselves comfortably, pretending we'll never die. Doping ourselves so as not to realise – and thinking the dope is all that matters.'

'So it is,' Edmund said, equably. 'Oh, yes, it is,' he affirmed, seeing his brother's face contract. 'Good thick dope. The stronger the better. So long as we never come out of it, and slide comfortably, unknowingly into the end. All right: frown. But don't you see that that's the only way anything can be achieved in this life – the only way, in fact, that the lot of mankind can be bettered? And what higher aim do you want than that? Believe me, Arthur (and stop digging holes in that carpet with your heel), it's stronger, it's more spiritual to ignore death and go ahead as if this present life were permanent than it is to throw up the material sponge and go ghoul-hunting.' ('God, what eloquence,' he added to himself.)

Lois swept in on them. Her perfume tantalised the air. She sat down on the sofa. 'And what are you two confabulating about so seriously?' she asked, idly. Without waiting for an answer, lowering her voice suddenly she said: 'Do you know, I believe Irina hardly sleeps at all. Last night was at least the fourth time that I saw light under her door at two o'clock.' There was silence at the mention of Irina: once more, that enigmatic woman appeared as the hub round which, like helpless spokes, the personalities of the household radiated. Edmund took a decision. He said in a deliberately normal voice: 'Lois, I don't think Irina is really our type of servant after all. She doesn't suit us – she's too high-class, or something. I think you'd better explain to her and give her a week's wages instead of notice. We'll always find some nice ordinary skivvy at the agency. Personally, I'd rather have my stomach upset than my soul. Hem,' he concluded, modestly, pleased with his phrase.

* * *

The train was not in yet. Arthur let down her heavy suitcases on the platform. She was wearing the black coat and hat in which she had first arrived; she looked the same. He talked rather noisily, to cover the straining silence that yawned between them. 'It won't be long now – these trains are always a few minutes late.' She did not say anything to that, and abruptly he asked her: 'What are you going to do when you get to London?'

She shook her head. 'I do not know. I will find something.'

He saw with painful clarity, with a sense of heavy, dragging responsibility, that as she stood on the bleak platform the pallor of her face was accentuated to a startling degree and her still, withdrawn eyes seemed to reflect nothing from within or without. In the thin wind she shivered a little; her coat was of poor material. He sensed now that she had, in the days passed among them, managed to construct some sort of spiritual shelter for herself; that in adopting the daily events of their lives she had managed, as it were, to clothe for a while in borrowed garments the nakedness of her spirit. And that (in the selfishness of self-defence) they had rudely torn these from her, sending her out again, naked. He felt the responsibility for that act sink into him, brand him.

The small local train rumbled to a halt. He helped her up the wooden steps to her carriage. 'Goodbye,' she said. For a moment – the first time – he held her thin hand in his. 'Goodbye,' he said, numbly. The train was whistling shrilly, sending up its white smoke against the dark winter sky. Doors slammed.

He did not wait. Without turning round, he left the small, empty station. His car was parked in the yard outside. 'Good evening, sir,' a porter said to him, passing with a lamp swinging from his hand. 'Good evening,' he replied, mechanically. He climbed into the seat. The engine stuttered, failed. 'It's the chill in the air does that,' said the porter, pausing to watch; 'the evenings are drawing in.' He went away. The words hung on the air; they echoed slowly.

Now he was driving back along the narrow country road. The fields were dim on either side, a slow mist rising from the ground. He shivered. He thought for a while of her sitting in that carriage, staring before her. At what? He had been intellectually convinced by Edmund; but at the same time, something in him wanted to repudiate this hearty, matter-of-fact attitude to life; this avuncular sanity. His thoughts harked back to the Russian woman, to his strange spiritual adventure with her, and it seemed to him that The Elms had suddenly become too small, too warm, too smug to house him comfortably.

He stared ahead. His twin arc-lamps shone forward, coring the moving darkness with a misty tunnel of light. It was cold driving. But he would be home in five minutes, now. Unconsciously, he pressed on the accelerator slightly. Despite himself (as the train bore her further and further away, further and further from his life) other images began to struggle back to their normal place; he saw the living room, the big fire leaping, warm, joyous; the supper cooking fragrantly in the kitchen. He gave a sudden deep sigh; an expression of relaxation, of adjustment that seemed to come not only from the body but from the mind. He pressed on the accelerator again. Darkness flew past.

Edmund, hearing the car, went to open the hall door. The light of the house, familiar, warm, and human, glowed forth. It fell on the upturned face of the boy as he came forward out of the gloom.

Edmund, sensing the night air, shivered: 'Brrh, it's cold tonight.' He looked at the eyes, bright, uncertain, young, that were raised to his. He smiled gently. 'Coming in?' he asked. They looked at each other.

A little sheepishly, Arthur nodded. 'Yes, I'm coming in,' he said.

The door closed behind the two of them.

THE RAINY DAY, THE GOOD MOTHER AND THE BROWN SUIT

Dorothy Canfield Fisher

(1937)

And yet she had done exactly what the books on child training assured mothers would ward off trouble on a stormy day. She had copied off the list of raw materials recommended by the author of 'The Happy Child is the Active Child': coloured paper, blunt scissors, paste, pencils, crayons, plasticine – she had bought them all, well ahead of time, and had brought them out this morning after breakfast, when the rain settled down with that all-day pour. But, unlike the children in the books, Caroline and Freddy and little Priscilla had not received these treasures open-mouthed with pleasure, nor had they quietly and happily exercised their creative instinct, leaving their mother free to get on with her work. Perhaps her children hadn't as much of that instinct as other people's. At least, after a little listless fingering of coloured paper Freddy turned away. 'Say, Mother, I want to put on my brown suit,' he said. Little did she dream then what the brown suit was to cost her. She answered casually, piling up the breakfast dishes, 'I washed that suit yesterday, Freddy, and the rain came. So it's not dry yet.'

He trotted back and forth after her as she stepped to and fro with the slightly nervous haste of a competent woman who has planned a busy morning. 'But, Mother,' he persisted. 'I *want* to put it on. I *want* to.' He raised his voice, 'Mother, I want to put my brown suit on.'

From the pantry where she had just discovered that the cream she had planned to use for the dessert was soured, she answered him with some asperity, 'I told you it isn't dry yet!' But she reminded herself of the excellent rule, 'Always make children understand the reasons for your refusals,' and added, 'It's hanging on the line on the side porch. Look out there, dear. You can see for yourself how wet it is.'

He did as she bade him, and stood staring out, leaning his forehead on the glass.

Yet a little later as she stood before the telephone, grocery list in hand, he tugged at her skirt and as Central asked, 'What number, please?' he said with plaintive obstinacy, 'Mother, I *do* want to put on my brown suit.'

She said with considerable warmth, 'Somerset three six one. For heaven's sake, Freddy, that suit is WET. Is this Perkins and Larsen? How *could* you put it on! What price are your grapefruit today? Freddy, let go of my skirt. Grapefruit, I said. No, no – G for glory, R for run –'

But when she turned away from her struggle with the clerk, Freddy plucked at her hand and whimpered in the nasal fretting tone she had sworn (before she had children) no child of hers should ever use, 'Mother, I waa-a-nt to pu-u-t my brown–'

'Don't whine,' she told him with a ferocity so swift and savage that he recoiled and was silent. She thought remorsefully, 'Oh, dear, to scold is just as bad as to whine.'

Going back into the pantry, she recalled with resentment that the psychologists of family life say the moods of children are but the reflections of moods of the mother. She did not believe a word of it. 'Did *I* start this?' she asked herself unanswerably, and, 'How can anybody help being irritated when they're so perfectly unreasonable!'

But she was really a very good mother. She remembered that the basis of child-rearing is to understand each child at all times, and went resolutely back into the other room, determined to understand Freddy, if it were her last act. Disconcertingly, it was not Freddy, but Priscilla who ran to take her hand, who said pleadingly, timidly, as if appealing from the cruel decree of a tyrant, 'Mummy, Fred *does* so want to have you let him wear his brown suit this morning!' The mother contained herself, collected the children – three year-old Priscilla, five year-old Fred, six and a half year-old Caroline – led them to the window and said, 'Now just look at that suit! How could I let Freddy wear anything that's as wet as sop?'

At least that was what she thought she said. What the children distinctly heard was, 'You're in the wrong, wrong, wrong. And I am right, right, right, as I always am. There's no use your trying to get around that!'

They stared gloomily out at this idea rather than at the wet clothes. Their mother went on, 'What in the world does Fred *want* to wear his brown suit for, anyhow? What's the matter with the suit he's got on?'

What the children heard was, 'No matter what Freddy said his reason was, I'd soon show you it was all foolishness.' They attempted no answer, shaken as they were by wave after invisible wave of her impatience to be done with them and at something else. Indeed she was impatient. Why not, with her morning work all waiting to be done. She held her children for a moment with the bullying eye of a drill-sergeant, and then said, challengingly. '*Well*–?' She meant, and they knew she meant, 'I hope you realise that I have you beaten.'

Something in Fred – it was something rather fine – exploded with a crash. His round face grew grim and black. He looked savagely at his mother, thrust out his lower jaw and, keeping his eyes ragingly on hers, kicked a footstool, viciously, as if he were kicking her.

'Fred-*dy*,' she said in a voice meant to cow him. But he was not cowed. He kicked again with all his might, looking at his mother and hating her.

And then – he was only a little boy – he broke. His hard defiant face crumpled up into despair. He crooked his arm to hide his suffering from his mother – from his mother! – and turned away to lean against the wall in the silent, dry, inexplicable misery which often ended what his mother called 'Fred's tantrums'. Little Priscilla began a whimpering. Caroline put her hands up to her face and hung her head.

Their mother thought, her nerves taut with exasperation, 'I'd just like to see one of those child-specialists manage *my* children on a rainy day! They'd find out a thing or two!' But she loved her children. She loved them dearly. With her next breath she was ashamed of being angry with them. The tears came to her eyes and an aching lump into her throat. Bewildered, dismayed, she asked herself, in the purest surprise, 'Why, how did we get into this dreadful state? What can the trouble be?'

She went back into the pantry, took a long breath, took a drink of water, tried to relax her muscles, cast her mind back to the book about what to do on a rainy day. But she could recall nothing else in it but that appeal to the creative instinct. She had tried that, and it had failed.

She heard the front door open. The voice of a young cousin, no special favourite of hers, cried, 'Ye gods and little fishes, what weather!' He slammed the door behind him. Although he was nineteen, he still slammed doors as if he were twelve. He had come as he sometimes did when it rained, to wait in the living room for the bus that took him to college. One of its stopping places was their corner.

Priscilla, the literal, asked. 'What does "gods and little fishes" mean?'

'Mean?' said the freshman, laughing and flinging his books and his raincoat down on the floor. 'What do you mean, mean? You mean too much, Prissy. What does this mean?' As she began to wash the dishes the mother could see that he had flung his heels in the air and was walking on his hands. 'He's too old for such foolishness,' she thought severely. And sure enough, out of the pockets of his adult suit of clothes, now upside down, little-boy junk rattled down around his hands.

The children squealed and made a rush towards the bits of string, dirty handkerchiefs, knives, fishhooks, nails, pieces of cork, screws and pencils. 'No you don't!' said he, returning his feet to the floor with a bang. 'Everything there is a part of an important enterprise.'

'What's a 'portant enter –' began Priscilla.

'Whatever I do,' he told her coolly, 'were it only to make a mousetrap. If *I* made mousetraps there'd be a four-strip concrete road to my door in a week's time, you bet. No mousetrap of mine would ever have let out Uncle Peter's mouse, believe me.'

'What? Who? What's Uncle Peter's mouse?' clamoured the children.

'Oh, surely you know that story. No child of our family gets brung up without hearing that one. No? Well, one morning when Uncle Peter and Aunt Molly came down to breakfast – Priscilla, do *not* ask who they were and where they lived, it's no matter – they found a mouse in their trap. It was the kind of trap that catches the mouse alive, so they got the cat, and they all went out on the porch to open the trap and let the cat catch the mouse. Priscilla, do *not* say this was horrid of them, it was, and I can't help it, but that was the way it happened and it was so long ago probably they didn't know any better. So there they all were' – he illustrated how tensely they stood, stooping over an imaginary trap – 'the two children and Uncle Peter and Aunt Molly. And the cat. She was scrooched right close in front of the cage' – he quivered and crouched with such vivacity of acting that the children began to laugh – 'while Uncle Peter s-l-o-w-l-y, s-l-o-w-l-y lifted the door of the trap till it was open enough for the mouse to get out.' He drew a long breath and made a dramatic pause. The children gazed at him, mouths open, eyes unwinking. 'And then –!' he sprang into the air, 'the cat jumped!' He clutched at Fred. 'Uncle Peter hollered!' He ran to Caroline and seized her arm. 'The children yelled bloody murder!' He flung the children to right and left. 'Aunt Molly shrieked!' He sank back on the floor. 'But the mouse was gone!'

He gazed with enormous solemnity at his spellbound listeners. 'The cat was prowling around, sniffing and lashing her tail' – he sniffed the air and getting up on his hands and knees lashed an imaginary tail – 'but – there – was – no – mouse.'

He sat cross-legged and earnest and went on, 'Well, Aunt Molly was terribly afraid of mice, and she always had the idea that all a mouse wanted to do was to run up folks' clothes, so she was sure the mouse had done that to one of them. So she took one child and then the other, shook them till their teeth nearly dropped out' – he shot out a long arm and seized Priscilla, Caroline, and Freddy one after the other, shaking them hard and setting them into giggling fits – 'and put first one and then the other inside the house and shut the door, quick! Then she shook herself hard. And went into the house and shut the door. Then Uncle Peter shook *him*self hard. And went in quick and shut the door. And then they all had breakfast, wondering all the while about where that mouse could have gone to. And after they'd finished breakfast, Uncle Peter stood up to go to the office and took hold of the lower edge of his vest to pull it down' – he seized the lower edge of an imaginary vest vigorously and stood appalled, a frantic expression of horror on his face – '*and there was the mouse!*' The children shrieked. 'It had been right under the edge of his vest and when he grabbed the vest he put his hand right around it, and when he took his hand away the mouse was in it, squirming.' He showed them how it squirmed, and then, speeding up to express-train speed, finished the story all in one breath, 'And he was so rattled he flung it right away without looking to see where, and it went spang into Aunt Molly's face and she fainted dead away – and the mouse beat it so quick they never did see it again.'

He grinned down at the children, literally rolling on the floor, as pleased with the story as they. 'Say, kids, what-d'you-say we act it out? Let's. Who'll be what? I'll be Uncle Peter. Priscilla, you be one of the children. Caroline, you be Aunt Molly – that's a swell part! You must yell your head off when I throw the mouse in your face. Fred, you be –'

'I'll be the cat,' said Fred, scrambling to his feet.

So they acted out the little drama, throwing themselves passionately into their roles, Caroline so magnificent with her scream and faint at the end that Priscilla said, 'Oh, *I* want to be Aunt Molly.'

So they did it over again, Priscilla screeching as though she were being flayed alive, and fainting with fat arms and legs outstretched.

'I'd kind o' like to be Uncle Peter,' said Fred.

'Okay by me,' said the student. 'I'll be the cat.'

By the time they had finished it again they were out of breath, what with screaming and running and laughing and acting, and sank down together on the floor. Little by little their laughter subsided to a peaceful silence. Freddy sprawled half over the knobby knees of the tall boy, Priscilla was tucked away under his arm, Caroline leaned against him. From the pantry where, unheeded, the mother washed the dishes, she thought jealously, 'What do they see in him? That story is nothing but nonsense.' And then – she was really an intelligent person – it came over her, 'Why, that is just what they like in it.'

Out of the silence, almost as though she were thinking aloud, little Priscilla murmured, 'Freddy was bad this morning.' There was compassion in her tone.

'What was eating him?' asked the student, not particularly interested.

'He wanted to wear his brown suit. And it was wet, and he couldn't. So he kicked the footstool and was bad.'

'What's the point about the brown suit, old man?'

The question was put in a matter-of-fact tone of comradely interest. But even so Fred hesitated, opened his mouth, shut it, said nothing.

It was Caroline who explained, 'It's got a holster pocket at the back where he can carry his pretend pistol.'

The mother in the pantry, astounded, remorseful, reproachful, cried out to herself, 'Oh, why didn't he tell *me* that!' But she knew very well why he had not. She had plenty of brains.

'Oh, I see,' said the student. 'But why don't you sew a holster pocket on the pants you've got on, boy? On all your pants. It's nothing to sew on pockets. You girls, too. You might as well have holster pockets. When I was your age I had sewed on dozens of pockets.' He took a long breath, and began to rattle off nonsense with an intensely serious face and machine-gun speed, 'My goodness, by the time I was fourteen I had sewed on five hundred and thirty-four pockets, and one small watch-pocket but I don't count that one. Didn't you ever hear how I put myself through college sewing on pockets? And when I was graduated, the President of Pocket Sewing Union of America sent for me, and –'

'But you've only just got in to college,' Priscilla reminded him earnestly.

(In the pantry, her mother thought, with a stab of self-knowledge, 'Why, is that *me?* Was I being literal, like that, about rainy-day occupations?')

'Priscilla,' said the college student, sternly, 'don't you know what happens to children who say "go-up-bald-head" to their elders – oh, but –' He clutched his tousled hair, and said, imitating Priscilla's serious little voice, 'Oh, but I'm not bald yet, am I?'

A horn sounded in the street. He sprang up, tumbling the children roughly from him, snatched his books. 'There's my bus.' The door slammed.

The children came running to find their mother. 'Oh, Mother, Mother, can we have some cloth to make pockets out of?'

She was ready for them. 'I've got lots of it that'll be just right,' she said, telling herself wryly, 'I can get an idea all right if somebody'll push it halfway down my throat.'

But for the rest of the morning, as the children sat happily exercising their creative instinct by sewing on queer pockets in queer places on their clothes, she was thinking with sorrow, 'It's not fair. That great lout of a boy without a care in the world takes their fancy with his nonsense, and they turn their backs on me entirely. I represent only food and care – and refusals. I work my head off for them – and the first stranger appeals to them more.'

Yet after lunch they put their three heads together and whispered and giggled, and 'had a secret'. Then, Caroline at their head, they trotted over to the sofa where their mother had dropped down to rest. 'Mother,' said Caroline in her little-girl bird-voice, 'wouldn't *you* like to play Uncle-Peter-and-Aunt-Molly-and-the-mouse? You didn't have a single chance to this morning – not once – you were working so.' They looked at her with fond shining eyes of sympathy. 'Come on, Mother! You'll love it!' they encouraged her.

A lump came into her throat again – a good lump this time. She swallowed. 'Oh, thanks, children. I know I'd like to. What part are you going to have me take?'

The secret came out then. They let Freddy tell her, for it had been his inspiration. He looked proudly at his mother and offered her his best. 'Ye gods and little fishes! We're going to let you be the *mouse!*'

She clasped her hands, 'Oh, children!' she cried.

From their pride in having pleased her, a gust of love-madness blew across them, setting them to fall upon their mother like soft-pawed kittens wild with play, pushing her back on the pillows, hugging her, worrying her, rumpling her hair, kissing her ears, her nose, whatever they could reach.

But Priscilla was not sure they had been clear. She drew away. 'You don't have to get caught, you know,' she reassured her mother earnestly. 'The mouse wasn't caught – never!'

NINE YEARS IS A LONG TIME

Norah Hoult

(1938)

It wasn't until October was well under way that she began to wonder that she had had no word from him. Even then she didn't actually worry. He had probably gone on some business trip. Men in a good position, like he certainly was, often went away on business looking after their affairs. He might have gone to London: he was a member of some swell club there. That she did know, for he'd let out one day something about an important call being put through to his club in town, and he had had to return to Rotherfield sooner than he had expected.

All the same, she found herself watching the posts, watching for the appearance of the telegraph boy – he usually wired. All the time she was watching. When she dusted the front room, or went to fetch anything from the cupboard, she would find herself come to a standstill in front of the window, and staring up and down the road. By the end of the month she admitted that it was a good piece over his usual absence.

Her husband thought it funny too. They had a talk about it one evening when their daughter, Irene, was out at her shorthand class.

She started the subject herself. She said: 'What do you think about it, Harry? What's your real opinion? You can say right out what's in your mind, you know?'

They were sitting in the kitchen over the fire. He took up the poker, and knocked the coal about with it making a better blaze, before he answered. Then he said in a very thoughtful voice: 'Well, of course, he might be dead.'

She nodded her head. 'I've thought of that myself.'

So she had. But to have it put into words from him made it more real. Like hearing a thunderclap, when before you had just wondered if there mightn't be a storm about.

He added, leaning back in his chair, and looking at her out of small eyes blinking over their comfortable creases: 'He could die sudden and you not a penny the wiser seeing that you don't know his name or address or anything about him.'

'I'll tell you this much,' she said a little sharply, 'if he did die, there'd probably be half a column at the least about him in the *Rotherfield Telegraph*. He'd be one of their leading citizens; there's no doubt about that. I wouldn't mind betting that he's the director of several companies.'

'Well, what of it? You'd be none the wiser, since you don't know his name. There's several leading Rotherfield men died lately; about his age, too. I don't know that you'd do much good if you went over to Rotherfield, and looked up the papers. You wouldn't know, see, would you?'

She looked into the fire. 'I suppose I wouldn't.' She thought a little, then she said: 'Tell you what. I wouldn't be surprised if his name started with a "Mac". He had a Scotch accent all right. Though he wasn't mean.'

No, he wasn't mean. Three pounds a time came in very useful to help out. She was going to miss it, if it stopped. And so would Irene, and Mr Scott. Mr Scott was how she always thought of her husband.

He agreed with her this time. 'Oh, no. I wouldn't say that he was mean. But reserved. Scotch people, of course, are like that. That was why he never let out a word about himself or his occupation.'

The flames from the fire were beginning to scorch the front of her legs. She rubbed her hands up and down them. Then, crossing one leg over the other, she hazarded: 'I often had the idea that shipbuilding was his line. Else, what brought him to Merseyhead so regular? I mean he came here before he met me.'

'Very likely,' said Mr Scott. 'Quite likely, I'd say.' He took out his pipe and his pouch, and began to press tobacco into the bowl.

She watched his red face bent forward with some hostility. If her Rotherfield friend didn't turn up soon, he'd feel it. He'd have to go without tobacco. All she had now was Irene's pound a week and about a pound profit on Miss Halpin, their paying guest, who had a good post as manageress of Bailey's, the big drapers. Two pounds a week didn't go far towards keeping them well fed, and with good fires. Seeing as he was the one who was out of a job, who didn't contribute nothing, it was only fair he should give up things.

'So that's what you think, that he's dead?' she asked, resuming the conversation, but as if she were attacking him.

He took a draw at his pipe, before answering. He was always one like that, one to take his time over things. It would annoy you if you didn't know him. It annoyed you when you did know him, too.

'I didn't say that he was dead, for I don't know. What I said was that he might be dead, for all you know, or that I know, or for all that we would know.'

He stopped and looked at her, as if hoping that at last she had got the position clear. Deciding to take no risk he added patiently, 'Because, you see, you are not in possession of his name, or of his address, or anything about him except that he lives, or lived, at Rotherfield. So that you can't find him, or satisfy your mind.'

'I know that. I don't need you to tell me that.'

'Well, then . . .'

'And I tell you, Mr Scott, you'll find it no bloody joke us losing three quid a month.'

'I know that.' His mouth pursed into lines of bitter resignation. 'How long is this going on, I wonder?'

What he meant was, how long before his father kicked the bucket? Before their two minds was a picture of an old paralysed man. Just sitting in a big chair holding on grimly to life. When he died there'd be money coming to Mr Scott as his only son. *When* he died. All over the world there were people waiting for other people to die, and settle their financial problems for them. And it seemed like that the longer you waited, the longer you had to wait.

Mr Scott said what they'd each of them said many a time: 'You'd think that with nothing to do, nothing to live for as you might say, he'd be glad to go. I'm sure I should in his place.'

She nodded her head. But that topic was threadbare. Her mind went back to her own problem. Why didn't her Rotherfield friend write? Wasn't she going to see him again ever?

The fire was too hot on her other leg now. So she reversed her position. Then she held out both legs in front of her. She used to have good legs; they were a little on the fat side now. She'd put on eight pounds this last year. Eleven stone ten was her weight.

'Do you think I've got to look much fatter lately?' she asked him.

Mr Scott looked at her indifferently. 'I don't know. Maybe you have.'

'My legs are fatter, aren't they?'

'You always had a good calf.'

'Yes, but my ankles were slim. 'I used to be able to get my thumb and middle finger to meet round. Now I can't.'

She showed him. There was a good inch of flesh-coloured stocking to spare over the squeezed flesh.

'Hmmm.' He stared. Then he said: 'Thinking of slimming or what?'

'Doctors say it's very bad for you. Besides, it wasn't as if I was a big eater. And heaven knows I get my share of exercise with all the housework.'

'I'd leave it. I don't think it makes much difference. Nature intended there to be two kinds of women, big and small. I like the modern slim woman myself.'

She had heard him say this till she was tired of hearing him. Whenever he came in from the pictures, he'd go on talking about some lovely slim little girl till you'd think he was daft. Getting into his dotage he was. Pinning pictures of girls up on his bedroom walls; just legs and scraps of lingerie. Sixty! An old man really. She could ask him, why he married her then? Of course she'd been slimmer then, but she'd always had a figure.

She said: 'My Rotherfield friend said he always liked a woman with a figure. Something to get hold of.'

'Some men do,' he agreed, nodding his head in deep assent, so that you could see the thin hair brushed neatly across the top. 'There was a time, I remember it well, when most men liked them big. Fashions change in women like they do in everything else. I think Edward liked them on the full-figured side. But I believe the Prince of Wales likes·them skinny.'

'Go on with you! What do you know about what the Prince of Wales likes in the way of women?'

'As much as anybody else, I suppose. Why only the other day I walked back from the library with a man who knew someone who knew . . .'

'You told me that bit before. Anyone can pretend they know anything, can't they? Well, I'd better get Irene's supper.'

She got up from her seat with a jerk. Anyhow it was no good worrying. Worrying never did any good. She might hear from him tomorrow.

But she didn't hear. Nor the day after. Nor the day after that . . .

A depression settled slowly and abidingly on her spirit. It was a bad time in the garden. You couldn't do anything with it just now but prop up the chrysanthemums against the wind. And the daily housekeeping round, making the list for Mr Scott to go to the shops, cooking meals, washing clothes, ironing, dusting, and for diversion talking to Miss Halpin – who was as dull as ditchwater, and had probably never had a man in her life – hung heavily. When she lay down after clearing up from the one o'clock dinner, she didn't go to sleep, but her thoughts went round in a dull painful question. It seemed to rain every day, so that you had no heart in you to go for a bit of a walk or up to see the shops. It was a pity, because they said there was nothing like a walk or a change to take your mind off things – and walking reduced the weight too.

What she was really missing was the change her Rotherfield friend made, she decided. It had been a sort of holiday when she got his wire or letter. Then Mr Scott knew that he'd have to manage everything himself. She'd be the rest of the morning having a bath, and dressing herself with special care. The last touch was a drop or two of Coty's Chypre, that was too expensive to use for any but very special occasions. Then after a light lunch – no steak and onions – off to the Queen's, where they always met. She liked sitting in the lounge of the Queen's, with well-dressed people about her, and having a drink and a chat, and then another drink before they went off to the hotel. They were nearly always able to have the same bedroom, with the red curtains and the alabaster vases on the mantelpiece, so that it was really homelike in its familiarity. Mrs Weston always had the gas fire lit for them ready.

It wasn't that her Rotherfield friend really attracted her in the way one or two men – no, really only one man in her life – had attracted her. But still a woman wanted to get into bed with a man now and then. It was only natural. She had always felt better in herself afterwards. Mrs Weston sent them tea up, or if they preferred they had it downstairs in the lounge. You'd see quite a good class of people having their tea, too; you'd be surprised. Mrs Weston knew some really famous theatrical people, like the time when Daisy Allen had stayed with her. Handy the place was. And central. Well Mrs Weston would be wondering what on earth had happened to her.

Almost every month – he'd missed now and again, of course – as regular as regular for nine solid years.

It *had* been a change. He went off pretty soon afterwards. Had some dinner engagement usually, he said. And she'd meet Irene coming out from the office, and they'd go off to the pictures, and have a little bit of supper somewhere afterwards. It always seemed to her that when she went into Spinetti's with Irene men used to look at her with increased attention. They looked at her a damn sight more than they did at Irene, pretty and slim and young as she was. Anyhow she always felt pleased with herself and warm and comfortable inside.

Now, if he never came to see her again, or if she never saw him again, life would just go on as if it were a wet November all the time.

She began to spend more time in front of her looking-glass. One morning she went out, and recklessly bought a special pot of expensive skin food. Irene saw it when she came back from the office.

‘What’s that? Is that yours?’

‘Yes. I treated myself for a change. Mrs Rosenbaum was telling me that it’s terribly good for the skin. Works marvels. So it should at the price.’

‘Well, I just hope to goodness, mother, you are not going to start making yourself up the way Mrs Rosenbaum goes on. I think it’s disgusting. An old woman like that.’

‘She’s not an old woman. ‘She’s only about fifty.’

‘Well, I do think there’s nothing more repulsive than to see a woman of that age trying to make herself look young. They never do; they just look repulsive, revolting. Why should a woman when she’s past forty go on fussing about herself?’

‘I suppose you’d like me not to use powder or lipstick, even?’

‘Well, I don’t say I mind a little powder, but . . .’

She stopped, and shrugged her shoulders. Standing there scornful and young, with her smooth skin and hard eyes. She was always bossing her now. Last time they’d gone out together, she’d said: ‘Mother, you’ve got too much rouge and lipstick on,’ rubbed it off herself. And she wouldn’t let her smoke on top of trams: when once she had wanted to light up – ‘Please don’t, mother. If any of the girls at the office should get on!’

The whole thing was that she was beginning to put on airs and graces, to fancy herself. But Irene wasn’t a bit like an ordinary girl, like she’d been when she was eighteen. She said she hated men. Once she had told her straight: ‘Well, if it hadn’t been for some of my men friends, *you’d* have had a thin time when you were a kid, I can tell you. It wasn’t your father supported you, and him at the war.’

Did her good to be told straight out. Of course, young people were like that, very intolerant. They thought no one should look nice but themselves. She said, and now there was anger in her voice: 'Well, if you think I'm going to look dowdy just to please you.'

'I don't want you to look dowdy. But if you have a lot of stuff on your face with your red hair – and honestly, mother, it suits you better if you'd stop hennaing it so much – if you put on a thick cream and lipstick with your hair and big figure, it makes you look conspicuous, that's all.'

'You're jealous. Because when we're out together more men look at me than they do at you.'

'I'm not at all jealous . . .' Irene looked at her mother as if she were going to say hard words, then she went out of the room with her lips tightly pressed together.

Mrs Scott sat down in front of the fire, holding the skin food in her hand. There was a pain at her heart which she tried to banish by getting up quickly and putting a record on the gramophone:

There's a lovely lake in London . . .

'Pom pom pom-pom pom pom pom-pom' she hummed to herself defiantly, but her thoughts went on all the same. So Irene thought she was too old to bother about herself, that she looked fast when she took a bit of trouble with her appearance. She wasn't too old. She tried to cheer herself up thinking of the story her Rotherfield friend had told her about the old man who was asked at what age sexual desire had left him. But the smile faded, because it took her thoughts back to him again. Why *hadn't* she heard from him?

Had he got tired? Might as well face it, Irene thought of her as old and fast-looking. Had he come to think that about her? She got up and took down the oval mirror that hung over the mantelpiece and examined her face intently; then she held it further away, so that it included the reflection of part of her figure as well.

She couldn't see that she looked so old. There was something cheeky and attractive about her face, especially when she made her eyes laugh. Experienced, of course. Well, why not? Well, wouldn't she be a fool at her age if she didn't look as if she had had something to do with men? Withering on the virgin thorn – somebody, not her Rotherfield friend, somebody else had used the phrase once, and she remembered it with satisfaction. That wasn't her line. Though it just about suited her lady lodger.

Of course she was on the plump side.That was upstairs. Her hips were still slim, and, thank God, she didn't stick out behind. And her friend had always said . . .

She heard Irene's steps in the hall, and replaced the mirror quickly. The hall door banged. She had gone back to work without saying 'goodbye'. Bad tempered. Not got over her buying something for herself. What she was going to do straight off was to go upstairs, and give her face a good massage with the skin food.

She came down to the afternoon cup of tea in a good temper. Her skin felt as soft as velvet to her touch, and the lines from her nostrils to the corners of her mouth showed a lot less. Even Mr Scott noticed it. He said: 'You do look smart.'

He said that because she had on her best satin blouse and men always liked satin. Satin or velvet. But he wouldn't have said anything, if she hadn't done her face up. They chatted amiably, and when he said: 'Do you know Bessy Morris is on at the Palace: I wouldn't mind seeing her,' she surprised herself by saying: 'Let's go.'

'But what about her ladyship's supper?'

'Let her have it cold for once. I'll do her up a nice salad and leave the coffee, so that it only wants heating.'

'And Irene?'

'It just won't do that girl any harm to get her own eats for once. She's getting above herself.'

'Haven't I said she puts on too many airs? Ever since she went to that office she's been a changed girl. And you always stick up for her.'

'Well, I did stick up for her. But as a matter of fact you're right for once. She's getting to think there's no one in the world but herself.'

'That's just what I've often said.'

'I know that, and I'm agreeing with you. See?'

Pleasantly they set off for the Palace. It wasn't often that she went out with her husband. Not likely. It was treat enough for her to give him the money to go to the pictures. But he didn't look so bad when he was dressed nicely, with his hat brushed and everything. Irene would think she'd gone off her chump going out with him. It would show Miss Scott that she wasn't everybody.

She did it in style, too. At the interval, she slipped him half a dollar, and they went into the saloon, and had a Scotch and splash. He passed her back the change, and it warmed you up, so that you enjoyed the second half better.

Still, wasn't it funny, even in the Palace, a place he'd never be likely to go to, unless compelled by some business function, she found herself looking for her Rotherfield friend. Once she really thought she saw him, looked a bit like at the back, and her hand stiffened, ready to clutch Mr Scott's arm. But when the man turned, it wasn't a bit like him really.

Bessy Morris sang one of her old songs. She sang: '*I don't want to get old; I don't want to get old; I want to stay just as I am . . .*' Running furiously up and down the stage, and making everyone die laughing. '*I want to come home at half-past four and have a row with the woman next door; I don't want to get old . . .*'

She laughed a lot; and she also laughed loudly at the jokes of the comedian who followed. Thank God, she had a sense of humour and could enjoy a saucy story. A man in front, a very nice looking, well-dressed fellow, too, kept looking round and trying to catch her eye. She didn't take any special notice: after all it wasn't playing the game to give a man encouragement when you were out with another – even if it happened to be only her husband, and she was paying for him.

All the same it just showed that she wasn't quite on the shelf whatever Irene thought. When they stood up for *God Save the King*, he just stared and stared at her. Mr Scott noticed it. He whispered: 'Would you like me to slip away quietly?' but she shook her head. No, she didn't feel like it, and after all she had given all that up.

When they were sitting in the tram, she slipped out the mirror attached to her handbag, and was satisfied. There was a green light in her grey eyes that beckoned. Putting it back she hummed: '*I don't want to get old; I don't want to get old . . .*'

The next day wasn't so good. To begin with she had found herself with the definite expectation that she would hear from her friend that morning, and by twelve o'clock, when nothing had come – he was considerate; he always let her know before twelve – her spirits went down, plop, and she as definitely decided that it was the finish, and that she might as well face the fact. She stood at the window, and told herself so in good round language. Then she stared up and down.

It was one of those not infrequent days when without actually raining, it looked as if it were going to rain, that it would rain if the weather wasn't too indifferent and spiritless to be able to do anything so positive. It *should* rain. A grocer's van passed; the woman from two houses up went by on her morning's shopping. Mrs Scott's eye followed her critically. What a way to go out, shoes all muddy, old mackintosh . . . oh, who cared! An errand boy wheeled by on a bicycle, whistling cheerfully. Let him whistle. He knew damn all about life.

Yes, he must be dead, and if he was dead, that was that, she couldn't do anything about it. Or he'd found another woman, younger and better looking than she was. But that didn't seem reasonable. After all if he'd stuck to her for nine years, when he could have any girl he wanted as any rich man could, why should he change now? Nine years showed that he was the faithful sort. Or he'd made it up with his wife; of course there was a wife somewhere; she knew that though he kept his mouth close. Perhaps she'd been in a lunatic asylum, and been let out cured. And he was sticking to her. That was another thing about married men. They might be ever so bitter about their wives, say they'd spoilt their lives, and all that stuff. And the very next thing, for the sake of his children, or for the sake of his home, or for the sake of his bloody position, or his bloody conscience, he'd turn you down as if you weren't flesh and blood at all.

Still, nine years was a long time, and she'd have thought he'd have done it before if he were going to do it.

Well, everything went in time, and it was no good moping about it. 'The best of friends must part,' as the old saying was. It wasn't as if she'd actually been in love with him, still you got used to having a man. At this very moment, she wouldn't mind . . . it was last night's outing, and being near her period. That was why she felt so depressed, too.

Depression or not, no good standing there. Mr Scott would be wondering when he was going to get his dinner. Dinnertime was what he spent all *his* morning waiting for. Like his blasted cheek, but there it was.

When they were sitting over a cup of coffee and Irene had gone back to work, Mr Scott said suddenly: 'Do you know when I was coming back I saw a telegraph boy cycling up the road this morning, and I made sure he was going to turn in here. He just went a few doors on: I think it would be for Tilson's.'

'Who the hell would be sending us a wire? The Sweep isn't on now. Did you think your father had died at last?'

'Not likely!' Mr Scott sniffed contemptuously through his nose. 'No, *he'll* never die. I thought it was from your friend, of course.'

'Well, you can give up thinking about him. It's over three months now.' She put her cup on the table, and then turning towards him, raised her voice emphatically. 'I shan't hear from him again. Not never. See?'

'I don't know. Christmas is coming. That might bring you something. Why are you so sure of a sudden?'

'I couldn't tell you why I'm so sure. I just know it today. I feel it in my bones. Somebody has been making mischief, saying that I'm a married woman, not a widow, like I told him, and my friend is so straight that he wouldn't go with a married woman. He told me that once, and I remember it now. Somebody might easily have seen me and him at the Queen's, and known us both. Or else he's dead. Or else . . . anyhow I just know I shan't see him again. So that's enough about that.'

Mr Scott looked at her face. She was getting quite worked up about it. He sought for sympathetic words. 'Well, no wonder you're upset. It must be – I was working it out in bed last night – must be a good nine years since you first ran into him – just by the Arcade, wasn't it? – and he turned out so lucky. Ah well, no use crying over spilt milk.' He waited for her to speak, but as she said nothing he went on tentatively: 'Dare say you could easily pick up someone else if you fancied?'

She gave him a hard look. 'Could I? Well, I might. But you know damn well that having Irene going to an office, I can't do what I please. Besides, after being so regular with just the one man . . .' She stopped and her lips began to be unsteady. Horrified, she comprehended in a lightning flash that she had got the habit of being faithful. Why, if that chap last night had spoken to her, and she'd been on her own, she'd have behaved like a silly kid and rushed away. She had just got out of the way of all that . . . pretty awful to think that she, Sally Scott, had dwindled into a Miss Prim and Steady for the rest of her life. Not a single man in her life, for you wouldn't count Mr Scott. Past work and past everything he was. She choked back a sob. That's what her Rotherfield friend had done to her. That's what a woman got for being so blasted loyal. She took out her handkerchief.

'Don't take on about it,' said Mr Scott, rising uncomfortably. ''Course I can understand your feeling sore. Nine years is a long time.'

'Oh, shut up, can't you? Don't you know any other words? Shut up, can't you?'

The tears were coming. She couldn't stop them. Aghast at herself, she got up; and turned her back, trying for self-control.

Mr Scott stood a few seconds contemplating her back, her downcast head. Her hair looked pretty when it caught the sun. It wasn't like Mrs Scott to give way. If it were Irene it would be different. She often threw fits about nothing at all. But, whatever her faults, Mrs Scott was generally a sensible cheerful woman. Why couldn't she see that she'd been lucky to keep her friend as long as she had done? Should he pat her shoulder? Better not. She might only fly out at him.

Mrs Scott put an end to his dilemma by saying: 'Hadn't you better put the kettle on for washing up?'

'Right you are,' said Mr Scott, and shuffled rapidly away into the scullery.

Mrs Scott replaced her handkerchief, and took out her compact. She dabbed her nose with powder, saying under her breath: 'That's that.' Then, moving briskly, she started to collect the dishes and bring them into the scullery.

THE TEST

Angelica Gibbs

(1940)

On the afternoon Marian took her second driver's test, Mrs Ericson went with her. 'It's probably better to have someone a little older with you,' Mrs Ericson said as Marian slipped into the driver's seat beside her. 'Perhaps last time your Cousin Bill made you nervous, talking too much on the way.'

'Yes, Ma'am,' Marian said in her soft, unaccented voice. 'They probably do like it better if a white person shows up with you.'

'Oh I don't think it's *that,*' Mrs Ericson began, and subsided after a glance at the girl's set profile. Marian drove the car slowly through the shady suburban streets. It was one of the first hot days of June, and when they reached the boulevard they found it crowded with cars headed for the beaches.

'Do you want me to drive?' Mrs Ericson asked. 'I'll be glad to if you're feeling jumpy.' Marian shook her head. Mrs Ericson watched her dark, competent hands and wondered for the thousandth time how the house had ever managed to get along without her, or how she had lived through those earlier years when her household had been presided over by a series of slatternly white girls who had considered housework demeaning and the care of children an added insult. 'You drive beautifully, Marian,' she said. 'Now, don't think of the last time. Anybody would slide on a steep hill on a wet day like that.'

'It takes four mistakes to flunk you,' Marian said. 'I don't remember doing all the things the inspector marked down on my blank.'

'People say that they only want you to slip them a little something,' Mrs Ericson said doubtfully.

'*No*,' Marian said, 'that would only make it worse, Mrs Ericson. I know.'

The car turned right, at a traffic signal, into a side road and slid up to the kerb at the rear of a short line of parked cars. The inspectors had not arrived yet.

'You have the papers?' Mrs Ericson asked. Marian took them out of her bag: her learner's permit, the car registration, and her birth certificate. They settled down to the dreary business of waiting.

'It will be marvellous to have someone dependable to drive the children to school every day,' Mrs Ericson said.

Marian looked up from the list of driving requirements she had been studying. 'It'll make things simpler at the house, won't it?' she said.

'Oh, Marian,' Mrs Ericson exclaimed, 'if I could only pay you half of what you're worth!'

'Now, Mrs Ericson,' Marian said firmly. They looked at each other and smiled with affection.

Two cars with official insignia on their doors stopped

across the street. The inspectors leaped out, very brisk and military in their neat uniforms. Marian's hands tightened on the wheel. 'There's the one who flunked me last time,' she whispered, pointing to a stocky, self-important man who had begun to shout directions at the driver at the head of the line. 'Oh, Mrs Ericson.'

'Now, Marian,' Mrs Ericson said. They smiled at each other again, rather weakly.

The inspector who finally reached their car was not the stocky one but a genial, middle-aged man who grinned broadly as he thumbed over their papers. Mrs Ericson started to get out of the car. 'Don't you want to come along?' the inspector asked. 'Mandy and I don't mind company.'

Mrs Ericson was bewildered for a moment. 'No,' she said, and stepped to the kerb. 'I might make Marian self-conscious. She's a fine driver, Inspector.'

'Sure thing,' the inspector said, winking at Mrs Ericson. He slid into the seat beside Marian. 'Turn right at the corner, Mandy-Lou.'

From the kerb, Mrs Ericson watched the car move smoothly up the street.

The inspector made notations in a small black book. 'Age?' he inquired presently, as they drove along.

'Twenty-seven.'

He looked at Marian out of the corner of his eye. 'Old enough to have quite a flock of picaninnies, eh?'

Marian did not answer.

'Left at this corner,' the inspector said, 'and park between that truck and the green Buick.'

The two cars were very close together, but Marian squeezed inbetween them without too much manoeuvring. 'Driven before, Mandy-Lou?' the inspector asked.

'Yes, sir. I had a licence for three years in Pennsylvania.'

'Why do you want to drive a car?'

'My employer needs me to take her children to and from school.'

'Sure you don't really want to sneak out nights to meet some young blood?' the inspector asked. He laughed as Marian shook her head.

'Let's see you take a left at the corner and then turn around in the middle of the next block,' the inspector said. He began to whistle 'Swanee River'. 'Make you homesick?' he asked.

Marian put out her hand, swung around neatly in the street, and headed back in the direction from which they had come. 'No,' she said. 'I was born in Scranton, Pennsylvania.'

The inspector feigned astonishment. 'You-all ain't Southern?' he said. 'Well, dog my cats if I didn't think you-all came from down yondah.'

'No, sir,' Marian said.

'Turn onto Main Street here and let's see how you-all does in heavier traffic.'

They followed a line of cars along Main Street for several blocks until they came in sight of a concrete bridge which arched high over the railroad tracks.

'Read that sign at the end of the bridge,' the inspector said.

'Proceed with caution. Dangerous in slippery weather,' Marian said.

'You-all sho can read fine,' the inspector exclaimed. 'Where d'you learn to do that, Mandy?'

'I got my college degree last year,' Marian said. Her voice was not quite steady.

As the car crept up the slope of the bridge the inspector burst out laughing. He laughed so hard he could scarcely give his next direction. 'Stop here,' he said, wiping his eyes, 'then start 'er up again. Mandy got her degree, did she? Dog my cats!'

Marian pulled up beside the kerb. She put the car in neutral, pulled on the emergency brake, waited a moment, and then put the car into gear again. Her face was set. As she released the brake her foot slipped off the clutch pedal and the engine stalled.

'Now, Mistress Mandy,' the inspector said, 'remember your degree.'

'*Damn* you!' Marian cried. She started the car with a jerk.

The inspector lost his joviality in an instant. 'Return to the starting place, please,' he said, and made four very black crosses at random in the squares on Marian's application blank.

Mrs Ericson was waiting at the kerb where they had left her. As Marian stopped the car the inspector jumped out and brushed past her, his face purple. 'What happened?' Mrs Ericson asked, looking after him with alarm.

Marian stared down at the wheel and her lip trembled.

'Oh Marian, *again*?' Mrs Ericson said.

Marian nodded. 'In a sort of different way,' she said, and slid over to the right-hand side of the car.

IT ALL BEGINS AGAIN

Helen Hull

(1941)

Mary Bristol had intended never to live with any one of her children. The decision had been automatic, full-formed even as she had sent the telegrams telling them their father had died suddenly. That had been fifteen years ago, she had been just past sixty, and her income (arranged cannily by Will in annuities so that no one would look hopefully for her death!) had been enough for independence and even for assistance to one or another of the children. Except for an appropriate and swiftly abandoned gesture from Vera, the children hadn't suggested that she live with them. Hugh, the youngest, ran through wives and jobs too rapidly to offer sanctuary to anything. She might have enjoyed an occasional visit with Tom, the middle child, but his domestic life was irregular, for all he was more faithful to his mistress than Hugh ever tried to be to any of his wives. And Tom had died, a few years after his father's death, the neat surgery job done on his interior after Verdun being inadequate for many years of service.

After Mary's serious illness in the late winter of 1940, Vera insisted that she must not stay alone. In the discussion, Vera let drop that if her mother would stay with them instead of going alone to some expensive summer hotel, they could open the Westchester house, Vera could take out a cook and second maid, Clement would stop his talk about selling the house, and the children would give up their ridiculous proposals for the summer – dude ranches, Heaven knew what! 'Why not say you need the money, instead of going on about my health?' Mary had asked. Vera's answer had been, 'When I'm so distressed about you – how would it look if you had a stroke or something all alone? – must you be carping?' Vera was like that, insistent and unsubtle in projecting upon someone else the necessity for doing what she herself wished. Mary liked showing her up, and perhaps one reason she didn't want to live with her daughter was that she knew she'd have to hold her tongue. It was one thing to catch Vera up in an afternoon call, when Vera could take her injured feelings home and forget them in some new scheme. But under one roof!

If Mary had been stronger, she might have given Vera a cheque for her summer and rejected the plan. But the pneumonia germ had been vicious, the climb back to health seemed scarcely worth the effort when the years left were of necessity so few. In a way Mary regretted her recovery; she felt rather silly about it, having been sure that she was through with life. Much like the state of mind of one who has stripped her house and packed her trunks for a long journey, only to find herself sitting on top of a locked trunk in an empty house with no place to go and no reason for going. Perhaps if she didn't unpack – all her concern about the family, all her interest in their affairs, all her amused, sardonic contemplation of them, perhaps if she perched on a locked trunk, aloof, ready for departure – she wouldn't have to wait too long. She had agreed to Vera's suggestions, so compliantly that Vera asked, 'You aren't feeling worse today, are you?' Maybe I am, thought Mary, to let you bully me. Vera had gone on in her high-pitched, quick voice, with talk of her problems. Clement was impossible, he was such a grouch, surely the market was better than he thought, in war times steel and wheat always shot sky-high. She would write at once to that woman who'd worked for them three years ago. Hilda, Vera's daughter, would have to drop her notion of getting a job for the summer, it was just an excuse to stay downtown where she could meet that boy, if he had any pride at all he would stop chasing Hilda, not a penny to his name. Mary had looked at Vera, smartly slender, well groomed, her silvery hair (she still called it prematurely grey) in soft curls under the thimble of cornflowers she perched over one eyebrow for a hat, her mobile face marked with sharp lines. She exaggerates everything, thought Mary; she uses her face too much, she has more wrinkles than I have. 'Is Hilda in love with this boy? What's his name?' Mary was fond of her granddaughter, she liked the girl's looks, fine-skinned, small-boned, intense.

'Oh, love!' snapped Vera. 'At her age? But she doesn't tell me anything. You simply can't imagine what modern children are like.'

'I seem to remember saying just that when you were young.'

'Things were simpler then.' Vera sighed. 'And you never had to worry about money.'

'We didn't have much to begin with,' said Mary. 'I haven't seen you starving or taking in washing.'

'It's much worse having to give up what you're used to than it is not to have it ever!' Vera's hasty kiss buzzed against Mary's cheek and she whisked herself away.

For the next few weeks Vera was so busy closing the apartment in town and opening the country house that she had little time for her mother. During those weeks Mary grew steadily stronger. She could walk about her rooms with her heart quiet in her breast instead of acting like a frightened, caged squirrel. She looked, she thought, like an elderly Alice in Wonderland, with a ribbon tied around her white hair to keep it back off her ears. No, more like the White Queen, the way her body had sagged and thickened. Her face had kept its structure, the dry skin taut over the fine, high brow, the eye sockets deep and cleanly modelled, for all the worn lids drooped over the dark eyes. She couldn't read for long, but she began to look at headlines, with an amazed anger at what was going on, as if Hitler had taken advantage of her illness to wreck the world she had known. Oh, my, she thought, I'm too old to reckon with another war! Holland, Denmark, Belgium, Calais. Yet no one seemed to pay much attention to it. When Vera telephoned, Mary said, 'What does Clem think about the war?'

'It's simply ruined the market,' said Vera. 'I don't even mention it to him any more. I'm calling from the country, Mother. I'm not coming in again this week, if I turn my back something goes wrong. Clem says he'll drive you out on Saturday. You can get a maid to help you pack, can't you?'

'I'm not helpless yet,' Mary had replied tartly. She didn't like to have Vera pawing over her personal belongings, exclaiming at your age, Mother, some quieter colour! Will Bristol had always liked her in bright colours, deep, dark red, yellow. As long as her public costumes were decorous enough, white in the summer, black with white in winter. But she tired quickly, and it was the chambermaid who packed for her. 'I don't want that – nor that –' Mary discarded recklessly; she might need nothing when fall came again. 'You can have them. Only they won't fit you.'

The woman gathered up the pile of clothes, looking at Mary with bleak eyes. 'There are some who can use them,' she said. 'If they still live. I do not know. I have not heard.'

'Your people?' asked Mary. 'Where are they?'

Farmers in Norway. 'For many weeks I do not hear. It is a great blackness not to hear.'

The words sounded in Mary's mind like a deep bell far under water. As she waited for Clem, she kept hearing them. A great blackness not to hear. If she sat very still, scarcely breathing, the sound might come more clearly, floating up and up through the waters of time. She must have been a child, she could feel herself spraddled over the edge of a high feather bed, trying to reach the floor with her bare toes, afraid of the darkness, compelled by the sound which had wakened her, a low moaning, broken by sobbing breaths, to extricate herself from the safe warmth of her bed and brave her way across the black room to the other bed where her mother lay.

'Is it another baby, Ma?' Her hand had found the heavy rope of hair, had moved up it, had touched the clammy wetness of the coarse pillow. Just a year earlier her brother had been born, right in this very bed. He whimpered in his crib. The moaning had ceased, her mother had said, 'Go back to bed, what are you doing up?' Then she had laughed, at least the sound was not crying. 'A baby? How would I get a baby!' She had reached out in the night and pulled Mary's head against her thin neck. 'I didn't mean to wake you up. You aren't old enough to know. Oh, God, if only I could hear from him! It is death not even to hear!' She had led Mary back to her own bed, had lifted her into the hollow of the feathers.

That was another war, thought Mary, and her mother wept for her husband. When he came back, he was a gaunt, bearded stranger Mary had never seen. He had been in a Southern prison, he must have been sick for a long time after he came home. They had given up the farm and moved into a village. Her father had a cobbler's bench in the shed off the kitchen; Mary could hear the tap of mallet driving in wooden pegs, and the dry rasp of his cough. He had done other odd jobs; she remembered clocks with their wooden wheels strewn over a table and the hot smell of soldering. She and Tom, the next younger child, had gone to the village school, and then she'd taken Jimmy when he was so little she had to carry him part of the way because her mother went out by the day, nursing, cooking, sewing. 'If I had died, I would have been a hero! And now look at me!' When had her father cried that out in a terrible voice? Mary could feel herself running away from the house dragging Jimmy with her, out of reach of the voices, her mother's sharp with flailing impatience, her father's like white torment. They were still young, her mother had been seventeen when they married, but Mary could not see them; her effort evoked only the image of an old tintype, her father in a stiff hat standing with his hand on the shoulder of her mother, long dark ringlets over the tightly fitted basque of the young girl who stared soberly out of the faded square. Well, she thought, I can't remember how I looked when I was twenty. Queer, as if time destroyed the image with the prototype.

She did remember that she had grown to share her mother's irritation with that increasingly silent, useless, ailing man. She had meant to get ahead, to make something of herself, to escape poverty and ignominy. Because she was the oldest, she would pull Tom and Jimmy up with her. Well, she had helped them, it was a long time ago, they were all dead now, all but her. Other women now were saying of their men, it is a great blackness not to hear, it is death not even to hear.

Odd, how vividly she could see her father, dying. Her mother had sent for her – she was lady principal in a high school in Northern Michigan that year. Will Bristol had driven to the station with her. He was a mining engineer who ate his meals at the boarding-house where Mary lived. 'Don't be gone long,' he had said. Tom, summoned from college, had met her. 'He's going,' he had said. 'Had another haemorrhage.' She must have sat beside her father's bed that night, she remembered the acrid odour of a kerosene lamp, the faint rale, the only sound of life in the figure propped on pillows. He had lifted papery eyelids, disclosing eyes brilliant with fever, and the line of his sunken, colourless mouth had altered into gentleness. 'Why, Mother!' he had said.

'It's me, Mary,' she had told him. But he had not heard her, he had pushed himself up, talking in a high, shrill voice, like a boy's.

She had not heeded his words, but now they sounded again. 'Don't cry! It's a grand new land where a man can be free, and his children after him! I'll be coming back to visit you, a great man driving high-stepping black horses and bringing you the grand gifts!'

The telephone jangled; it was like silver trappings on black horses. The sound scattered the images of the past, just before she might have found out what they meant. What had set her digging into those old years? She hoisted herself stiffly to her feet, the desk clerk said that Mr Clement Lawler was on his way up.

Then Clement was at the door, an artificial brightness in voice and manner. Well, well, how was Mother? Fine she could spend the summer with them, were the bags ready? He seemed to turn on his manner and retreat behind it into protective colouration; grey hair, eyebrows, eyes, suit, skin. He had been an amiable fellow who wished to please, but having failed to do so he now wished chiefly to avoid unpleasantness. Vera's worn him to the bone, thought Mary, and then forgot him in an exasperating search for purse, gloves, spectacles. 'Just stop and think,' said Clem, blinking. 'Just stop –'

'If you'd stand still,' cried Mary, 'maybe I could think!' The ineptitude of age irritated her, it made a husk between herself and the small affairs with which she had to deal. The porter shook out her coat, and there lay the missing articles. 'I knew I'd put them somewhere!' She gathered them triumphantly, and headed the procession toward the elevator.

She was sorry there were not more people in the lobby to witness her departure. Going away was, after all, exciting, once you surmounted the inertia of staying where you were. Clement helped her into the front seat of the elderly family car and sat beside her, clearing his throat anxiously as the starter zoomed twice before the motor caught. 'It's really a good car yet,' he said. 'A very good engine.' Mary thought, Clem really drives well when Vera isn't telling him how, and then she looked contentedly out at other cars, at the curve of ramp up to the highway, at the river wide and ruffled in the hazy sunlight. An aeroplane sounded overhead, she saw its shadow over the water, she thought, we don't have to scurry for shelter. After a moment Clem said, 'Lord, if they'd only get it over with and let a man go about his business in a normal world!'

'That would be nice, wouldn't it?' said Mary, drily.

Clement peered at her, his eyelids twitching. 'I mean, look at us, nothing's happened here, business ought to be good. Ought to start big production, factories running double shifts. Do they?' The car rolled on in spurts, fast, slow, fast, slow, as if Clement beat time with his foot. 'No. Everyone's scared, everyone's waiting.'

They had reached the toll bridge, and Clem, fumbling for a coin, let the motor die. By the time he had it started, his ears were scarlet and he had forgotten larger issues. 'It's the mixture,' he muttered.

Mary's hat slid backwards on her spun-glass hair, she moved a little from the window, and Clem smiled at her, inquiringly. 'You all right?'

'Yes, I am.' She wouldn't be like Vera, wanting windows open and then shut and then half open – 'Clem, what is a normal world, anyway?'

'Why, you know! The kind I grew up in, the kind you grew up in!'

'We grew up quite a while apart.'

'You know what I mean. A world where you knew what to expect, where you could make a living for your family. Why, look at Father Bristol, that's what I mean, climbing straight up. He had a good life, he made a lot of money. The kind of world we've tried to get back to, ever since 1918. Instead of this – this headache.'

'Perhaps headaches are normal.' Mary spoke testily. 'Just because you can't make a fortune!'

'A fortune? I can't make a cent.' The words rasped. 'But I – I didn't mean to get on that subject.'

'The trouble was, you made too much too easily to begin with,' said Mary. 'Put notions in Vera's head.'

'She's ambitious – for the children,' said Clement, hastily. 'You mustn't blame her. She's had a difficult time.'

'Pooh!' said Mary. 'Pooh! If she is my own daughter, I know her. You never should have let her bully you out of your own profession. Why didn't you go on being an architect?'

'I'd be no better off if I had. They've had a bad time, too.'

'You might have enjoyed it.'

'You know how it was, after those years in the army. I didn't want Vera to go on working, we wanted to settle down, raise a family.'

'You were very handsome in your uniform.' Mary chuckled. 'Too bad you couldn't go on wearing it, you might have managed Vera.'

Clement's teeth worried at the lower lip. Like a rabbit, thought Mary; I'd like to shake some spunk into him!

'No,' he said. 'You'd have to have all the bands playing for a uniform to count. Weren't we the idealistic young fools? Making the world safe for democracy. Sounds pretty silly now, doesn't it? They'll have to think up better slogans for this generation. They know all the answers. Or worse, they know there aren't any answers.' Clement slowed for construction signs, a labourer with a flag waved him into a bumpy detour.

'Half slave and half free,' said Mary, as she jounced.

'What? I'm sorry, be out of this in a minute.'

(A slogan good enough for her father. She'd never thought of it quite that way, her father as a boy, seeking a land where a man could be free, finding a slogan – And his children after him.)

'There.' Clement relaxed a little, having reached smooth pavement. 'What was I saying? Oh, slogans. Well, this isn't our war. Let them have it out. Look, back in the seventies, when the Prussians got to Paris, you didn't worry about it, did you? It's this damned radio stuff, calling off the scores as if it was a game in the Yankee Stadium. Keeps us in a state of nerves.'

Mary's head jerked forward, she slid down in her seat, her hands folded over her wide, soft body. When Clem got started in that light, monotonous voice, quotation marks humming like bees among his words – She would have said she did not sleep, her mind dropped a few stitches, and picked up its knitting again as the car stopped.

'Here we are,' said Clem, gently. 'Feel tired?'

He's nice, thought Mary, warmly. He means well. His shoulder was a fulcrum to pry herself out of the car, but as she stood up, her feet firmly on the grass, she brushed him away. 'I can walk,' she said. 'I'm just stiff.'

'Sitting so long.' Clement was anxiously animated. 'Good trip, not much over an hour. Old bus comes right along. Now where's Vera?'

Mary went slowly along the flagged walk to the front door, a gracious door with fan and lights. The house, which represented Vera's successful attempt to spend a great deal of money (in the late twenties) looked down at the heel. The shrubbery massed against the grey stone of the first storey needed clipping, the white clapboards above had rain stains from the faded shutters. But the shadow of trees lay crisp on the cropped lawn, and there was pleasant colour in the garden around the small pool down the slope of the hill. Clem followed her with some of the luggage. 'Ring the bell, will you, Mother? Where's everybody?'

A plump, elderly woman opened the door. 'How do you do, Mr Lawler, and Mrs Bristol. Mrs Lawler is out. She left word she had to go to this bridge tournament, it's for the Red Cross. No, Mr Lawler, the young people are out, I couldn't say where they are.'

'That's a nice note,' said Clem, mildly. 'Walking out on us. Where's the girl, what's her name, Anna?'

'It's her afternoon out, Mr Lawler. That is, Thursday is her afternoon, but with the plumbers and all she couldn't take it. We did have quite a time with the plumbers, Mr Lawler.'

'So I heard. A nice kind of welcome for you, Mother.' Clem's eyelids twitched. 'Everybody gone but the cook.'

'That's good,' said Mary. 'I don't have to talk to anybody. Good as a hotel.' It wasn't, really. At a hotel, as weary as she was, she'd go to bed and no one would disturb her until she rang. A long sigh for independence lost lifted her breast. Clem said, 'Which room, Effie? You take those bags, will you? I'll get the rest of the stuff.'

'Mind your step,' said Effie. 'It's Mr William's things from college. He said he'd be back to see to them, I wasn't to touch them.' She started up the wide stairs, and Mary stood for a moment, hand on the mahogany rail, gathering determination for the ascent and looking over her grandson's college deposit. Tennis rackets in a press, a musical instrument in a black case on the carved Italian chest; skis, boots, a radio, a pile of records, leather coat, bulging laundry bag, suitcases. Bill, home from college. Mary hadn't seen much of her grandson since he had been a little boy. Preparatory school, summer camps, college. He'd been a funny little boy. She began to climb, her heart creaking as she lifted her weight from step to step. When she got up she'd stay!

'Did you see all that junk?' Clem was at her heels. 'That's what my money goes for. If I say a word, I'm a brute. When I was his age, I knew what I wanted to do!'

'Well,' said Mary, shortly, 'you didn't do it, did you?' She was sorry she had said it, Clem looked so suddenly deflated.

'At least I did something,' he said, with dignity. 'Effie!' He raised his voice. 'Which room is it?'

'It's here, Mr Lawler.' Effie appeared at a doorway. 'Right here.'

Mary looked about with the experienced eye of a traveller. 'This used to be the nursery,' she said.

'Did it, Mrs Bristol? Mrs Lawler thought it would be the quietest room for you, with the young people running in and out the way they do.'

'Don't you like it, Mother?' Clem peered at chintz curtains and silver-striped wall paper. 'If you don't, speak up. Plenty of others.'

'It's all right.' Mary settled into an armchair. Vera knew she liked a double bed, but probably there wasn't one in the house. That shade of lavender in bedspread and rugs was one she despised. Vera had no doubt picked it especially for her, something appropriate to age.

'What would you like? A spot of sherry? Tea? That's it. Effie, bring Mrs Bristol some tea.' Clem balanced uneasily in the doorway. 'Want a paper to read?'

'No,' said Mary. 'I have to unpack.'

'Well, I can't help you with that.' Clem teetered a moment. 'Take it easy. Vera ought to be home any minute.' He turned to go.

'Clem!' Mary's voice halted him. 'I needn't have said that.'

'Oh, I know. I ought to do something – take steps – instead of grousing.' He glanced at her. 'I don't know how anything's coming out. I wake up at night in a cold sweat. I thought if I could give them a start – the children – but what are they to start *at,* in a world like this? And you know, they aren't even happy! You'll see.' His newspapers slipped from his elbow and crackled about his feet. He stooped for them, and as he straightened, automatically read the leaders across the sheets. 'Look at that! If Paris falls, that'll fix the market all right.' On the stairs sounded Effie's deliberate step. 'Here comes your tea. Do you more good than my ranting.' His quick smile was apologetic. 'You know what Vera thinks? She thinks if she ignores the war long enough it will come to an end from chagrin. Little boys showing off and no one looking at them.'

'Known as the ostrich technique,' said Mary. 'Have some tea?'

Clem didn't drink tea, or coffee, either. He had this pain in his stomach, the doctor couldn't find anything, he thought he'd worry less if they could find something definite, no matter what.

'Ticker tape-worm,' said Mary. 'That's what ails you.'

'What? Oh, yes. Yes.' Clem's lips jerked into a smile.

'Go read your market reports. Tea would do you less harm.'

Clem edged away. 'I'll be on the terrace, in case you want me.'

Mary drank her tea, three cups. When I was his age, Clem had said, and Mary had jumped on him because it might have been Will Bristol talking about Tom, their son. Only Will bellowed when he was angry. 'When I was your age,' he had roared, 'I had to work my way through college. I tended furnaces for a corner of a cellar to sleep in, and I cooked my own food, what I had.' Mary had tried to defend her son, he was just a boy, Will didn't want him working himself to death the way he had – not skis and radios and cars in those days; what had it been? Girls, even as early as that. Frat parties. Liquor. The same words, when I was your age. How we repeat ourselves, she thought! There must be an archetype for all we say, the pattern repeats itself endlessly. Tom had gone back to college on probation, his senior year, and before Christmas he had enlisted. Perhaps, after he finally came home, he had used his wounds as an excuse – Will always thought so, and Will had died before Tom, so he hadn't known. 'Such a pity they sewed me together again. A gold star would be much less annoying.' Dear God, the same thing her father had said! If I had died, I would have been a hero.

She wished Tom hadn't died. She would like to talk to him. He always made her laugh. Her eyelids lifted in long folds, she felt a mild astonishment to see this unfamiliar room around her. She ought to unpack some of her dresses, instead of prowling through the past. Queer the way the past kept pushing aside the present, the dead voices sounded louder in her mind than those that spoke today. Almost as if she were searching for something, knowing neither its shape nor colour. But when I find it, I'll know, she thought, nodding softly; I'll know.

Vera's voice preceded Vera as she hurried along the hall. 'Oh, Mother, I'm so sorry I wasn't here when you came.' At the door she stopped. 'Mother! You aren't sick again?'

Mary cocked her head forward from the pillows. 'No. I'm not. I'm just comfortable.' Vera leaned over the bed, investigatory fingers on Mary's forehead before she kissed her cheek, the brim of the wide hat clipping Mary on the head.

'You don't feel feverish,' said Vera.

'I'm not. You look very smart.'

'I picked it up at a sale at Bergdorf's.' Vera's fingers brushed the heavy white silk. 'Good, isn't it? But why are you in bed if –'

'Well, I'll tell you. It was accidental.' Mary pushed the full, fine lawn sleeves of her nightgown up from her hands. 'I started to unpack. I laid out my toilet case. I thought I'd take off my dress so I could rest a little, and the first thing I knew, here I was, all ready for bed.' She chuckled. 'So I just went to bed.'

'I suppose the trip tired you.'

'I was thinking about something else,' said Mary.

'Heaven knows I'm dead!' Vera drew a chair near the bed. 'What an afternoon! Really, some of the women I played with! Bridge, you know. For the Red Cross. Anyone could come, just by paying, and anyone certainly did. You know, women who don't belong to the Country Club. They wanted to see the inside of it, I suppose, and the members. Awful people!'

'What's wrong with them?' Mary's tone was innocent enough.

'Why, you know! Simply common. Why, at one table –' Vera stopped, at a sniff from her mother. 'Of course,' she went on, hastily, 'we did clear quite a nice sum. And Mrs Poole – you know, *the* Pooles – asked me to serve on her committee to organise a stronger chapter. We've got to get women knitting again, and rolling bandages –'

‘It’s awful,’ said Mary, ‘to think what common folks may wear them.’

Vera made a startled grimace and then laughed uneasily. ‘Now, don’t be difficult, Mother. You know perfectly well what I mean.’ She got to her feet. ‘You’re sure you won’t come down for dinner? Peter Willoughby’s coming in, quite informally. I wanted you to meet him, I thought you might help me with Hilda. She’s beginning to be reasonable, I think. He’s just enough older and more experienced. As I told Hilda, after all the advantages we’ve given her, she’s not going to be content –’

‘Willoughby?’ asked Mary. ‘Is he the divorced one?’

‘Just incompatibility. After all, he’d know better what he wanted the next time, wouldn’t he?’ Vera listened. From the lower hall rose the sound of discussion, Clem’s voice, and another voice like Clem’s, but more impassioned. ‘Bill’s home. He simply must clear away that litter from the hall, it looks like an annexe to Abercrombie’s.’ Vera moved with determined haste from the room, pulling the door shut after her.

Now she did that on purpose, thought Mary, so I couldn’t hear. Vera had got around Hilda and her poor little love affair. Talked her down. Oh, my, thought Mary, I can’t be bothered with them! I’m too old. All I want is a little peace. Peace? I came not to send peace, but a sword. And a man’s foes shall be those of his own household. She couldn’t remember how the sonorous phrases continued. His terrible swift sword. Transformed now into bombers and tanks. Vera tired her with her jittery talk. After all, Hilda was old enough to decide for herself. Or was she? Certainly no one could have pried

Mary away from Will Bristol. She couldn't remember why she had been so sure, the beginning of love was overlaid with all their years together; did a tree remember the seed from which it grew? If Will were here today, he would be troubled, too. Perhaps he would know what she was searching for. He might give her the word to set in order the kaleidoscopic jumble of thoughts and recollections which had beset her all day.

She reached impatiently for a book face down under the scarlet afghan across her knees, and looked at the corpse that sprawled on the bright jacket of the book. *The Case of the Missing Surplice.* A waste of time, when she had so little left, reading mysteries. Let's see, she had decided the minister hadn't committed the murder, the author was too obvious about him. She was so absorbed that a knock on the door and Hilda's entrance left her not a second to hide the book.

'Hello, there, Grand-Mary,' said Hilda, darting toward her, the skirt of her white evening frock swinging around her slim waist. 'Aren't you the lazy one?' She touched her fingertips to her scarlet lips and brushed them over Mary's cheek. 'Promise of a kiss. Don't want to smear you all up.' She perched on the edge of the bed, arms locked around a knee. 'Look at the gore!'

'At my age, too!' Mary mimicked Vera's reproachful voice. 'How nice you look.' She forgot how beautiful young bodies were! Skin with a tinge of gold, like pollen over the smooth surface, fitting so perfectly over fine bones, exquisite in their articulation, that hollow at the base of the throat, the spring of shoulder blades like hints of wings, delicate flow of young, firm muscles down to the elbows, down to the narrow wrists. 'That dress is a starched petticoat and not much else!'

'Um.' Hilda looked at her arms against the stiff whiteness. 'I ought to be a darker shade of tan, to be effective. But the sun lamp blew out all the fuses and the man hasn't come to fix it.'

'Even your sunlight isn't real,' said Mary. 'Synthetic sunburn.'

'Why not?' Hilda looked at her grandmother, a wary restiveness in her face. 'You can turn it on and off yourself. At least, you can after the electrician comes. And what do you mean, *even*?'

'Figure it out,' Mary said. She could feel resistance in the girl's body, a harder thrust of foot on the floor.

'You mean me, I suppose. Mother's been talking, hasn't she? Did she tell you about the wonderful Peter Willoughby?' Hilda crossed the room to a window, and one hand swished the long curtain against the floor. 'You know what he's like, Grand-Mary? A ripe banana, soft and plump and just that colour, and his clothes fit him elegantly like the peel. Rich as mud. Squashy.' She jerked at the curtain. 'Here I had my mind all made up – you have to be practical, don't you? What's unreal about that? Oh, I didn't want to come in to see you, you always find out about things.'

'My goodness,' said Mary, 'why did that get under your skin?'

Hilda turned, her slight body held rigid. 'Because it's true. It's what he said – John.'

'John who?' asked Mary. 'I never heard of any John.'

'He said I was selfish and spoiled and afraid of reality. I wish you'd tell me why when it's something unpleasant, like being poor, people call it real, but having money or position isn't real at all. After all, Peter Willoughby's quite important. He's in a bank and everything.'

(She's not talking to me, thought Mary. She's wrestling with herself. All I need to do is keep still.)

'It will be years before John gets anywhere. He's a doctor, that is, he's an intern now. He's perfectly unreasonable, he says if I got a job and helped support us now, he'd take care of me when I got to be an old lady. That's not when I want things, I want them now. It's much better, anyway, if you aren't too crazy about a man, isn't it? You can manage him better. Peter's mad about me, and so he does everything I want him to. But John –' Her face had sharpened; it was like the face of a girl drowning, seen through still clear water, thought Mary. 'Oh, well, I'll get over him. I won't go on feeling this way. Anyway, look at the people who fall in love and get married and what happens to them? Look at Mother, she was in love, wasn't she? I mean, she's fond of Father, of course, but –'

'The trouble with your mother is that Clem never asked enough of her. She managed him, the way you think you'll manage this Peter. You're setting out to be just like her, a taker and not a giver. That's death for a woman. Dry rot. He who would save his life must first lose it. In love, above all else! Love of a man, or a country.' (A land where a man can be free, and his children after him!) 'You're afraid you'll lose yourself, your hard little comfort-loving pinpoint of a self!'

Hilda looked at her grandmother with strangely expressionless eyes. Through the window burst the notes of a French horn.

'Peter,' said Hilda. 'In his chariot. Coming for to carry me home.' She stood beside the bed, digging a finger into the soft wool of the afghan, twisting it round and round. 'You and John ought to get together. You'd have a wonderful time. If that's the way I am, why, that's the way I am, isn't it?'

'Not quite,' said Mary, quietly. 'Not quite. You're scared, but you're still breathing.'

'Just a mess!' Hilda drew herself erect with a shiver as something crashed against the door. 'Maybe we all are in this house! That's my darling little brother you hear! He's another.' She moved quickly to fling open the door. Skis tumbled in past her, and Bill on his knees frowned up and went on picking up bits of phonograph records. 'What *are* you doing?'

'What the heck d'you open that door for just when I leaned my skis there? Smashing my best pieces lugging my traps out of your way and why? Because that louse of a Peter –'

'You make it delightful for Grand-Mary,' said Hilda sharply.

'Gee, I didn't know you were in this room!' Bill brushed Hilda aside and strolled in, dropping the broken discs on a chair. His face was surprisingly young, looking down from his tall, loose body, his grin was ingenuous and ingratiating. 'Hi, Gramma, what'd they put you to bed for? I was just going to stow my gear in here. Changing things around like this! How are you, Gramma?'

‘She was all right,’ said Hilda, ‘till you knocked down her door.’

‘Say, beat it, woman! Your boyfriend’s champing around below!’

‘You can’t come to dinner looking like that!’ Hilda disappeared.

‘The fuss they make about this droop Willoughby,’ said Bill. ‘I thought Christmas time Hilda’d ditched him. You can’t tell about women, can you? Of course he’s lined with money. But Hilda’s a good kid – I dunno – well, we all could use a little. Money, I mean.’

‘Sit down,’ said Mary. ‘You’re up so high I can’t see your face.’ He was restless, in a hurry to be off. He had to speak to her but he really didn’t see her; she was just an old woman, labelled Grand-Mary. There might be traces in his face of the child who had liked her, in the shape of the head, the long dark lashes over the blue eyes; but his affection now was nothing but a recollected form.

‘Well, I can’t stay, see? I got a lot of things to do.’ He drew a chair near her and folded himself down upon it, hands dangling. ‘You – you staying long?’

‘I don’t know.’

‘I just noticed you hadn’t unpacked.’

‘I just came this afternoon.’ What was he leading up to, meeting her eyes with quick, speculative glances?

‘You haven’t got a radio, have you? How about me setting mine up in here? I could get along without it.’

‘I don’t want it.’ Mary smiled. ‘What is it you want, Bill?’

‘Gee, I was just thinking it’s lucky for me you’re here. You’d understand if a fellow asked a favour, wouldn't you?' He dropped his voice into husky confidence. 'Here I come home, no kick at all. Do I get any credit? Dad lands on me the minute he sees me. Why, half the fellows flunked the same courses I did! But while he's sore like that is no time to be trying to collect a bill, now is it! This guy says he won't wait any longer, tonight's the deadline, I wouldn't speak of it only it's an emergency, see! I was driving this other fellow's father's car –' Bill rolled his eyes toward the door, his furrowed forehead flushed, even the parting of his crisp brown hair was scarlet.

'Whose father's car?' Vera frowned at the clasp of a bracelet she was fastening. 'What car?'

'I was just telling Grand-Mary a little story.' Bill scrambled to his feet. 'See you later, gotta rush now.'

'You might hurry,' Vera called after him. 'Your father's cross enough already.' She vibrated a moment in the doorway. 'Was he asking you for money? You mustn't give him any. He's so cute, the way he tries to get around you.' She sighed. 'Clem's furious at him, I told him he was just a boy. The trouble is just that Clem is upset. You'd think Paris was his home town, the way he's taking it. Of course it's the market that worries him. He got it on the radio.'

'Got what?' asked Mary. 'The way you jump around!'

'I said very plainly that they were evacuating Paris.' Vera spoke with dignity. 'I don't jump, although I might, the way everything piles up. I don't know where Hilda's gone. I heard her on the telephone, but I can't find her. If she's going to be difficult again about Peter! Goodness, I envy you! I'll have Anna bring up a tray, do you eat a heavy dinner at night?'

'Yes, I do,' said Mary, with emphasis. 'I'm hungry.'

Vera sighed, slid her bracelets up her thin arms with a nervous gesture, and went quickly away, trailing grey chiffon.

Mary settled into the pillows, her eyes closed. Her heart seemed to have slipped down so that it was beating in her stomach, each thud loud and disturbing. The trip had tired her, the family had tired her, she was glad the twilight was deep enough now so that her eyelids could shut her into darkness. Her heartbeats seemed very far apart, and between them silence and darkness, and all the recollections, the impressions, the images of the long day rolling at last together into the meaning she had sought.

A land where a man can be free, and his children after him, she thought. Free? We have thought the world was run for us, that we could go on turning always in these narrow, petty, selfish cells. We are losing them again, peace, freedom. We had them only as a promise. My father, my sons, and now these children. They have lost them, having no dream to hold them safe, to strive to keep them. They are blind and empty, passionless – I must tell them this, perhaps Hilda heard me, it may not be too late. She thought, it all begins again, the old struggle. She could not lift her eyelids, her heart climbed up into her throat, it floated away like a bright and burning word. When you have the word, it is too late to speak. It all begins again.

DEFEAT

Kay Boyle

(1941)

Toward the end of June that year and through July, there was a sort of uncertain pause, an undetermined suspension that might properly be called neither an armistice nor a peace, and it lasted until the men began coming back from where they were. They came at intervals, trickling down from the north in twos or threes, or even one by one, some of them prisoners who had escaped and others merely a part of that individual retreat in which the sole destination was home. They had exchanged their uniforms for something else as they came along – corduroys, or workmen's blue or whatever people might have given them in secret to get away in – bearded, singularly and shabbily outfitted men getting down from a bus or off a train without so much as a knapsack in their hands and all with the same bewildered, scarcely discrepant story to tell. Once they had reached the precincts of familiarity, they stood there a moment where the vehicle had left them, maybe trying to button the jacket that didn't fit them or set the neck or shoulders right, like men who have been waiting in a courtroom and have finally heard their names called and stand up to take the oath and mount the witness stand. You could see them getting the words ready – revising the very quality of truth – and the look in their eyes, and then someone coming out of the post office or crossing the station square in the heat would recognise them and go toward them with a hand out, and the testimony would begin.

They had found their way back from different places, by different means, some on bicycle, some by bus, some over the mountains on foot, coming home to the Alpes-Maritimes from Rennes, or from Clermont-Ferrand, or from Lyons, or from any part of France, and looking as incongruous to modern defeat as survivors of the Confederate Army might have looked, transplanted to this year and place (with their spurs still on and their soft-brimmed, dust-whitened hats), limping wanly back, half dazed and not yet having managed to get the story of what happened straight. Only, this time, they were the men of that tragically unarmed and undirected force which had been the French Army once but was no longer, returning to what orators might call reconstruction but which they knew could never be the same.

Wherever they came from, they had identical evidence to give: that the German ranks had advanced bareheaded, in short-sleeved summer shirts – young, blond-haired men with their arms linked, row on row, and their trousers immaculately creased, having slept all night in hotel beds and their stomachs full, advancing singing and falling singing before the puny coughing of the French machine guns. That is, the first line of them might fall, and part of the second, possibly, but never more, for just then the French ammunition would suddenly expire and the bright-haired, blond demigods would march on singing across their dead. Then would follow all the glittering display: the rustproof tanks and guns, the chromiumed electric kitchens, the crematoriums. Legends or truth, the stories became indistinguishable in the mouths of the Frenchmen who returned – that the Germans were dressed as if for tennis that summer, with nothing but a tune to carry in their heads, while the French crawled out from under lorries where they'd slept maybe every night for a week, going to meet them like crippled, encumbered miners emerging from the pit of a warfare fifty years interred, with thirty-five kilos of kit and a change of shoes and a tin helmet left over from 1914 breaking them in two as they met the brilliantly nickelled Nazi dawn. They said their superiors were the first to run; they said their ammunition had been sabotaged; they said the ambulances had been transformed into accommodations for the officers' lady friends; they said '*Nous avons été vendus*' or '*On nous a vendu*' over and over, until you could have made a popular song of it – the words and the music of defeat. After their testimony was given, some of them added (not the young but those who had fought before) in grave, part-embittered, part-vainglorious voices, 'I'm ashamed to be a Frenchman' or, 'I'm ashamed of being French today', and then gravely took their places with the others.

There was one man, though, who didn't say any of these things, probably because he had something else on his mind. He was a dark, short, rather gracefully made man, not thirty yet, with hot, handsome eyes and a cleft chin. Even when he came back without his uniform and without the victory, a certain air of responsibility, of authority, remained because he had been the chauffeur of the mail bus before the war. He didn't sit talking in the *bistro* about what he had seen and where he had been, but he got the black beard off his face as quickly as he could, and bought a pair of new shoes, and went back to work in stubborn-lipped, youthful, almost violent pride. Except one night he did tell the story; he told it only once, about two months after he got back, and not to his own people or the people of the village but, as if by chance, to two commercial travellers for rival fruit juice firms who were just beginning to circulate again from town to town in the Unoccupied Zone. They sat at the Café Central together, the three of them, drinking wine, talking about the anachronism of horse-and-mule-drawn cannon in Flanders and the beasts running amok under the enemy planes, and saying how they had all believed that the French line was going to hold somewhere, that it wasn't going to break.

'At first we thought it would hold at the Oise,' one of the travelling men said. 'We kept on retreating, saying the new front must be at the Oise, and believing it too, and then, when we dropped below the Oise, we kept saying it would hold at the Marne, and believing it, and then we thought it would be the Seine, and even when we were south of Paris we kept on believing about some kind of a line holding on the Loire. . . .'

'I still don't know why we stopped retreating,' said the other commercial traveller. He sat looking soberly at his glass.

'We can't talk about the Italians any more. I still don't see why we didn't retreat right down to Senegal. I don't see what stopped us,' he said. Then the quiet-mouthed little bus driver began telling them about what had happened to him on the Fourteenth of July.

It seems that in some of the cities the enemy hadn't taken or had withdrawn from, processions formed on the Fourteenth and passed through the streets in silence, the flagstaffs they carried draped with black, and their heads bowed. In some of the villages the mayor, dressed in mourning, laid a wreath on the monument to the last war's dead while the peasants kneeled about him in the square.

'I was in Pontcharra on the Fourteenth,' said one of the travelling salesmen, 'and when the mayor put the wreath down and the bugle called out like that for the dead, all the peasants uncovered themselves, but the military didn't even stand at attention.'

'By that time none of the privates were saluting their officers in the street anywhere you went,' said the other salesman, but the bus driver didn't pay any attention to what they said. He went on telling them that he'd been taken prisoner near Rennes on the seventeenth of June, and that there he saw the tracts the Boche planes had showered down the week before. The tracts said, 'Frenchmen, prepare your coffins! Frenchwomen, get out your ball dresses! We're going to dance the soles off your shoes on the Fourteenth of July!' He told the commercial travellers exactly what use they made of the tracts in the public places there. He was more than three weeks in the prison camp, he said, and on the night of the twelfth of July he and a *copain* made their escape. They went in uniform, on borrowed bicycles. They kept to the main road all night, wheeling along as free and unmolested in the dark as two young men cycling home from a dance, with their hearts light, and the stars out over them, and the night air mild. At dawn they took to the side roads, and toward eight o'clock of the new day they saw a house standing alone, a little in advance of the village that lay ahead.

'We'll ask here,' the bus driver had said, and they pushed their cycles in off the road and laid them down behind a tree. The house, they could see then, was the schoolhouse, with a sign for '*Filles*' over one door and for '*Garçons*' over the other. The *copain* said there would be nobody there, but the bus driver had seen a woman come to the window and look at them, and he walked up to the door.

The desks were empty because of what had happened and the time of year, but the bus driver said he knew it must have been the schoolmistress who was standing in the middle of the room between the benches, a young woman with fair, wavy hair, eying them fearlessly and even sharply as they came. The bus driver and his *copain* said good morning, and they saw at once the lengths of three-coloured stuff in her hands and the work she had been doing. They looked around them and saw four French flags clustered in each corner of the classroom and great loops of bunting that were draped along three sides of the room. The first thing the bus driver thought was that she ought to be warned, she ought to be told, and then, when he looked at her face again, he knew she knew as much as or more than they.

'You ought to keep the door locked,' he had said, and the schoolmistress looked at him almost in contempt.

'I don't care who comes in,' she said, and she went on folding the bunting into the lengths she wanted to cut it to drape across the furthest wall.

'So the village is occupied?' the bus driver said.

'Yes,' she said, but she began cutting the tricolour bunting.

'There's one thing,' said the *copain,* looking a little bleakly at the two others. 'If you give yourself up, at least you don't get shot.'

The schoolmistress had put her scissors down and said to the bus driver, 'You'll have to get rid of your uniforms before there's any chance of you getting through.' She glanced around the classroom as though the demands of action had suddenly made it strange to her. 'Take them off and put them in the cupboard there,' she had said, 'and cover yourselves with this stuff while you wait,' and she heaped the blue and white and red lengths upon the desks. 'In case they might come in,' she said. She took her hat and *filet* off the hook as she said, 'I'll come back with other clothes for you.'

'If there would be any way of getting something to eat,' the bus driver had said, and because he asked this, the tide of courage seemed to rise even higher in her.

'Yes,' she said. 'I'll bring back food for you.'

'And a bottle of *pinard,*' said the *copain*, but he didn't it say it very loud.

When she was gone, they took their uniforms off and wrapped the bunting around themselves, doing it for her and modesty's sake, and then they sat down at the first form's desk, swathed to their beards in red, white, and blue. Even if the Boche had walked into the schoolhouse then, there probably wasn't any military regulation made to deal with what they would have found, the bus driver said: just two Frenchmen in their underwear sitting quietly inside the colours of their country's flag. But whether he said the other thing to her as soon as she brought the bread and sausage and wine and the scraps of other men's clothing back, he didn't know. Sometimes, when he thought of it afterward, he wasn't quite sure he had ever got the actual words out, but then he remembered the look on her face as she stood by the tree where the bicycles had lain and watched them pedalling toward the village just ahead, and he knew he must have said it. He knew he must have wiped the sausage grease and the wine off his mouth with the back of his hand and said 'A country isn't defeated as long as its women aren't' or 'until its women are' or 'As long as the women of a country aren't defeated, it doesn't matter if its army is' – something like that, perhaps saying it just before they shook hands with her and cycled away.

That was the morning of the thirteenth, and they rode all day in the heat, two what-might-have-been-peasants cycling slowly hour after hour across the hushed, summery, sunny land. The war was over for them, for this country the war was over; there was no sound or look of it in the meadows or the trees or grain. The war was finished, but the farmhouse they stopped at that evening would not take them in.

'Have you got your bread tickets with you?' the peasant

said, and even the white-haired sows behind his legs eyed them narrowly with greed.

'We're prisoners escaped, we've got a bit of money,' the bus driver said. 'We'll pay for our soup, and maybe you'll let us sleep in the loft.'

'And when the Boche come in for the milk they'll shoot me and the family for having taken you in!' the peasant said, and the bus driver stood looking at him bitterly a moment before he began to swear. When he had called the man the names he wanted to, he said:

'Look here, we were soldiers – perhaps you haven't got that yet? We haven't been demobilised; we were taken prisoner, we escaped. We were fighting a little war up there.'

'If you'd fought it better, the Boche wouldn't have got this far,' the peasant said. He said it in cunning and triumph, and then he closed the door.

They slept the night at the next farm, eating soup and bread and drinking red wine in the kitchen, and when they had paid for it they were shown up to the loft. But they were not offered the side on which the hay lay; the farmer was thinking of next winter and he told them they could lie down just as well on the boards. They slept heavily and well, and it was very light when they woke in the morning, and so that day, the day of the fourteenth, they did not get far. By six that night they were only another hundred kilometres on, and then the *copain*'s tyre went flat. But a little town stood just ahead and they pushed their bicycles toward it through the summer evening, and down its wide, treeless street. They hadn't seen the uniform yet, but they knew the Germans must be there. Even on the square in the heart of town they saw no sign, but still there was that unnatural quiet, that familiar uneasiness on the air, so they pushed their wheels through the open doors of a big garage, past the dry and padlocked gas pumps, and stood them up against the inside wall. There, in the garage's half-security and semi-dark, they looked around them; twenty or more cars stood one beside the other, halted as if forever because of the lack of fluid to flow through their veins. Overhead the glass panes of the roof were still painted blue; the military and staff cars parked in the shadowy silence still bore their green-and-khaki camouflage. The war was over, everything had stopped, and out beyond the wide-open automobile doorway they saw the dance platform that had been erected in the square, and the dark, leafy branches twined on its upright beams and balustrade, and the idle people standing looking. There were no flags up, only this rather dismal atmosphere of preparation, and it was then the bus driver and his *copain* had remembered it was the Fourteenth.

'It's a national holiday and we haven't had a drink yet,' the *copain* said. He stood there in the garage with his hands in the pockets of the trousers that didn't belong to him, staring bleakly out across the square. Even when two German soldiers who were putting electric wiring up in the dance pavilion came into view, his face did not alter. He simply went on saying, 'We haven't had the *apéritif* all day.'

The bus driver took a packet of cigarettes out of his jacket pocket and put one savagely on his lip. As he lit it, he looked in hot, bitter virulence out to where the Germans were hanging strings of bulbs among the fresh, dark leaves.

'"Frenchmen, prepare your coffins!"' he had said, and then he gave a laugh. 'They've made only one mistake so far, just one,' he said, and as he talked the cigarette jerked up and down in fury on his lip. 'They've got the dance floor and the decorations all right, and they've probably got the music, and maybe the refreshments too. So far so good,' he said. 'But they haven't got the partners. That's what's going to be funny. That's what's going to be really funny.'

He sat there in the Café Central telling it to the two commercial travellers, perhaps because he had had more to drink than usual telling the story, or perhaps because it had been weighing heavy on his heart long enough. He told them about the dinner the garage owner gave him and his *copain*: civet and fried potatoes and salad and four kinds of cheese and armagnac with the coffee. He said they could scarcely get it all down and that then their host opened a bottle of champagne for them. That's the kind of man the garage owner was. And during the dinner or afterward, with the wine inside of him, it seems the bus driver had said it again. He had said something about as long as the women of a nation weren't defeated the rest of it didn't matter, and just as he said it the music struck up in the dance pavilion outside.

The place the garage owner offered them for the night was just above the garage itself, a sort of storeroom, with three windows overlooking the square. First he repaired the *copain*'s tyre for him, and behind him on the wall as he worked they could read the newspaper cutting he had pinned up, perhaps in some spirit of derision. It exhorted all Frenchmen to accept quietly and without protest the new regulations concerning the circulation of private and public vehicles.

'Without protest!' said the garage owner, taking the dripping red tube out of the basin of water and pinching the leak between his finger and thumb. 'I'll have to close the place up, and they ask me to do it without protest!' He stood rubbing sandpaper gently around where the imperceptible hole in the rubber was. 'We weren't ready for war and yet we declared it just the same,' he said, 'and now we've asked for peace and we aren't ready for that either' and when he had finished with the tyre he showed them up the stairs.

'I'll keep the light off,' he said, 'in case it might give them the idea of coming up and having a look,' but they didn't need any light, for the illumination of the dance pavilion in the square shone in through the windows and lit the rows of storage batteries and the cases of spare parts and spark plugs with an uncanny and partial brilliance. From outside, they heard the music playing; the exact waltz time and the quick, entirely martial version of swing.

'Somebody ought to tell them they're wasting their time,' the bus driver had said, jerking one shoulder toward the windows. He could have burst out laughing at the sight of them, he explained, some with white gloves on even, waiting out there to the strains of music for what wasn't going to come.

The garage owner shook out the potato sacks of waste on the floor and gave them the sacks to lie down on, and then he took one look out the window at the square and grinned and said good night and went downstairs. The *copain* was tired and he lay down at once on the soft rags on the floor and drew a blanket up over him, but the bus driver had stood a while at one side of the window, watching the thing below. A little group of townspeople was standing around the platform where the variously coloured lights hung, and the band was playing in one corner of the pavilion underneath the leaves. No one was dancing, but the German soldiers were hanging around in expectation, some standing on the steps of the platform and some leaning on the garnished rails.

'For a little while there wasn't a woman anywhere,' the bus driver told the commercial travellers. 'There was this crowd of people from the town, perhaps thirty or forty of them looking on, and maybe some others further back in the dark where you couldn't see them, but that was all,' and then he stopped talking.

'And then what happened?' said one of the travelling men after a moment, and the bus driver sat looking in silence at his glass.

'They had a big, long table spread out with things to eat on it,' he said in a minute, and he didn't look up. 'They had fruit tarts, it looked like, and sweet chocolate, and bottles of lemonade and beer. They had as much as you wanted of everything,' he said. 'And perhaps once you got near enough to start eating and drinking, then the other thing just followed naturally afterward – or that's the way I worked it out,' he said. 'Or maybe, if you've had a dress a long time that you wanted to wear and you hadn't had the chance of putting it on and showing it off because all the men were away – I mean if you were a woman. I worked it out that maybe the time comes when you want to put it on so badly that you put it on just the same whatever's happened, or maybe, if you're one kind of a woman, any kind of a uniform looks all right to you after a certain time. The music was good, it was first class,' he said, but he didn't look up. 'And here was all this food spread out, and the corks popping off the bottles, and the lads in uniform, great, big fellows, handing out chocolates to all the girls. . . .'

The three of them sat at the table without talking for a while after the bus driver's voice had ceased, and then one of the travelling men said:

'Well, that was just one town.'

'Yes, that was just one town,' said the bus driver, and when he picked up his glass to drink, something as crazy as tears was standing in his eyes.

GOOD EVENING, MRS CRAVEN

Mollie Panter-Downes

(1942)

For years now they had been going to Porter's, in one of the little side streets off the Strand. They had their own particular table in the far corner of the upstairs room, cosily near the fire in winter, cooled in summer by a window at their backs, through which drifted soot and the remote bumble of traffic. Everything contemporary seemed remote at Porter's. The whole place looked as though it had been soaked in Madeira – the rich brown walls crowded with signed photographs of Irving and Bancroft and Forbes-Robertson, the plush seats, the fly-spotted marble Muses forever turning their classic noses hopefully towards the door, as though expecting to see Ellen Terry come in. The waiters were all very old. They carried enormous napkins over their arms and produced the menu with a special flourish from the tails of their old-fashioned coats. The waiter who attended to the corner table looked as though he could have walked on as a senator in a Lyceum production of *Julius Caesar*. Leaning protectively over them, he would say in a hoarse, fruity voice, into which

Madeira seemed to have seeped too, 'The steak-and-kidney pudding is just as you like it today, Mr Craven.'

Every Thursday evening, wet or fine, they would be dining in their corner under the bust of Mrs Siddons, talking quietly, sometimes holding hands under the tablecloth. It was the evening when he was supposed to have a standing engagement to play bridge at his club. Sometimes he called for her at her flat; more often they arrived separately. Out of all their Thursdays she loved the foggy winter evenings best, when the taxi driver growled, 'Wot a night!' as she fumbled in her purse for change, when she ran coughing up the stairs into the plushy warmth and light and their waiter greeted her with a 'Good evening, Mrs Craven. Mr Craven's waiting at your table. I'll bring along your sherries right away.'

She would go over to their table, sit down, and slide her hand palm upwards along the sofa seat until his hand closed round it.

'Good evening, Mrs Craven,' he would say, and they would both laugh.

They always enjoyed the joke that the waiter supposed they were married. It went with the respectability of Porter's that any nice couple who dined together continuously over a long period of time should be thought of as husband and wife. 'We're one in the sight of God and Mrs Siddons,' he said, but although she laughed, it wasn't a joke with her. She liked being called Mrs Craven. It gave her a warm feeling round the heart, because she could pretend for a moment that things were different and that he had no wife and three fine children who would be broken in bits by a divorce. He had long ago made her see the sense of this, and now she was careful never to make scenes or to sound the demanding note which he hated. Her value for him was to be always there, calm and understanding. 'You smooth me out,' he said sometimes. 'You give me more peace than anyone in the world.' She was a wonderful listener. She would sit watching him with a little smile while he told her all the details of his week. He often talked about the children. At her flat, standing in front of the mirror tying his tie, he would tell her proudly how clever eight-year-old Jennifer was, or how well Pete was coming on at school. On these occasions the little smile sometimes grew a trifle rigid on her lips.

They never went anywhere but Porter's. In a queer sort of way, although he was known by name, he seemed to feel safe and anonymous there. 'None of the people one knows comes here,' he said, by which he meant none of the people his wife knew. More men than women ate at Porter's. Very occasionally he was greeted by a business acquaintance, who would nod and call across the room, 'How are you?' Then he would call back heartily, 'Fine! How are *you*?' but he would be a little uncomfortable all through the meal. If she slid her hand towards his knee, he would pretend not to notice, and he would talk in a brisk, cheerful way which, at a distance, might look like the kind of manner one would use when dining with a female cousin up from the country or a secretary one had kept working late and taken along for some food out of sheer good nature.

Sometimes she felt that she would like to put on a low-cut gown and go somewhere where there were lights and dancing, where she could walk in proudly, with him following her without taking a swift, surreptitious look round the room first to see who was there. But she knew how worried he would look if she suggested it, how he would say, 'Darling, I wish we could, but you know it's impossible. Someone would be sure to spot us. We've got to be careful – haven't we?' By now she had learned exactly how to dress for their Thursday evenings. The clothes had to make her look beautiful for him, but they must be on the unadventurous side so that no one would cast an interested remembering glance from an opposite table. She often wore brown, and sometimes she had a funny feeling that she was invisible against the brown wall and the faded prints of the Prince of Denmark and the noblest Roman of them all.

When the war came, he got a commission in a mechanised regiment. Their Thursday evenings were interrupted, and when he got home on leave things were often difficult. There was a family dinner party, or the children were back from school. 'You know how it is, darling,' he would say ruefully on the telephone. But every now and then he sent her a telegram and came dashing up to London for a few hours. Porter's still looked the same except that most of the men were in uniform, and the old waiter always saw to it that they got their usual table. 'Good evening, Mrs Craven,' he would say shambling forward when he saw her. 'You're expecting Mr Craven? . . . Ah, that's fine. The pigeon casserole is just how he likes it today.'

They dined together just before he went to Libya. There were two men drinking port at the next table, one with white hair and beautiful, long hands who looked like a Galsworthy family lawyer, the other round and red.

'Don't think I'm being stupid and morbid,' she said, 'but supposing anything happens. I've been worrying about that. You might be wounded or ill and I wouldn't know.' She tried to laugh. 'The War Office doesn't have a service for sending telegrams to mistresses, does it?'

He frowned, because this sounded hysterical, and glanced sharply at the old men at the next table, who went right on drinking port and talking in their tired old voices.

'Darling,' he said, 'don't start getting ideas like that into your head. If anything did happen – but it won't – I'd get someone to let you know right away.'

She had a wild impulse to ask him how this would be possible when he would be lying broken and bloody, alone in the sand. With an effort, she remembered that he loved her because she was calm, because she was not the kind of woman to make scenes or let the tears run down her face in public.

'I know you would,' she said. 'Don't worry about me. Remember, dearest, you don't have to worry about me one little bit.'

'Good night, Mrs Craven. Good night, Mr Craven,' said the old waiter, hurrying after them as they went out.

A long time after he left, his letters began to arrive. They were not very satisfactory. He wrote in the same hearty style that he put on at Porter's for the business acquaintances' benefit, and she had the feeling he was worried the censor might turn out to be his wife's second cousin. She worked hard at a war job and lost a lot of weight. The girl who washed her hair said, 'My goodness, aren't you getting grey!' and she longed foolishly to be able to tell her about it and get her sympathy. There was no one to confide in; all these years she had been so careful that she had hardly mentioned his name to anyone else. She went out with other people, but she imagined that she wasn't so amusing or attractive as she used to be and that they noticed it. She began to stay home most evenings, reading in bed or writing him long letters. Before he left, they had settled on various little code words which would give her an idea of where he was, so she was able to tell when he was up in the front lines or when he had gone back to Cairo for leave.

After a while his letters stopped, but she wasn't seriously worried at first. She knew that the mails were often bad; there had been long gaps before. But this time hard fighting was going on in Libya, and she had a terrible premonition that something had happened. She found that she could hardly sleep at all, and when she came home in the evenings, her hand shook as she put the key in the door. She made herself take the letters out of the box and look through them very slowly. Afterwards she would go into the living-room, sit down, and stare blankly out of the window at the barrage balloons glittering in the late sunlight.

One evening she came in after a hard day's work, and as she stood getting the key out of her purse, she knew that there would be a letter or a cable waiting for her. She was so positive of it that she was tremulous with relief as she got the door open and stooped to the mailbox. There was nothing except a bill for a repair to the radio set. She stood, feeling cold and stupid, then she went swiftly to the living-room telephone and looked up a number in the book. As she dialled it and then listened to the bell buzzing, it seemed odd to her to think how many times he must have heard it ring through that unknown house.

When a child's voice, high, and carefully a little overloud, answered, she was slightly taken aback. She said, 'Is this Mrs Craven's house?' The child's voice said, 'Yes. This is Jennifer. Do you want Mummy? . . . I'll get her.'

After a pause she heard footsteps on a hardwood floor, and then a new voice said, 'Hello? Yes?'

She had thought out what to say, and she made her voice crisp and friendly.

'Good evening, Mrs Craven,' she said. 'I do want to apologise for troubling you like this. You won't know my name, but I'm an old friend of Mr Craven's, and I've only just heard that he's in Libya. I thought I'd like to ring up and see if you've had good news of him.'

'Why, that's nice of you,' Mrs Craven said pleasantly. 'To tell you the truth, I've heard nothing very recently, but I try not to worry. He'll cable me when he has a minute. Judging by the papers, I shouldn't think any of them have a minute.'

'No, I don't suppose they have,' she said. She could hear the little girl calling out, as if to a dog. She knew that there were two dogs, and that there was French Empire furniture in the room, and on the mantelpiece stood a little Chinese figure in white porcelain with a scroll in its hand. She had helped choose it one Christmas. Mrs Craven sounded calm and unfussed. She could picture her standing at the telephone, smiling slightly, secure in the middle of her own familiar things, maybe watching the child abstractedly out of the corner of her eye while she dealt courteously with this well-meaning stranger.

The pleasant voice said, 'Luckily, I'm tremendously busy myself. That helps to keep one's mind off things, doesn't it? I'm so sorry, I don't think I quite caught the name.'

She mumbled a name that might have been anything and added lightly, 'Just someone Mr Craven used to know a long while ago. Goodbye, Mrs Craven, and thanks so much. I hope you hear good news very soon.'

She hung up the receiver and sat for a long time without moving. Then she began to weep bitterly. The tears poured down her face, and she rocked her body backward and forward. 'I can't go on,' she sobbed, as though he were there in the room with her. 'I can't, can't go on. You'll have to break them up – I don't care. I just can't go on this way any longer.' She thought of his wife sitting in their home on the other side of town, and the contrast seemed too bitter to bear. All those years of Thursday evenings seemed like a pathetic game of make-believe – two children playing at housekeeping in a playhouse with three walls. After a while she grew quieter. She sat thinking of him, wondering whether, wherever he was, he would have had a sense of something breaking sharply in two, coming apart with a hum, like a snapped wire. Already she could feel the relaxed tension, as though whatever had been holding her taut all these years had suddenly gone limp.

Tomorrow she would write and tell him, but not now. She couldn't remember when she had felt so tired. She went into the bathroom to bathe her face, and then came back and began taking off her dress. There was a brooch pinned at the neck, and she undid it and stood looking at it for a moment. It was a discreetly beautiful thing of dark, old garnets – diamonds, he had pointed out, were too likely to cause comment, and didn't suit her, either. She put down the brooch and finished undressing. Maybe, she thought, she would wait until after tomorrow to write to him, for she had a feeling that tomorrow there would be a letter from him. She was sure of it. She could see it lying in the mailbox, addressed in that small, neat, familiar hand. If it wasn't there tomorrow, it would be there the next day. She would go to Porter's for dinner, sit at their table, and read it over and over. 'Good news from Mr Craven, Mrs Craven?' the old waiter would say as he leaned protectively over her. 'Ah, that's fine, that's fine.'

She began to smile, but suddenly she closed her eyes for a minute. She had had a queer sensation of falling, of the room slipping away and of herself falling, falling, as one does in a dream, without being able to stop and without wondering or caring what lies at the bottom.

SUBJECT FOR A SERMON

Elizabeth Berridge

(1944)

She leaned forward on her toes, white-gloved hands clasped. In her navy uniform, with hair cut close about her ears, she looked like an earnest schoolgirl.

'You know,' she was saying with controlled frankness, 'I shall enjoy the second part of this programme so much better, having spoken.' The hot faces in the little church hall relaxed into grins of sympathy. Not that she hadn't enjoyed the *first* half, Lady Hayley explained, but – an expressive gesture completed the sentence for her. She glanced disarmingly towards the sides of the platform. Reproachful faces stared at her from slits in the odd curtains that formed the wings, curtains now bulging with the jostling bodies of those who had already performed. *And* she was touched by the efforts they had all made, organisers, performers, everyone in the small village had contributed – done their bit. Her voice grew deeper and more fluent. *Her* thanks, she said, were nothing compared to what the men would say when they came home. It meant such a lot to them to know that *everyone* – men, women, yes, *and* children, was doing something to bring victory nearer.

Miss Pollett nodded, looking round at her Guides. She was standing with one foot on the platform steps to balance them. She nodded and looked at her girls. Then she motioned some little boys away from the platform edge. One of them had already sat on the curtain and now it hung in a perilous loop above where Lady Hayley would have to step down from the platform. And Miss Pollett felt possessive towards Lady Hayley, she was taking her home to spend the night. She glanced round the hall, it was crowded. With relief she noted the vicar at the back, he would keep order on the windowsills – how boys loved climbing up on to them. She tried to catch his eye, but he was looking intently at the speaker.

'. . . so I know you won't let me down, will you?' Her clasped hands were coming forward now, in a pretence of anxiety. The speech was coming to an end.

Judging her moment, Miss Pollett sprang up on to the platform so that Lady Hayley could not get past her to the steps. She held up a hand against the dying applause.

'I just want to say,' she began, hand now tucked familiarly into her belt, 'that we have a special reason for thanking Lady Hayley for being with us tonight.' She paused, and her distinguished visitor looked down at her black polished shoes, a shy gesture. 'It is this. Yesterday she learned that her son was coming home on embarkation leave. I told her she must not think of coming, but – Lady Hayley won't mind me quoting her words – she told me over the phone, "I've always said the Red Cross comes first, now's my chance to prove it." And as her train left the station, her son's train pulled in.' Miss Pollett stopped and involuntarily caught the Vicar's eye. He wore an expression she knew well; he had found a subject for his sermon – she must have just given it to him. In his joy he was leading the renewed applause and there were murmurs of sympathy. Lady Hayley smiled and blushed, led the way off the platform and the concert went on.

As they drove home after dropping the last Brownie, Miss Pollett started to talk. It was as if the tiredness of her body, the excitement of having Lady Hayley to herself in the dark, rattling car released some suppressed verbal energy. But as her companion continued silent, her eyes closed and remnants of the vivacious smile wan on her mouth, Miss Pollett found herself talking faster than she had intended. Her voice became louder, she put overtones and undertones into it; sometimes she gestured with one hand on the wheel, laughed excitedly. She did not want to talk about the concert, but almost involuntarily she told how the whole thing was the Guides' own idea – she had nothing to do with it except sell a few tickets and, of course, get Lady Hayley down to bless the occasion as County Organiser. The parents had trained the small Brownies, made all their dresses – no-coupon muslin, of course, weren't they wonderful . . .?

As she at last eased the car through the garage doors her voice ceased as automatically as the engine, and for a moment she savoured the healing silence, felt the echoes of talk dying in her head. Then she turned to her companion. Lady Hayley's face was quite blank, a little crumpled. After a pause the charming voice spoke out of the darkness and they went from the garage to the house, but Miss Pollett could not help feeling a silent judgement had been passed on her.

They drank the coffee that had been kept warm on the hearth, wrapped in blue flannel, and although Lady Hayley said, 'Wonderful, I think they are all simply wonderful,' Miss Pollett could no longer respond. She had nothing more to say. It was as if the party were over, everything flat. Also she had a strange feeling that if the other coffee cup had not been on the table, the cap beside it, she could have believed herself alone in the room. And to allay the disturbing feeling that she could never get past that quick smile – to prevent it pushing her away – she asked about the morning train. The 7.30 was the earliest, if she was not too tired . . .

'I must get that one,' replied Lady Hayley, 'I have a meeting at noon.' Then, as if some expression on the other's face made her remember something, she added quickly, 'John will understand.'

* * *

John Hayley sat outside the stables, cleaning an old gun of his father's. The mists were curling away from the other side of the valley and there was a promise of heat. Round three sides of the house the pines and firs were still wet from the night rain, their heavy foliage curiously unseasonable. As the sun grew hotter the scent of early wallflowers dispersed the tang of the trees, and the old sunk cobblestones of the yard dried patchily.

He called over his shoulder to someone inside: 'This double summertime certainly lets you in on the dawn,

Griffiths.' He spoke in Welsh and without waiting for a reply, ducked his head, for he was a tall youth, and went through the low door into the gloom where an old man sat among harness and guns.

Almost caressingly Griffiths answered him. 'A pity there's no horse now for you on mornings like this.' He looked through the door of the harness room down into the long, cool stable and nodded to each empty stall. 'Glendwyr, Gwyneth, Mad Robert – ' he shook his head and rubbed at the saddle he was working on.

'Hand me another,' said John abruptly as he laid the gun he was carrying on the rough table by the window. The old man selected one for him and with a frown the lad said: 'This needs oil very badly,' and going outside he started to look it over with care. After a while he became aware of the sun on his face and smiling for the first time that morning, he rose, stretched, and with the gun still over his arm, strolled off to the front of the house.

Here everything was startlingly different. The ground sloped abruptly away in lawns to the winding road below. There were no trees and the wide glass windows drank in the sun. He glanced in at the front door, placed at the side corner to protect the hall from the direct heat that would beat down once the sun was fairly up over the far mountains. The oaken hall seemed always to be cool and dark. It was long as a corridor and the stuffed victims of his father's gun were quiet in their glass cases, and until a door was opened somewhere inside no gleams were struck from the unsheathed swords and sabres hanging high up near the ceiling.

After a moment's hesitation he set off down the main drive. The little train had just passed through the station, leaving its fragmentary signature against a blue sky. The rhododendrons were a sight, he thought, picking one idly as he went on to the main gates. A pity he had missed the daffodils, they must have flowered early. As he saw his mother coming up the slope from the station he felt irritated at missing the daffodils and cut at the withered brown trumpets and drooping leaves with his gun. Then she waved and he threw the gates open ceremoniously and ran to meet her.

'You look tired,' he said accusingly, after they had kissed and were walking up together, she on his arm, her fingers light on the rhododendron flower.

'Why did you not come to the station to meet me?' she asked, looking up at him almost girlishly.

'I might almost ask why you – ' but her hand was over his mouth, her eyes reproachful.

'John, dear.'

He laughed against his will. 'You always know what I'm going to say,' he said half-sulkily. 'All the same . . .'

'There's no ammunition in the house now,' said his mother, catching sight of the gun. 'Did you want to go off shooting?'

'Oh, later, perhaps,' he replied carelessly, 'actually I scrounged some before I came away, hope it'll fit.'

She said nothing to this, but disengaged her arm quickly as the telephone bell rang out through the open door. She took off her cap when just inside the hall and ran firm fingers through her hair. As she moved to take up the telephone John picked up the cap and idly swung it round on one finger. His mother was only a moment: she made brief replies. 'No, no difference at all. Of course I shall be there. Yes, yes. Goodbye.' Then she made small pencilled notes on a pad near her hand.

'You know, darling,' he said as she rang off, 'I hate you in this cap. It's absurd somehow.' He glanced at her in sudden appeal. 'Look, won't you change into one of your frocks, come for a walk, early lunch and . . .'

Lady Hayley took the cap from him playfully and then with one turn of her strongly-knit, almost dumpy body, was on the first stair. With a little laugh she called back: '*I'm* not on leave, if you are, silly billy!'

When she came down again it was to find him smoking moodily on the terrace. She took his arm confidentially.

'I'm going to rest here a little if you will bring out a chair. Sit by me, I want to see how changed you are.'

She had combed out her hair, and relaxing with her feet up John could imagine her, summers ago, in one of her green linen frocks, enjoying the sound of a lawnmower somewhere below, and the hot energetic ping of unseen tennis balls.

'Well?' he asked at last, almost rudely, as he found her watching him.

She laughed and held out her hand for a cigarette. When he had lighted it she glanced down at the neat gold wrist-watch, half-hidden beneath her navy cuff.

'We shall have to start in about an hour,' she said. 'So we've time for a nice talk.' She closed her eyes, but her son said nothing. 'That is, if you haven't forgotten how to ride a bicycle.' Her voice was light and teasing.

'Where to?' asked John, beginning to tap on the gun-barrel with long fingers. His mother tried to keep her eyes away: she hated any purposeless movement.

'There is a blood transfusion meeting,' she said evenly. In the strong sunlight her face looked tired, as if the skin was stretched by too many smiles, too many alert, interested nods. 'We have made ourselves responsible in this county for at least two hundred and fifty donors. I thought . . .'

'You want me to talk to them? Tell them how the fellows appreciate it, eh?'

His mother looked at him. 'I don't care for your tone, John,' she said drily. No doubt the army had coarsened him. 'Sometimes I think you have inherited your father's most unlovable traits.' In spite of a distaste for his drumming fingers and sprawled legs, she touched his arm. 'John, I know you've been through a lot. I know you are on leave, going abroad soon. But don't you see that for people like us duty is never finished? We can never relax, it is our privilege to lead. You are a lieutenant – '

'Captain now,' he murmured.

'And you never said a word!'

'Wanted to tell you last night. I was quite pleased about it then. But this morning – it doesn't seem important any more.'

'Well!' his mother leaned back. 'It is just that sort of attitude that is wrong. Always you see things in the wrong perspective. There are many things *I* do not like doing

– Miss Pollett frays my nerves. I dislike long journeys undertaken in uncomfortable circumstances, I am nervous when on a bicycle. But if *I* did not do these things, who would? It is expected of my position – our lives are not our own, John.'

Her son looked at her curiously, and the set of her shoulders, the impenetrable reason moulding her face, set up a wonder in him. This wonder had been stirring for months, a half-understood, uncomfortable thing. What would she do, what would the people like her do, if they once realised that their lives were indeed their own? Had she, had they, the courage to take them up and see?

Impulsively he said, 'That's just it, mother, that's just where I feel you're wrong. You wouldn't dream of letting the people round here organise their own schemes. And you don't really care about them; you don't want to *know* them, they're just a mass of faces in a church hall to be talked at, and exhorted. You're only interested in maintaining your own position, and seeing that they keep to theirs. They're fair game for pennies, but you wouldn't recognise one of them in the street afterwards.' He looked angrily at her. 'I've lived among them, mother. I know what they think about people like us. I know what they're like and what they want – and it's nothing we represent. We've had our chance as leaders of society, and lost it.'

His mother made a great noise with her feet as she lifted them down from the stool to make room for the tray of coffee a maid brought out. From habit he remained silent until the girl had disappeared again round the stone coping. 'You can't believe they're fed up with us, can you? Even if Gwen had poured the coffee down our necks? But I tell you that when the war ends, that's the end of our kind, too. They'll just sweep us away and choose their own leaders.'

He took up his gun again and began tapping it lightly on the ground between his legs. He was cold with a sudden fear; never before had he spoken to his mother like this. But she only looked amused.

'I suppose you still allow yourself the luxury of cream and sugar in coffee, my boy?' He went a dull red and threw the gun on the ground. How many times in his childhood had she spoken to him in exactly that controlled, bantering tone? Usually it effectively silenced the jerky spasms of talk that had marked the beginning of the queer, groping independence and sudden insight of his adolescence.

'I can do without it, if that's what you mean,' he said ineffectually. 'In the Naffy – '

'Oh, come. No boasting, John.' She handed him his cup with a slightly raised eyebrow, and he knew he was being invited to laugh with her at himself, at his boorishness. Laugh, maybe kiss her and give in. But he merely scuffled his feet and took the cup gracelessly. Lady Hayley watched him, her face settling into a frown.

'Don't worry, John,' she said, her voice hard. 'They'll never sweep *me* away. Why, you make me feel like a bad old Russian landowner wielding a knout! Do be sensible and realise that this fancy of yours to be – shall I say – one with the people is just a phase; like Dora what's-her-name at Castle Mount wanting to be a nun. Young people are all the same, only when I was young all the girls wanted to be like Mrs Eddy or Sylvia Pankhurst. And the boys ached to go to Paris, affect flopsy ties and a French mistress, then come back talking languishingly of *fin-du-siècle . . .*'

Perhaps it was the carelessness with which she pronounced the phrase that roused John. It seemed to sum up, even more than the use of the weary cliché, her tolerant, humorous dismissal of anything new, anything foreign. Out of shame for her careless mispronunciation he retorted that times were changed; that he was twenty, not sixteen like Dora what's-her-name, and that dilettantism had died a natural death after the Great War, that –

'Oh, how dreary, all this talk of the times!' exclaimed Lady Hayley. 'If you're serious – which I doubt, no young man is *ever* serious at twenty – then *go* to the people, become one of them. Eat their fish and chips, drink their cocoa. Wear a muffler and learn to lounge against a lamp-post. But I warn you that if they don't accept *me* for what I am – a leader with generations of experience behind me – how much less will they accept you, trying to be something that does not exist. A canary let out among sparrows!' She put the tray decisively on the ground and replaced her legs with a sigh. 'No, my boy. We've got to make a stand. And you must take up your difference with courage, otherwise you'll find you're a misfit. And there's nothing so boring as that.' She looked at him oddly, then went on, 'I noticed a book on the French Revolution in the dining room, you'd been reading it. Well, there's a good lesson for you. The aristocrats didn't really lose, because the mob could only cut off their heads. And ultimately that's such a small thing.' Glancing at her watch, she rose to her feet. 'I must go now, I can see you don't want to come with me. But think about what I've been saying. You can't shirk the issue, John.'

Quickly she turned from him, left him sitting there.

* * *

That afternoon before she came home from the meeting John wandered round to the stables again. But they were empty, the harness room neat with the saddles back on their nails and smelling of the polish Griffiths had used. He was suddenly warmly grateful to the old man for this unnecessary task, then, looking round idly, he saw his fishing rods stacked in one corner. For the first time it struck him as strange that they should not be in what used to be his father's study – for after all, they were originally his father's rods, left to him. Then he remembered that this was now being used as a drying room for herbs collected and brought in by volunteers. All the same, it was somehow disquieting to find them outside the house altogether . . . perhaps they were only being overhauled. It might be a good idea to do a bit of fishing. More than ever he felt the need to be voluntarily submerged in the silence and invulnerability that, as a fisherman, he could cast about himself.

Once settled in the woods, however, beside the river, the fine day turned to rain, and hunching up his shoulders, he shifted into shelter to watch the shimmer of the two waters meeting: rain and river, from now on indivisible. Once again he was feeling bitter towards his mother. Thinking: at least my collection of flies is intact. It's a wonder she hasn't presented them to the Prime Minister on his birthday. As the rain cleared he cast in his line, but the peace he hoped for was not to be found in this stream, in these woods. Perhaps not in this time at all. Funny, he had known this leave was going to be all wrong from the moment he had looked out of the train on to the empty platform – of course, old Jones the stationmaster was there. Good old Jones, with the silver plate in his head, nineteen-sixteen relic.

He sat watching the river, his mind clogged with rancour. Tidying him away, just like his father – that's what she was doing. His rod trembled and he drew it up; the hook and fly were gone. Carefully he wound up his line and started back through the woods. He wished he had a dog at his heels.

His mother was already at the table when he came in, and they spoke very little during the meal. He wanted to bring up the matter of the rods, but feared to be soothed by her reasonable explanations. Instead he watched her, wishing she would ask him eagerly, curiously, what the strange half-world of the army was like. He wanted her to make tentative enquiries as to the girls he had met. He wanted to hear the anxious 'I hope, John . . .' which would make him into a man of the world, not a boy on his school holiday. But she did not speak, and as John looked at her, across the planned expanse of table, he pondered how strange it was that one never thought about one's parents as separate people until they were dead, or it was too late to have a relationship with them anyway. Did they always see their children as beings from a different, a nursery world?

Lady Hayley moved into her favourite low chair by the window, and picked out a pack of patience cards that were always in a box on a small table there. She had wanted to tell him about the meeting, but his closed face stopped her, reminded her of his absurd and irritating mood of the morning.

'What did you do this afternoon, John?' she asked, laying out the cards neatly. One, two, three, face down. Yes, tonight it would be Sevens. 'By the way, the dean is coming . . .' she paused, a tiny hesitation which conveyed her meaning exactly. John had strolled over to the windows, and was standing as he had done a hundred times before, to watch the slow evening procession of clouds above the valley. Ponderous, impersonal, they passed in the form of ghost-porpoises, rolling snails, wisps of fish and formless old testament heads with their drifting, drowning beards. When he spoke, it was in the dean's social voice, which sounded as if he were discreetly gargling with the best port. 'Home is the hero, eh? Dear lady, you must be proud – '

He broke off abruptly as his mother swept the cards up. It was impossible to concentrate in such an atmosphere.

'John, I've never heard you speak this way before. Is it the men you've been mixing with?' Her voice held the first definite note of enquiry since he had come home.

He did not turn from the window.

'Not only mixing. Thinking as well,' he said.

Still he did not turn and face her, and a little dully Lady Hayley recognised the exact stance of her husband; the same stretch of neck, the same unwilling tone of voice. As if he were half expecting defeat and the sentence was therefore not worth completing. But John went on speaking.

'I came across a picture in one of my billets,' he said. 'You know, where those women are throwing themselves between the spears of the two armies. Now they *did* stop that war. Funny, isn't it? The picture was stained with damp. Hauled down from the attic, I suppose, to hide a bad patch of wallpaper. It's nothing to do with what we were talking about this morning, I know. But it set me off thinking along different lines, somehow. Instead of just accepting things like war and unemployment and all the rest, I began to wonder *why*, and if it couldn't be prevented. Then I thought of you – '

'Well?' Lady Hayley's face wore the expression she used for particularly obstinate or stupid subordinates who failed to rally their districts to target level.

'Well,' he said, facing her at last, 'I know you wouldn't have done a thing like that – ' his mother made a gesture of impatience '– and that there were hundreds like you, who called themselves leaders of the nation. *They* wouldn't either. They wouldn't try to stop a war, stop their men being killed. No! They wanted to be in on it. Organise it.'

'You don't know what you're saying, John. For one thing, women don't declare war. It's not their responsibility.'

'That's not fair,' he broke in. 'This morning you were saying that the people looked to you – to us. That's responsibility, isn't it? And surely it's time we led them into peace and security at home, rather than to death and poverty abroad?'

Lady Hayley made no further attempt to argue with her son; indeed, his statements were so wild and illogical, not to say utterly unfamiliar, that she could not follow them. Instead, she rose to her feet. 'Come into the oak room,' she said, 'I want to show you something.'

John turned from the window in surprise, then followed as she went from the room. Already he was regretting his words: he should have waited until these things were really clear in his mind. He knew from experience that however unassailable a conviction seemed when it was safe in his own head, directly he tried to express it he was lost in a confusion of words.

As they went through the door at the end of the silent hall he was wishing despairingly that he had thought more when days and weeks and years had been his as certainly as the clouds moved over the mountains. One spent so little time alone; looking back it was a lifetime of chatter. The army had made him remember every wasted minute of that former existence. Hours that could have been spent in the school – and later, the university – library. He thought with nostalgia of the polished perfection of the Bodleian. Austere tables and scholastic chairs, the ranged books; so much clear and penetrating thought between covers, evidence of quiet minds in slow-paced centuries.

They were in the oak room now, and he noticed that his mother was standing in the middle of the floor, waiting for him. It was a long, large room, entirely panelled in oak, with an old well-trodden oaken floor. The windows on one side reached down to within a foot or two of the floor and beneath their sill ran a polished hollow window seat. As a child John had kept his odd small treasures in it. Now it was quite empty; he had looked when he first came home. The light that came through these tall windows made the room an effective gallery for the ranged family portraits. Beneath these were ancient weapons such as were usually found in the homes of peace-loving English gentlemen – curious intricacies of seventeenth-century Italian craftmanship, sheathed scimitars, swordsticks, old heavy pistols; and criss-crossing one corner, two red-tasselled halberds.

But Lady Hayley was pointing to the portrait of a grave and shadowed man.

'Your grandfather,' she said.

'Very bad,' John commented, looking up. His hands were in his pockets. 'And if you don't mind my saying so, Mother, I think they are all in extremely bad taste. For one thing, the painters are worse than second-rate.' He gestured to another painting. 'Look at great-uncle Horace embracing that marble fountain as if it were the baronetcy he prayed for all his life. And anyway, why so many rose arbours and stone seats? I think factory chimneys would be more in the family tradition, don't you? Don't forget what great-grandfather made out of the industrial revolution. We're still living on the interest today.'

Lady Hayley's face began slowly to take on a rather ugly expression. To the boy it was painful to see all charm twisted out of it. At the same time it gave him some satisfaction to know that this face was not known to many people – probably only to his father and himself.

'These are your ancestors,' she said. 'Your cheap remarks won't alter that fact.' She walked slowly round the walls and paused before a portrait here and there – a man in heroic stance, a woman serenely resigned to wealth. 'These relations of yours, at least a good many of them, died for their country. Died for *you*. They made England what she is. It is your duty to carry on that tradition.'

'I didn't ask them to bequeath me their tradition,' said John, 'I don't like it.' An old, submerged obstinacy was stirring in his voice. 'I wasn't born then, so how were they fighting for me? You mean they fought for an idea handed down to them; for their own position. Then they fought for *you*, for grandmother and great-aunt Anne; they had to fight, it was expected of them. Well, grandmother and great-aunt Anne are dead now, so what's the odds? They're all dead.'

'Dead, yes, they're dead!' cried his mother in a suddenly vibrant voice. 'We all die. I know that. And yet they live in the very air you breathe! They have passed on their tradition to you – '

'Tradition again! What is it exactly? An obligation to lead the people continually into war? Quote time-honoured clichés at them? Glory, honour? Dust is more glorious!'

'Oh, you are too unutterably callous, John! I can't – no, I can't talk to you.' For a moment Lady Hayley stood and gazed at the walls while the evening sun crept round the house and suddenly spilt into the room, making every metalled object dart tiny fires. In that moment her son looked at her with immense pain, for in her dignity and belief she *was* the past generation. He began to speak, to try once more to explain, but he was alone and the sound of his mother's low-heeled shoes came clopping back in echoes as she walked away from him down the hall, away and back to her patience.

* * *

After that his leave passed swiftly. Lady Hayley went to her meetings, and her son bicycled and fished, visited the Laceys and other neighbours, and one afternoon even went for a walk with his mother – each preserving the polite impersonality of a confirmed difference. Sometimes before going to bed he lingered in the shadow of the stable door, the day's defences down, heartsick for the soft blown breath of Owen Glendwyr in the darkness, the intimate rustle of straw. He began to long for the army, his new life.

On his last day a letter came for him. It was from a friend of his, a man in his own Company. He was in London on twenty-four hours' leave, and suggested that John come up and join him. 'Let's meet in the Long Bar for lunch,' he wrote, 'we'll have a jolly good bust to finish off, old boy. Once back, we don't know what they've got in store for us – or do we?' John handed the letter across to his mother; they were finishing breakfast.

'But on your last day!' she exclaimed. 'Surely – ' But at the expression on his face she stopped. 'You want to go up, don't you?' she asked.

He nodded quite briefly, already thinking of train connections. Could he make it?

'But the early local has gone,' said Lady Hayley, watching

him with a flicker of emotion stirring her face. 'It connects with the fast London train, you remember – ' she glanced at her watch, ' – the next one isn't until this afternoon, and then from Dempsey to London it stops at every station.'

'But the express from Dempsey doesn't leave until ten-twenty,' John said, 'don't you remember the wait we always had on that chilly station? I've got an hour – I'll just do it if I take the car. Will that be all right?' He half rose, his mind racing ahead, his mouth dry with the dread of obstacles.

His mother almost flinched. 'Take the car on an unnecessary journey! I should think not . . . and who would drive it back from Dempsey?'

He paused at the door, bewildered; catching at the last part of her sentence. 'Who – but you, of course – '

His mother shook her head. 'You have made this sudden plan, John. What about *my* plans? I have kept this afternoon and evening free on account of it being your last day, and now – '

'But it's too late!' If he had not shouted the words he would have sobbed them. 'Too late, Mother! – you're so busy ministering to the needs of a thousand unknown men that you forget the one who's here. *I'm* the reality, but you won't see it, won't believe it . . . you've got the energy of the heartless.' He was trembling, aware of the seconds passing, but powerless to go until he had spoken, until the bitter unhappiness had poured itself out in revenge. 'I shall take the car. It's the only damned bit of leave I've got left to enjoy and you're not going to spoil it!'

He raced upstairs (knowing it was not only himself, John Hayley, aged twenty, who had spoken; it was John Hayley the baby, the child, the schoolboy, the adolescent) and threw his things together. No time for goodbyes, that was just as well. He was leaving more than the house behind him this time.

To his surprise he did not find his mother guarding the garage doors. He wondered where she was as he got into the car and checked up on petrol; just enough and a bit over to get him the twelve miles into Dempsey. As he backed out of the garage he saw nothing before him but the crowd in the Long Bar, the queer folded positions people got into as they leaned on the counter and drank. He looked ahead to the gates and saw they were open – that would save a minute or two, anyway. He noticed that the rhododendrons were now in full flower, soon they would shrink and fall off, lie in heaps on the gravel.

Then he realised why the gates were open. His mother was ahead of him on her bicycle. He watched her with no trace of the red devouring rage of ten minutes ago. Now his mind was clear, he felt almost happy: he wanted to sing. Doggedly her blue uniformed figure pedalled and pedalled, and she looked dumpier than ever; solid and somehow impressive. But it was a stranger cycling, someone with a purpose alien to his own. He slowed down as he approached her, let down the window and called to her. But she did not turn her head, nor move her hands from the firm hold she had on the handlebars. He accelerated, raising dust; and was speeding past her. He listened for her voice, but only air rushed in through the window. Thoughtfully he wound the window shut again.

Soon Lady Hayley could see her car no longer. On and on she went, methodical and untiring, wondering why she had not opposed him – it would have been easy to lock up the garage – yet knowing that unlike his father, unlike *himself*, this time he would not have given in. She could imagine him smashing the locks with his gun. Heartless, that was what he had called her. Heartless, it seared up at her from his incoherence; familiar because it was an old accusation, one she could never understand. Her husband and her son, why had they always impeded her? Of course, her husband had been a failure, and failures were always touchy and arrogant, humble and admiring in turn. John was the same, although too young to be a confirmed failure yet. She smiled a little, with relief. Turning up the lane to the village hall, she thought, 'Of course he will write, say he's sorry. I shall keep all his letters . . .'

She found the women assembled, shook hands with some of them, smiled at the others. She had come to judge war-time recipes: cakes, puddings, biscuits, all containing some measure of soya flour. Miss Pollett, whose idea this was, led her round the entries. 'When does your son go back?' she asked, as they walked together to the platform.

'Today, this morning,' replied Lady Hayley.

Miss Pollett's eyes widened. 'And you found time to come – oh, Lady Hayley, you're *too* good!' Enthusiastic as was her tone, it flattened strangely into doubt.

After the prizes had been distributed, Lady Hayley spoke of the honour they had done her in asking her to judge the entries. She emphasised the need for the solidarity of women – it would be needed even more after the war, with all the men coming back, changed and strange to the forgotten ways of peace. War, she said, tested a woman even more than a man. A man, after all, had only one way before him, it was only a question of acceptance. A woman had to add to her usual roles of companion and mother, that of organiser. Naturally this involved sacrifices, loss and pain. It was a struggle all the time, with no medals at the end.

Just before she stepped down from the platform, she clasped her white-gloved hands and said, 'Do you know, more than ever I feel so much – so much at *one* with you all.'

Mechanically Miss Pollett smiled and found herself wishing with all her heart that Lady Hayley really meant it.

WEDNESDAY

Dorothy Whipple

(1944)

Mrs Bulford, as she still called herself, kept passing and repassing the double wooden doors, standing wide open to make a gap in the garden wall. Every time she passed she glanced in at the house. She did no more than glance, but with every glance she saw a little more. She saw something else; a hoop lying on the lawn; Elsie as she stood at the kitchen window examining her nails in the pause between the courses in the dining-room. Mrs Bulford, Elsie's former mistress, knew how particular Elsie was about her nails, how she brooded over every little break or blemish, blaming her work, threatening to leave, insisting on the best soap if ever she had to wash anything.

Passing again, Mrs Bulford saw Elsie going past the passage window with a tray. She must be taking the pudding in now. Perhaps it was the children's favourite: Queen's Pudding with meringue on the top. Pat used to bang his spoon on the table with joy when this pudding came in; but probably he was too old for that now. Mrs Bulford hoped it wasn't Queen's Pudding today because the children ate it so slowly, making it last.

They wouldn't hurry, she feared, even though they knew their mother was waiting outside the gate.

Preoccupied with the innocent cruelty of her children, Mrs Bulford walked quite a long way beyond the house before she turned back. The trees hung over the garden walls, making a pleasant irregular shade. There were the familiar drowsy summer sounds; the doves cooing from the Watsons' roof, the faint sound of someone's wireless, far away from the hum of the city.

The road was empty. The families living in the pleasant houses were all within, having lunch. Parents and children sitting round the table, the subdued clatter of spoons and forks, intimate small talk. 'Don't spill, darling.' 'I got all my sums right this morning, Mummy.' 'I saw Mrs Parsons in town. I haven't seen her for ages.' 'Please may I have some more?'

Mrs Bulford laid her hand on the wall as she walked. Behind this it was all going on as before. She alone was shut out. She was shut out of the house, waiting for her children to finish their pudding at a table presided over by Cecil's new wife. Another woman sat in her place, did her hair at her dressing table, slept in her bed, bought clothes for her children.

She was shut out of the town too, because she shrank from being seen in it. She had taken rooms in a village on the outskirts, just far enough away not to be known, she had fancied. But by this time, everyone in the village knew all about her; she saw it in their eyes.

Half the time, she couldn't believe that such a thing had happened to her. She would lie in bed, her arms behind her head, looking round at the cottage bedroom, at the pink-washed walls, the yellow furniture with white china knobs on the drawers, and think, 'It can't be. How have I got here?'

She had the wholly unwarranted feeling that she might be able to go home sometime. She was like an exile waiting all the time to go home, devouring news of the place she longed to be in. She bought the Beddingworth papers, morning and evening, and read every word, even the advertisements. She knew who was born and who died or was married, she knew who wanted domestic help or houses. Every train that passed through to Beddingworth, she felt she ought to be on it. If anyone so much as mentioned the name of the city, a pang went through her. Though when she lived there, she had taken little interest. She had other things to do, she had so much . . . Now she had nothing. She did nothing but wait for the first Wednesday of the month; the first Wednesday, fixed by Cecil's lawyers as the day when she, not a fit and proper person to have custody of her children, could, as a concession on Cecil's part, nevertheless see them for a few hours in the afternoon.

The children were quite used to these Wednesdays now, that was why they didn't hurry out. After all, it had been going on for almost eighteen months. The separation had grown less painful for them; more painful for her. But it was better that way. Anything was better than that first terrible Wednesday when they hadn't been able to understand, at the end of the afternoon, why she couldn't go back into the house with them. They had tried to pull her inside the gate, crying: 'Why don't you come in, Mummy? You must come in. Don't go away again. Don't go, Mummy. Come in . . .' She had seen the alarmed faces of Elsie, the daily woman, and Cecil's new wife at the windows. Then Elsie came out to get the children in, and she had to tear her skirt from their hands and go away, weeping. She could hear them calling after her as she went.

She thought she could never face another Wednesday after that. It would be better to go right away, never try to see them again, she decided. But on the first Wednesday of the next month, she could not help herself. She was at the gates, walking up and down, waiting for them as she waited now.

Passing the house again, she saw that the nursery windows were thrown wide; she was glad of that. She saw there were new curtains at her bedroom windows. Perhaps everything was new there now. When she had come to sort out the things that were hers, to take away, they made such a pitiful collection that she had left them. Keep them, keep them, she had cried to Cecil. He had kept them and presumably his new wife had them now.

He had married the very week the decree was pronounced absolute, and she didn't know who his wife was. That was what was so extraordinary; she didn't know where he had got her from. During her life with Cecil, she had never heard of anybody called Sheila. Yet he must have known her all the time he was getting the divorce. He had always been secretive. He had always known how to hide things, even the most trivial, and she herself never had, or she would not have been walking up and down outside the wall now.

He must have been watching all the time. He must have seen the affair with Jack dawning, developing and giving him his opportunity. He edged her into adultery, set the trap and watched her fall into it. He could not afford misconduct himself; he was a lawyer and his practice would have been ruined. Her idiotic infatuation for Jack was the chance he must almost have despaired of, because she had never given way to, or even felt, such a temptation before.

It had all been very short-lived. It was over in three days. She had pretended to go to Aunt Julia's, had gone to London with Jack instead, and after three days, the private detective got them.

It had been a temporary madness, induced by loneliness, the cold withdrawal of Cecil, the approach of middle age. She felt her looks were going, she made a last grab at the romance she had missed. She felt that if she didn't get it then, she would have missed it for ever, and how sad to die without having loved or been loved. As it stood on the horizon like the sun about to go down into night, love seemed the most important thing in life and Jack, to her almost incredulous happiness, seemed to love her as Cecil had never done.

He was good-looking, several years younger than she was, weak and frightened of life. She felt she made him strong by her love, but it had all been an illusion. When they were found out, his horrified family came and bore him away to safety; the safety of not having to marry her. As if she would ever have married him! She was deeply hurt that he should have thought she would try to make him marry her.

Anyway, he had gone abroad. The suit was undefended. The whole affair rebounded to her shame and hers alone. It was all heaped on her and she accepted it. She was so overwhelmed by it that she never looked up to see what Cecil was doing. She accepted the proceedings as her due; she told herself that she deserved the worst and made no protest.

For several months she felt this. But afterwards she had seen more clearly. She saw that Cecil had calculated everything; and sometimes as she brooded in the cottage bedroom, she felt that if there was fairness anywhere, not in this world, but in what she vaguely thought of as 'afterwards', she felt he would be faced with a meaner sin than hers.

As she reached the gates again, she saw the children passing the staircase window, going up to put on their outdoor things. Cecil and his wife were standing together in the garden, admiring the sweet peas. She saw the sun shining on the girl's fair hair. She was young.

The whole thing was oriental really, thought Mrs Bulford. Ageing wife got rid of, young one put in her place. But since nature discriminates against women, why should men do otherwise?

When she found herself on the verge of middle age, she should have dug herself in, she thought grimly, and kept her children, kept her place in the house and in the world. Instead, she had gone gallivanting after Jack and lost everything. What a spectacle she had made of herself! What an ugly, exposed thing to do! It was like one of those bad dreams where you find yourself in a public place with nothing on but your vest. Only from this dream there was no waking.

She was still walking in the opposite direction when the children came out of the gate, Pat, aged six, examining with absorbed interest a toy aeroplane in his hand. She turned and saw them and came hurrying, a stout figure in a tight coat and skirt; in spite of her suffering, she grew steadily fatter.

'Darlings,' she said breathlessly. What happiness to kiss their round, smooth cheeks. They let her, and she kissed them over and over again, greedily, until Pat drew off, frowning a little, and gave his attention to his plane again.

'Mumsie's going to buy me a Comet when she goes out this afternoon,' he announced.

'Is she, darling?' said Mrs Bulford brightly. 'How nice of her.'

That was how it had been arranged. She was 'Mummy' and her supplanter was 'Mumsie'. The children had jibbed at it at first. They wouldn't say it. But they said it now without a thought, she could see.

Mrs Bulford took Susan's hand and drew Catherine's arm through hers. She blinked back the tears of happiness and emotion that had come into her eyes, and saw Susan looking up at her with curiosity. Nine-year-old Susan wondered why anybody grown-up should cry. Surely when you were grown-up and could do as you liked, you had no need to cry?

Mrs Bulford squeezed Catherine's arm against her side and smiled lovingly at her tall daughter. Catherine smiled in a constrained way and looked across the road. She let her arm lie in her mother's for several minutes. Then she withdrew it. Mrs Bulford went on smiling and pretended not to notice. But a pang went through her. Perhaps somebody had said something. Catherine was thirteen, she was beginning to know what her mother had done. She was beginning to judge her with the ignorance and intolerance of the young.

‘Now what would you like to do this afternoon?’ asked Mrs Bulford brightly. ‘Where would you like to go?’

‘The Little Park,’ said Pat. ‘I want to fly my plane on the grass so if it makes a crash landing it won’t matter.’

‘Would you like to do that, girls?’ asked Mrs Bulford.

They nodded.

‘We’ll go to the Little Park then,’ said Mrs Bulford. ‘But wait a moment, Susan, let me do your hair again.’

No one could do Susan’s hair but her. The child had looked a sight ever since she left her. She took a pocket comb from her bag and the little group halted on the pavement while she combed out Susan’s thick fair hair. That woman would never learn that Susan’s hair should be tied securely almost on the crown of her head. She would let the bow dangle heavily over the child’s ear, ruining the effect.

‘There you are, darling,’ said Mrs Bulford, passing her hand over Susan’s head like a blessing.

They walked on, Mrs Bulford in the midst of them. For the next few hours they were hers.

‘Now tell me all you’ve been doing since last month,’ she said, drawing Catherine’s arm within hers again. It might have been her fancy that Catherine withdrew it last time. Perhaps there was nothing wrong really. She knew how apt she was to look for slights and coldness now.

Catherine, her arm lying inertly along her mother’s, shrugged her shoulders and said she didn’t think she’d been doing anything. Pat was too absorbed to answer. What did he care about last month when he had this plane in his hand today? Susan remembered she had lost a tooth and showed her mother the gap.

'Oh, did it hurt?' asked Mrs Bulford with concern.

'No. Mumsie pulled it out. I only felt a little tweak. Mumsie gave me sixpence for being brave.'

Mrs Bulford felt a sharp pang of jealousy, which she tried to suppress. She knew she ought to feel glad that Cecil's new wife was kind to her children. And it wasn't the girl's fault that Cecil had married her. If it hadn't been her, it would have been someone else. Mrs Bulford told herself these things; but remained jealous.

Catherine, murmuring that there was something wrong with her belt, removed her arm from her mother's, fiddled with her waist and did not replace the arm.

'So there is something wrong,' thought Mrs Bulford.

They reached the Little Park, a bright, new, open place with an artificial stream running over a cement bed, looped by hump-backed cement bridges. On the cement shores of a shallow lake, blue, red, green and yellow boats were drawn up. Everything was miniature, Walt Disneyish, except that in a caged enclosure sat one solitary monkey quite out of key, forlorn, flea-bitten and, in spite of the heat, shivering. The children were always sorry for this monkey. Catherine held out her hand and murmured tenderly.

She has pity for the monkey, thought Mrs Bulford, but not for me.

If I'd been an animal, she thought, people would have been kinder.

The children asked for money to buy nuts. The monkey

received one or two with a listless air and dropped them to the floor of the cage. Susan looked as if she might cry, so Mrs Bulford suggested they should go in the boats. The two younger children seized more money and ran off. Catherine didn't want to go in a boat, but when she realised that she would otherwise be left alone with her mother, she hastily said she would take one too.

The boats, safe, flat-bottomed affairs, were only for children; sixpence each for half-an-hour. So Mrs Bulford waited half-an-hour, watching Pat and Susan enjoy themselves, and Catherine drift moodily on the water. She sat on a hard little bench in the sunshine, surrounded by stiff bright flowers in the flowerbeds.

When the half-hour was up, the children clamoured to ride on the miniature railway. They were with one who would give them anything they asked, so they took every advantage of it. Mrs Bulford packed her stout form in with them and rode round the Park bulging over the side of the little wooden wagon.

When that was over, they wanted ice cream. They bought little tubs with cardboard spoons and sat on a bench with their mother, scooping out very small tastes of ice cream to make it last. Even Catherine was a child again, thus engaged. When they had finished the ices, they sat looking about them for further opportunity for pleasure.

'Susan, how is that toe of yours?' asked Mrs Bulford. 'Is it better?'

'It hurts sometimes,' said Susan.

'Take off your shoe and sock, darling, and let Mummy see,' said Mrs Bulford.

‘Oh, you can’t,’ said Catherine. ‘Not here, what will people think?’

‘You mustn’t mind so much what people think,’ said her mother.

‘I think it’s better to,’ said Catherine in a low voice, turning her head away.

Mrs Bulford took Susan’s soft little foot into her hand. The feel of it moved her unbearably. What a loss – not to be able to touch her children every day, any time of night or day as she used to, not to know their limbs, their bodies any more. Once she had known them better than her own. She closed her fingers over Susan’s foot and could hardly see it for a moment.

But she repressed her tears. She knew how mystified and oppressed the children were by signs of adult grief. She spread Susan’s toes out, soothing the small pink mark that showed on one.

‘You must always be very careful about your shoes, Susan,’ she said. ‘You must ask – Mumsie – to see that this toe has plenty of room. You have feet like mine, the third toe is as long as the second. So many shoes don’t allow for that.’

‘D’you remember how we used to play “This little pig went to market” when we came into your bed in the mornings?’ asked Susan, laughing up into her face. She said it without any sadness; she said it as if all that wasn’t over, but could be resumed at any time.

‘Yes, I remember,’ said Mrs Bulford. ‘Now, let’s put your sock on again. I think it must be time for tea.’

‘Hurray,’ said Pat, sliding off the bench at once. ‘I’m hungry.’

Tea was the crown of the afternoon, not only for the children but for Mrs Bulford. Sitting like any other mother with her children at the table, pouring out tea for them, spreading Pat's bread and butter with jam, wiping his fingers, entering into indulgent co-operation with the waitress to give them all they wanted, Mrs Bulford almost had the illusion that she had never left them.

Pat, his aeroplane out of sight and mind under his chair, was able to give his mother his attention. He was getting what he wanted, she was giving him things. She was letting him have another cream bun, so, his chin only an inch or two above his plate, he beamed on her.

'You *are* kind, Mummy,' he said with sudden fervour. Then added, as if to explain this to himself: 'But I are a little bit your boy, aren't I?'

Mrs Bulford put the teapot down on the provided tile with a slight crash.

Susan was disgusted with her brother.

'Of course you're Mummy's boy. She *borned* you,' she said. 'She doesn't live with us now, but she's still our Mummy, aren't you, Mummy? Can I have another cream bun, too?'

Mrs Bulford passed the plate of buns with a smile. They couldn't help it. They didn't understand. She didn't know which hurt most, Pat's confusion, Susan's matter-of-fact acceptance, or Catherine's judgment.

Everything seemed to have a barb in it today. But probably every Wednesday would be worse than the one before. The children would grow further and further away from her. They would become used to 'Mumsie', to the situation, they would come to look upon her as a nuisance, their own affairs would absorb them increasingly. So long as she could provide entertainment they would come happily with her perhaps, but when they could find entertainment for themselves, would they want her?

She paid the bill. It came to quite a lot. But that didn't matter; she had three weeks to save in for the next Wednesday. It was perhaps as well that she was not allowed to see the children oftener; she couldn't afford to.

'Are we going home now?' asked Pat eagerly. 'P'raps my Comet is there now. P'raps it's waiting. I think Mumsie will be back now.'

'Yes, you're going back now,' said his mother.

Heartless little boy, she thought. But why blame him for the mess she had made of her life? What had a child of six to do with the emotional tangles of a middle-aged woman?

The little party returned along the leafy road, Mrs Bulford setting a slow pace to keep them with her as long as possible.

Then, turning the corner, walking towards them arm in arm, came Cecil and his new wife.

Mrs Bulford, her eyes fixed upon them, came to a standstill. She could not face such an encounter. But Pat, breaking away from his mother, ran towards them shouting: 'Mumsie! Did you get it? Did you get it, Mumsie?'

Susan raised her eyes to her mother. 'May I go too?' she asked.

'Certainly, darling. But kiss Mummy goodbye first,' said Mrs Bulford.

Catherine stood awkwardly with her mother.

'You'd better go too, dear,' said Mrs Bulford. She kissed the girl's smooth brow. 'Goodbye. I'll see you on the fourth, won't I?'

Catherine nodded.

'Goodbye,' she said.

The group had reached the gate. Cecil raised his hat to the woman he had lived with for fifteen years. Pat disappeared with his parcel; Susan waved vigorously, Catherine with restraint. Then they were gone.

Mrs Bulford turned and walked back the way she had come. She could not bring herself to pass the house yet.

But later when the dusk was deeper, she passed it on her way to the bus. Elsie had just come out to pick up the hoop on the lawn. Upstairs someone was drawing the curtains, first at one window, then at another. They were all gathered in for the night. Everything was very quiet. Even from the gate she could smell the sweet peas. She walked away down the road.

SPADE MAN FROM OVER THE WATER

Frances Towers

(1947)

Mrs Asher was having tea with Mrs Penny when the telegram came. She was leaning back, with her two long feet on the fender, talking and waving her lovely hands, that seemed to go about with her like attendant doves and to lead an independent existence, swooping and perching in gestures that dramatised her share of the conversation and made even her chance remarks sound significant. They settled to rest on her knee when Mrs Penny opened the telegram, but rose and fluttered towards that lady when she uttered a little cry.

'My husband! He'll be home on Friday,' said Mrs Penny, looking suddenly transparent with happiness.

'My dear, I do so rejoice with you,' said Mrs Asher, recalling her hands, that had seemed to wish to bear her joy straight into Mrs Penny's breast.

'I wonder . . . Oh, Mrs Asher, I do hope that you and he will be great friends!'

Mrs Asher's dark eyes went to a photograph on the

mantelpiece. 'I know *I* shall like *him*,' she said. 'He looks everything that your husband should be . . . So *kind*,' she said, giving the word a sonorous quality that made kindness into a rare and knightly virtue, 'and *fastidious* . . . and *sensitive*.' As if she were playing a little tune, she emphasised each adjective on her knee with a different finger. 'Proud, too,' she added. 'Oh, there is integrity in that face! One would trust him on sight.'

'But,' cried Mrs Penny, with a look of dismay, 'that isn't Rupert! It's a cousin of mine, Arnold Cross. He's a dear, as you say, but not the very least like my husband. Whatever made you . . . ? I can't think how such a mistake could have come about.'

She was profoundly shocked. Mrs Asher, that understanding woman, to have been entertaining all this time so erroneous an idea! Why, if she herself were to meet Mrs Asher's two little boys in the street, she would recognise them instinctively. She knew by sympathy exactly what they were like. She liked Mrs Asher so much, she seemed to know her husband too; though he had never been mentioned between them.

Mrs Asher had a deep sense of tragedy, as people have whose sense of humour is very keen. That was what made her so precious as a friend. Having once found her, you couldn't bear the thought of ever losing her. She was, like poetry, one of the things that do not fail. If the loss of Mr Asher had stricken her so deeply that she could not speak of him, it was because she was of heroic stature and had to drain to the dregs the cup that lesser mortals dare only to sip. Mr Asher, Laura Penny was convinced, was like Charles Lamb – Mrs Asher's favourite writer. He must have hated dying and going off into the dark without her.

'Oh, Mrs Asher!' said Laura, 'I thought you would have known that Rupert is . . . well, a very *magnetic* kind of person. I still sometimes think that it's all a dream, my being married to him. Isn't it absurd – after nearly a year?'

Mrs Asher looked about her in a hunted kind of way. But there was no other photograph in the room.

'Oh, dear!' she said, 'and I thought I saw the marriage likeness between you, as the gypsies say. He looks,' she said, 'like the man you *ought* to have married. But, never mind! I must readjust my ideas.' She twisted her mouth in that expressive way that seemed to make it the seat of her emotions, and added, laughing, 'I suppose you really married the Spade man from over the water!'

Laura gave a little start. A dark man from over the water . . . a stranger. He had walked into the hotel in Bloomsbury to which she had gone, all lost and bewildered, when her father had died and left her, entangled like a desiccated fly in the abandoned web of his existence. Her father had been paralysed for ten years, and she had had to be paralysed too, all the time, every minute of the day. Even now, sometimes, she groped in the night for her dressing gown, dreaming that she heard the remorseless thumping of his stick.

And then memory came flooding back, and she sank into the pillows as into a rosy cloud. Being loved by Rupert made you feel as beautiful as Helen of Troy. He had the darkest, most shining eyes in the world, and when he looked at you, you felt as helpless as a rose rifled by bees.

Oh, it was very odd that so intuitive a person had not felt the rare quality of Rupert's charm! One couldn't speak of him in just an ordinary voice, because to mention his name was to hear the sound of trumpets, to smell red clove carnations, to feel a warmth as of wine in one's veins.

Mrs Asher's past might lie beyond a closed door. She might have come into one's life as down a long corridor of time, but she had brought her memories with her. They were behind her eyes, looking out of them, and in the tones of her voice, causing vibrations like those of a bell when its peal has died on the air. One felt her memories like a presence. Soon Laura was thinking of Mr Asher as a person she had known in the flesh. She imagined them as so much part of one another that they could answer each other's unspoken thoughts, their love so deeply rooted that he could drop a kiss on that delicate hollowed cheek of hers without disturbing her thoughts. He was the sort of man who would bring her the first white violets, or a dead bee, or a young fir cone; and she the sort of woman to run to his study crying, 'Charles (was that his name, after all?), listen to this poem I came across'; or 'Charles, come quickly and see the light in the sky.'

Would the time ever come for Laura to be unaware of Rupert's kiss? To think her own thoughts in his presence as tranquilly as if he were the air she breathed? Or would he always make her feel in his arms as if the world had spun away from beneath her feet? Would she ever meet that dark, mocking gaze without a shyness that was exquisite pain?

'So prim,' he said, with the chuckle that seemed to come from unplumbed depths of humour in him, 'and chilly, like a snowdrop. It always was my favourite flower.'

There had been a break in the continuity of her existence. It was almost as if Rupert had created a new Laura. Drawn into his orbit, one could but revolve dizzily round him in the void. She had lost touch with her past self. She was wildly happy, but there was this queer feeling of disintegration.

It was Mrs Asher who gave her back the self she had lost, the self that first her father and then her husband had filched from her, the Laura who had loved to be alone to think her thoughts, to dance to the tunes she heard in her mind. For Mrs Asher was as good as solitude. Laura could hardly have paid her a greater compliment. It was strange that so restless and nervous a person should create so deep a tranquillity about her. All Mrs Asher's tricks, her gesticulating hands, the twisting of her mobile mouth, the way she was always losing things and having to search for them, but served to emphasise the sense of inward peace one felt in her company.

She had moved into the house over the way on the very day that Rupert went abroad. He had allowed Laura to choose the country to live in because the nature of his work took him away quite often, but he hadn't let her have the empty house she had fallen in love with – a tip-tilted black-and-white cottage, with the date 1590 carved into the lintel and the intriguing name 'Miss Lemon's Cottage' painted on the gate.

'Too dilapidated. And damp, I shouldn't wonder. It's been empty for years,' he said, 'and nobody's likely to take it, thank God! Fields on either side and a derelict house opposite

– what could be better! No one to run in and out – a thing I can't stand. Why, we could play at Adam and Eve in our garden, and not a soul to spy. Besides, your home is in my heart . . . isn't it, isn't it?'

So they settled into their modern house, and she made it very fresh and gay with cretonnes and limed oak from Heal's to match its newness. On the days he went to London, the house seemed strangely empty – like a beach when the tide goes out. When he returned, it glowed and sang, as if life had come pouring back into it.

Mrs Asher came over to borrow some matches. She looked terribly tired. Her furniture was standing in the road, amidst the litter of straw and sacking disgorged by the pantechnicon. The pieces looked forlorn, as if they felt the wrench from the past and were suffering in the east wind. Looking at them, one felt a little dubious of Mrs Asher's good taste. No Chippendale, no elegance.

But one's heart went out to her instantly, as it might go out to a giraffe at the Zoo because of its limpid eyes and its awkward grace.

'You've taken the house I'd set my heart on,' said Laura.

'Then, please, make it yours,' Mrs Asher said, with a queenly gesture. 'Please run in and out as you like.'

How trusting and generous, thought Laura, with a little pang, remembering Rupert's prejudices. He had only just quitted the house. It seemed still to vibrate with his presence. She hadn't had time to look into the abyss of the three months' parting that yawned at her feet.

Mrs Asher gave her no time.

'Come and help me,' she said, as if to an old friend.

And in a little while, 'Miss Lemon's Cottage' seemed as much Laura's as Mrs Asher's.

It was extraordinary the way the heavy mahogany snuggled into it with an effect of integrity and permanence, an air of being valued not for aesthetic reasons, but for something that had to do with the heart's affections. The house was one in which light bloomed softly like a great golden rose. The smell of newly-baked bread and roses greeted one's nostrils, even though the year was too old for roses, and the incongruous things in the drawing-room achieved a harmony that was completely satisfying, because of Mrs Asher's instinct for reconciling one colour with another, one period with another, by placing in juxtaposition to the discordant elements some object that beautifully resolved their differences.

'I shall live and die here,' she said, with a contented sigh. 'There will never be any reason to move again.'

In the chances and changes of life with a rover like Rupert, it was comforting to think that 'Miss Lemon's Cottage' would always be there, with its golden light and its quintessence of rose.

She had come, Mrs Asher said, because of the ancient Grammar School. Her little boys were at boarding school till the end of term, but next term they would live with her and go to the Grammar School.

'Oh dear!' she said, coming upon a small, very dirty eiderdown in a chest. 'Here is Gavin's downie, his totem-rag. He couldn't bear to be parted from it, couldn't sleep, or come downstairs, or face strangers without hugging his downie.

I suppose it gave him a feeling of protection. I must give it a good wash and put it on his bed,' she said, her eyes lit with tenderness.

Somehow, Laura couldn't mention Mrs Asher in her letters. She knew very well how irksome Rupert would find the thought of a woman on his doorstep, and one, moreover, who was wholly unaccustomed to the idea of intrusion. It would be better, she thought, to break to him gently the astonishing fact that in his absence she had formed a friendship which would last as long as life lasted.

Not that she would put it like that, of course; Rupert's mind was still an unexplored country. Once she dreamed of being lost in the dark in some strange landscape and of hearing a sound of gurgling water. 'That's Rupert's laughter; but I don't know where it comes from,' she cried in her dream. She felt a terrible urgency to find the source of the chuckling water, and set off on one of those perilous and futile dream-journeys, when one's legs seem weighted with lead and intangible obstacles block one's path. When she woke, the dream seemed to have lasted all night. It left her feeling physically exhausted and a little frightened.

The truth was that Rupert didn't really like people; though people fell for him . . . old ladies in hotels and young women in the train, and tradesmen and bus conductors and charwomen.

'Your starchy Cheltenham relations – let's keep them at arm's length,' he said. And when Arnold Cross sent that photograph from India – 'Good Lord, what a prig! So long as he stays in Delhi and doesn't come bothering us . . .'

From the depths of her armchair, little Mrs Penny looked at Mrs Asher consideringly, the colour coming and going in her cheeks. She was trying to see her friend with Rupert's eyes. It was terrible – like seeing a distorted reflection in a train window which bestows a foreknowledge of the friend beside you in extreme old age, or even in death. And then, as you turn with relief to the contemporary, the real, face, Laura saw once more the face of *her* Mrs Asher, and vowed to herself that neither Rupert nor any other force should come between them.

The winter afternoon had closed in. The sky still held a watery yellow light, faint as primroses, and pools of heliotrope shadow lay under the trees. The withered bines of the clematis on the wall were ropes of silver. In the myrtle bush beyond the window a ghost fire was fantastically burning. How lovely! And there was the back view of a ghostly Mrs Asher sitting on the frosty grass, like Keats's ghostly queen of spades. ('A Spade man from over the water,' she had said, with her little hollow laugh.)

Mrs Asher was still looking pensively at Arnold's photograph, her chin cupped in her hand. But probably her thoughts were far away.

'Wait!' said Laura. 'I have a snapshot of us on our honeymoon, feeding the pigeons in Venice.'

She got up and searched in a drawer

'Here it is!'

She handed the bit of pasteboard to her friend with an expectant look, as if she were waiting for a little sound of surprise.

‘It’s getting dark. I must take it to the window,’ Mrs Asher said, rising in her leisurely way.

‘We’ll have the light.’ Laura put out her hand to the switch, but on Mrs Asher’s protesting that she loved the twilight, she poked the fire instead.

Mrs Asher’s tall, straight figure at the window quenched the fire in the myrtle bush. The warmth and cosiness inside were no longer projected into the grey and silver world without. The light had died in the sky and a greenish star shone, faint as a glow-worm, over the thin black poplar.

Mrs Asher seemed to be peering at the snapshot as if she couldn’t quite see.

‘As I’m to meet him at Greenock,’ said Laura, waiting, ‘I suppose I shall be away a couple of days.’

‘Yes,’ said Mrs Asher, turning at last. ‘No doubt you will want to spend a night in London. He is a very handsome man, my dear.’ She gave her soft little laugh. ‘No wonder you were surprised at my . . . *absurd* mistake!’

She gathered her furs about her, stooped, and for the first time kissed Laura’s cheek. She was not a demonstrative woman, and a kiss from her was as sweet and surprising as a gift of chill Christmas roses.

Laura caught her hands. ‘Oh, my dear, how glad I am that Fate sent you my way! But you’re not going yet? Do have another cup of tea.’

‘You must have much to do. And so have I,’ said Mrs Asher. Yes, of course; she was expecting the boys home. How nice that Mrs Asher, too, had happiness to look forward to.

She would like Rupert, of course. Oh, everyone had to

succumb to that compelling charm of his! And he? If one were very tactful, if one didn't rush things, if one let her dawn on him, as it were, gradually, oh! surely Rupert would take to her unique, her delightful Mrs Asher. Laura wouldn't, at first, say a word. Indeed, she knew very well that her thoughts would be too much in a whirl, and for him alone.

But, as they approached 'Miss Lemon's Cottage', he might notice, perhaps, that it was inhabited. Golden light would be shining out through the curtains, smoke coming from the chimneys. 'Hullo!' he might say. 'So the house opposite has been let.'

That would be her chance. 'Yes,' she would reply, in a light, unconcerned voice; 'but to a quiet, unassuming kind of person – a Mrs Asher. You'd like her, I think.'

But when the time came there was no golden light, no smoke. 'Miss Lemon's Cottage' was as dark as the tomb, as hollow as a forsaken nest. A house agent's sign creaked in the wind. Some wisps of straw were blown to Laura's feet, then lifted and whirled away with a faint rustling, like a desolate word whispered in the ear. 'Treachery,' her lips repeated soundlessly, over and over again, 'treachery, treachery.'

'But whose?' asked a little, lost, cold voice from nowhere.

MINNIE'S ROOM

Mollie Panter-Downes

(1947)

Minnie was an ugly little Londoner who had been cook to the Sothern family for twenty-five years. She had come to them 'just a raw girl', as Mrs Sothern was fond of explaining. The way she said it made Minnie sound like a lump of something dreadfully unappetising that Mrs Sothern's skill had converted into a masterpiece of a dish. The words seemed to imply that the Sothern ladies, between them, had taught Minnie everything she knew. The truth was that Minnie was that extremely rare thing among the English, a natural magnificent cook, who would have found her medium and her style whatever happened. Before the war, her dinners were memorable, and Mr Sothern would say to his wife that though Minnie's cooking was, of course, nothing like the French, when it came to something solid, like a roast bird or a perfect bit of salmon, you couldn't beat the English. He was a big man, leaning, with Minnie's assistance, toward corpulence. All the Sotherns were substantially built, and their house in Bayswater was veiled with muffling plush curtains and full of large, softly curved objects filled with down, covered with rosy glazed chintz, or padded with leather. Even the china figures in the drawing-room cabinets contributed to the overstuffed effect, representing, as they did, bonny, plump shepherdesses and well-fed sheep. When you entered the front door and planted your feet on the thick Turkey carpet, you breathed comfortable virtues in the air along with a whiff of whatever delicious food Minnie was cooking.

Since the war, the Sotherns had visibly shrunk. The ruddy skin of Mr Sothern's face began to hang loosely here and there, like a too large overcoat worn by too small a man. Mrs Sothern was the only member of the family who was still stout – stouter, if anything – for she had developed heart trouble and was an invalid. Her daughter, Norah, did everything – changed the library books, stood in the queues, and exercised the cairn terrier in Kensington Gardens. In the old days, City friends of Norah's brother, Maurice, had sometimes looked at his sister thoughtfully as they leaned back after one of Minnie's excellent dinners and accepted a cigar from the old man. But now her big-boned figure had a settled, spinsterish look as she came back from her walks through the leafy squares, the little dog at her heels, to the Sothern house, which had escaped the bombing but looked somehow deflated, shabbier, like its owners. When she turned the key in the lock and opened the front door, the cairn ran in happily, knowing no comparisons, feeling no difference in the air as he trotted upstairs and jumped up on the faded glazed roses at Mrs Sothern's feet.

One day in May, when the square was alight with lilac and laburnum, the little dog trotted upstairs as usual and bounded to his place on the sofa, but the expected caress did not come. Surprised, he turned his little brindled snout toward the more expressive end of Mrs Sothern, who, taking no notice of him, flung out her hand toward Norah, entering with the shopping basket.

'One might as well talk to a stone!' she cried.

Norah set down her basket. 'You've spoken to her, then?' she said.

'Spoken!' Mrs Sothern's plump, ringed hand pawed the air, and emotion worked her flushed face. 'My dear girl, I've been practically on my knees. I put everything up to her – my health, the way you have to slave already, the fondness we all have for her. "Mr Sothern is devoted to you, Minnie," I said.'

'She seems to have made her mind up, all right,' Norah said, calmly enough. She lit a cigarette. There's nothing for it now, she thought, but to close this place and go to live in a hotel. But it will kill them, she thought. Mother will be lost without her big bedroom, with its familiar mahogany bed, the family photographs in silver frames, the curtains blowing out toward the smell of lilac and the sound of a barrel organ playing in the square, and Dusty curled up in his basket by the brass fire-dogs. And poor Daddy, who likes the feeling that he can walk around the house blindfolded and lay his hand on his cigars, his boot trees, and his Dickens – how can he turn into one of the anonymous old men one sees uneasily drinking tea at little wicker tables in hotel lounges?

‘Maurice must talk to her this evening,’ Mrs Sothern was saying. ‘She’s always adored Maurice.’

‘I don’t think it will make any difference, somehow,’ Norah said. ‘After all, she always said this would happen, didn’t she?’

‘As though one ever took her seriously!’ moaned her mother.

Minnie was leaving them. The unbelievable had happened. Her beautiful dinners were long ago a thing of the past, of course, but she was still an artist with what there was to cook. Mr Sothern sometimes observed that when one dined out in restaurants, everything tasted the same and one got up as hungry as one sat down, but at home Minnie managed to make food taste like food. Though the dry, red skin was loose now on Mr Sothern’s jaw, he did well enough. The other maids had gone long since, and Minnie and Norah did the work between them. Everyone envied the Sotherns for having Minnie. She had her one little oddity, though, her harmless bee in the bonnet. She had often told Mrs Sothern that if she had not married by the time she was forty-five, she intended to leave private service and take a room of her own somewhere. The family had laughed occasionally about Minnie’s room. ‘Someone will marry her, confound him, for her apple pie alone,’ Maurice had said lazily one Sunday lunch before the war as he poured cream over his second helping. But no man had asked for Minnie. Even during the war and the blackout, when London was full of lonely men thousands of miles from their women and looking hungrily for any waist to circle, any bosom to lean their heads against, Minnie had trotted home on her evenings out with no footsteps following, halting, and following hopefully again behind her. Fortunately for the Sotherns, no hint of her superb ability to keep a man's digestion tranquil and his temper perfect appeared in her tiny, sad marmoset's face. 'Poor Minnie, we are really her whole world,' Mrs Sothern had said one day to her daughter, sighing with compunction as they paused and listened to the radio floating up from the basement, a vast, Victorian catacomb, in which the solitary Minnie seemed to rattle about.

However, only the night before this lilac-tossing, perfect May afternoon, Mrs Sothern's assumption proved to have been false. It was Minnie's birthday, her forty-fifth, and in the evening, after dinner, she came upstairs and tapped at the door of Mr Sothern's study, where he was sitting doing the *Times* crossword. It was for fear of upsetting Mrs Sothern's heart that she came to him first, Minnie explained. If it would suit them, she said, she would like to leave at the end of June, when the room for which she had spoken would be empty. She looked at him at one moment as though she were contemplating saying something about her feelings for his family and their long time together, but it was no good; she had no means of expressing herself except through those lyrical meals that she had been creating for them for twenty-five years. She withdrew to the catacomb. Forgetting Minnie's prudence, Mr Sothern charged upstairs to find his wife, who was already in bed. Norah came up; Maurice came down, attracted by the uproar, from talking to one of his friends on the extension telephone in his bedroom. He was still unmarried, and lived a life of which his family knew very little. 'Good Lord!' he said. 'So she really meant it!' Hard luck on the parents, he thought. He assumed immediately that, without Minnie, the house must go. He could dig in somewhere; only the other day Miles Carrington had asked him to share a flat with him. But what would the parents do? Hard luck on poor old Norah, too, he thought, looking at his sister's worried face and the grey in her hair under the electric light. She was tied to the old people forever; she hadn't a hope now. 'A room of her own!' Mr Sothern was saying angrily. 'Hasn't she a room here, perfectly decent and comfortable? She must have gone out of her mind!' Yes, wailed Mrs Sothern from the bed, Minnie was plainly demented. How could she keep herself on her own, for one thing? 'By daily cooking,' growled Mr Sothern, and there was a stricken silence. It was an unfurnished room, he added, in a district too far from Bayswater to make it even possible that Minnie would come to them by the day. She had been getting things together for it, piece by piece, for years, tucking away every penny and every present they had given her, cherishing every chipped and battered remnant of furniture that had been thrown out from the upstairs world and had found its way down to the basement.

In the middle of the confusion, Dusty began to scratch urgently on the door, as a signal that it was past his time for a stroll to the letter box. Rather glad to escape, Norah went down with him. As she passed through the hall, she heard Minnie's radio playing a dance tune, loud and gay. One knows nothing about anyone, thought Norah. It had been raining lightly. She stepped out into the twilight after the pattering small dog and strolled under the trees, enjoying the quiet and the smell of the damp earth beneath the lilac bushes after the agitated scene in her mother's bedroom.

It was the next morning that Mrs Sothern decided Maurice must talk to Minnie, but it made no difference, as Norah had foreseen. He was perfectly amiable about 'having a try'. He lounged down to Minnie's quarters after dinner, which had been a melancholy meal, but he returned with scant comfort for the gloomy little party in the drawing room. Minnie had said, he reported, that she would be sorry to leave them indeed and that she realised what a fix she was putting them in, especially Miss Norah. 'Well?' said Mr Sothern impatiently. That, said Maurice, was exactly what he had asked. 'Well?' he had said to Minnie hopefully, and though he did not enlarge on this to his family, through his head had suddenly shot the possible explanation of her decision to leave them. By Jove, he had thought, has she got a man somewhere? It seemed incredible. She was such an ugly little devil. But nothing in that line, after all, should surprise one. He had amused himself with his idea as he sat there on the edge of the kitchen table, listening to Minnie's answer, which he later translated for the benefit of his relations. If a woman got to a certain age without finding a husband and kids, Minnie's philosophy stated, she ought to have something of her own, even if it were only one room that belonged to nobody else. She had made up her mind to it ever since she could remember. 'I wouldn't never respect myself again if I didn't stick to it, Mr Maurice,' she had said. He had nodded, still playing with the notion that it might be a man, after all. Though he knew it was really preposterous, it made him feel somehow warm and friendly toward Minnie, and his smile was almost knowing as he said, 'Well, good luck, whatever you decide,' and went upstairs again with his tidings to the desolate outpost in the drawing-room.

The next few weeks were rather dreadful ones for the Sotherns. Norah, who had determined to keep the house going at any cost, visited employment agencies and explained the Sotherns' needs to unimpressed women presiding over dog-eared ledgers that had a disconcerting look of being theatrical props, full of false names. Mrs Sothern was more than usually querulous; nothing was right, and Norah's heart sank when she thought what it would be like after Minnie left. One day, at Minnie's invitation, she accompanied her to inspect the new room. It was at the top of a gaunt house on the south side of the river. Minnie proudly introduced Miss Sothern to the present tenant, a quavering old woman who was going to live with a newly widowed daughter in the suburbs. 'Oh, I suppose you would have thought it rather awful,' Norah said that evening to her mother, but she had been struck by Minnie's large and opulent air of showing her around a mansion. There was a big lime tree growing in the street, just opposite the window. 'In the hot weather, I shall get the smell lovely,' Minnie had said. Mrs Sothern brightened faintly for the first time after hearing Norah's description. How could anyone put up with one sordid room, she suggested, after having the run, more or less, of the Sotherns' large, comfortable house. Given a month or two, Minnie would certainly be back. Norah was silent.

The last dinner Minnie cooked for the Sotherns was a memorable meal, with every member of the family's pet weakness remembered. It had the awful solemnity of a final sacrament, and nobody could swallow it, though, as Maurice sensibly reflected, this was probably the last decent food they would see in the house for some time. He had made arrangements to live with a friend, so that it would be lighter for poor Norah, but he would be coming back two nights a week to see how the old people were getting on. During a particularly oppressive silence, he observed, 'After all, everybody's got the right to live the life they want to.'

'Damn it!' exploded Mr Sothern. 'We ought to be life enough for her! She oughtn't to need anything else.'

His words were the naked, shameless expression of what they were all secretly thinking, and they felt as though the master's goaded bellow had stripped them as bare as a party of Greek marble statues sitting around the mahogany board. They avoided each other's eyes. After the appalling meal was over, Norah slipped away to the kitchen. She had fetched from her room a small Sheffield tea caddy, which she had bought the day before in an antique shop near Paddington. It was to be her parting present to Minnie, who burst out crying when she received it.

'I'm going to miss you all terrible,' she said.

She dried her eyes and looked with pleasure at the little box, from which she promised to make tea for Norah any time Miss Sothern felt like taking the bus ride over. For a while, Minnie would not need to work, for she had saved up a bit. Norah could imagine her sitting in the summer twilights, the tea caddy beside her, looking out of the open window at the green cloud of the lime tree. The kitchen windows were open now, and people's footsteps echoed on the pavements as they passed the railings. Norah could see a woman's short, bare legs hurrying along, a man's longer stride keeping up more leisurely. Minnie stood holding her tea caddy, facing Norah across the kitchen table.

'I'll be thinking of you all tomorrow evening,' she said.

For a moment, Norah had the most extraordinary emotion, a frightful pang of purest envy. She could hardly trust her voice to speak in its usual pleasant accents. As soon as she could finish with Minnie, she hurried from the kitchen. It was a warm evening, and the big, overcrowded house seemed very stuffy. Nostalgic Chopin sounded from the drawing room floor; Maurice played rather well. Mr Sothern, his back turned to the room, was staring gloomily out into the square. On her sofa, Mrs Sothern was going through the motions of setting out a game of patience, but she dropped the cards as Norah entered.

'You've been talking to Minnie?' she said. 'Any hope, dear?'

Maurice stopped playing; Mr Sothern half turned his head, but only for a moment. Poor old Norah, thought Maurice, it's really hard luck. He returned to his Chopin, and the music continued for some time to sigh and murmur and ask the bewildered, plaintive questions they were all asking themselves, in their own ways, as dusk came in from the square, where the dusty lilacs were purple and white no longer.

THE ENGLISH LESSON

Margaret Bonham

(1947)

When Miss Maurer remembered she had to take IVa for English at three, there was no more pleasure in looking out of the staffroom window at the bare trees etched on a winter sky. She turned away towards the fire and her hands were already cold with apprehension. I've got to be firm with them she said in silence, I've got to be, it's not too late to start. She watched how, over a book, the science mistress bent half-smiling, fresh from IVa's biology lesson with not a hair out of place, not a hair stirred by a breath or a movement from the class. Miss Maurer thought in desolation, if I smile they get worse than ever, and if I am stern they laugh behind the desks. A bell rang, and with her stiff, cold fingers she picked up her books and went into the icy corridor that led to the classroom.

All the seventeen children in IVa were sitting on desks and windowsills and arguing passionately about cakes; it was Prue Leigh's birthday and her mother was taking her out to tea. They said, 'Oh, Prue, you don't want to go to Lostriffs'; Lostriffs' are awful.' 'They don't have any with chocolate on.'

‘The Bay Tree have jam puffs with sticky on top. Gosh, they’re absolutely –’ ‘Oh, Anna, those are *foul*.’ ‘Helen, they’re *not* foul.’ Miss Maurer heard it from the passage. ‘Shut up, she’s coming.’ ‘Oh, Lord, *English*.’ ‘*Shelley*.’ Touching the frozen brass of the handle, the lunatic desire came to her again, to walk away down the corridor and down the stairs and out of the iron gates at the end of the path and along and away and on down the road. She held the knob for a second, and turned it, and went in.

Every time Miss Maurer faced IVa it seemed to her not possible that they should be no more than seventeen; in dozens, in scores she saw the pure immature lines of their faces turned towards her, their eyes clear or the deceiving light on glasses, scorn and amusement in their mouths and noses, hair impertinently curling or limp with approaching boredom. She touched the desk with her frozen fingers and set her books side by side on the slope. Beyond the window the hills were lighter with snow than the iron sky with the promise of it, and lighter than this malicious dusk in which thirty-four hands shuffled at notes and pencils and Things behind the lids of desks. ‘Please,’ she said, ‘please be quiet at once.’ Something in Prue’s corner made a noise like a saw; but who would bring a saw to a lesson on Shelley?

Prue said, ‘Oh, please, Miss Maurer, I can’t see to read.’

‘Turn the light on, Mary; I said *Mary*. Helen and Susan, go and sit down.’

‘Oh, Miss Maurer, it’s awful with the light on.’

‘Oh, shut up, it isn’t.’

‘Shelley,’ said someone very low, ‘gives me a pain in the . . .’

'Anna, you are *awful.*'

'Neck.'

'Oh, Anna, you *weren't* going to –'

'Page eighteen,' said Miss Maurer; she felt her brows contract, her mouth stretch in a helpless disciplinary mask. 'Mary,' she said. In a quite flat and expressionless voice, as if it were a seed catalogue, Mary began to read.

O Wild West Wind, thou breath of Autumn's being
Thou from whose unseen presence the leaves dead
Are driven . . .

Almost before the bell had stopped ringing, Miss Maurer passed the child who held open the door; the child contrived, simply by standing on one leg and sliding a sideways glance, to convey both insolence and relief. Once in the corridor, her fingers warmed and unflexed on the books, she walked with elegance; from one hand she swung a small saw. That was over and she looked forward to Blake with the Sixth, whose hands lay quiet on their desks and who had a good maturing respect for their own language; and then, she thought, I will go out to tea by myself for once, somewhere rich and warm.

Prue went to meet her mother by the Abbey gates, running across the already darkening square in the importance of her birthday, hair curling out and speckled with snow under the round, dark-blue hat. Against the icy flakes in the wind her mother was only two oval dark eyes between the fur of her cap and the fur of her jacket; in fur-lined boots, her feet stamped an expensive pattern on the stones. Like a Czarist lady, she smelt of cold and Cuir de Russie.

When they opened the door of the teashop the warmth, the rosy light, the rich smell of cakes struck almost solid on their faces, almost pressed them back into the street. They sat on gilt chairs against the sweep of petunia curtains shutting out the snow. Prue said, 'I'd like to *live* in a place like this.' 'Vulgar, darling, but at least warm,' said her mother, shedding gloves and furs with the graceful assurance Prue admired but never managed to copy. 'I wish I had a fur coat,' she said. 'A white one.' She looked sideways at the cakes on the tables round them. 'Mary said they didn't have chocolate ones here, and look, it's crawling with them.' 'Chocolate what?' said her mother. 'Darling, did you have a nice day at school?'

'Lousyish,' said Prue; 'well, I mean it was all right. English was quite fun.'

'What did you do in English?'

'Oh, I forget; some sort of poetry, Shelley, I think. I meant we were ragging Maurer.'

'Dearest, I do get them so mixed up; which is Maurer?'

'Oh, Mamma, I've told you; the new one. She's one of those hags – well, she's quite kind and all that, I suppose, but people simply shouldn't *let* themselves, should they? I wouldn't, would you?'

'Let themselves what?' said her mother vaguely.

'Be ragged around with. I mean, if they didn't show it, nobody would, would they? Mamma, you aren't listening.'

'Darling, I'm sorry; I was staring rudely at someone very beautiful and it took my mind off. Do say it again.'

‘Oh, where? Mamma, let me see,’ said Prue, turning inelegantly.

‘The girl over near the door, but you don’t have to go into contortions; do sit down.’ Prue half rose from her chair, the cups rocked; she peered over and around the intervening heads. ‘Oh, Lord, Mamma, there *is* Maurer; how awful. She couldn’t hear what I said from there, could she? She does look pretty cheesed off. What on earth do you think she’s doing here? Mamma, I can’t see anyone beautiful near the door.’

‘Well, never mind; which is Maurer?’

‘Well, that one – the hag by herself next to the pillar, with no hat.’

‘Darling, that’s the one I mean. In a black coat.’

With the overdone surprise so irritating in the very young, Prue sat down and stared speechless at her mother. ‘Mamma,’ she said at last, ‘you *must* be dotty, you must have made a mistake. You can’t possibly mean Maurer. I mean, I told you, she’s quite awful. It couldn’t –’

‘You can’t be expected to have any taste at your age,’ said her mother maddeningly. ‘I suppose you think anyone is plain who hasn’t got golden curls. I suppose I did too. Maurer is very beautiful indeed, and you’ll have to take my word for it.’

‘But, oh gosh, what’s she *got*? I mean, anyone can see she’s a hag; her hair’s straight.’

‘I know one does at your age, but do you really think people with straight hair are plain just like that?’

‘Well, I mean I’ve got eyes; and, Mamma, she’s so *dull*. What on earth *can* you see in her?’

'Choose your cake and let's stop arguing, it's no use at all. Darling, what a pity – you may never see a face like that again; by the time you're old enough to appreciate it, she'll be teaching some other horrid children, or having broods of her own, and getting wrinkles, not that in her case it would matter a great deal. Do you want the chocolate or the jam?'

'Both, please,' said Prue almost absently. 'Couldn't you ask them to get us some more, Mamma?' she said. 'I still think you're dotty.' Tilting back her chair to an angle from which she could see Miss Maurer's profile colourless in pale and dark against the gilt and petunia wall, she ate steadily through the cakes.

Miss Maurer's tea took her mind off IVa at the time, but in the cold morning she was no more inclined to teach them English grammar than she had been to face them with Shelley the day before; when she sat in the staffroom window at break she could, indeed, hardly bear the thought. Snow had fallen through the night and the glass framed in white feathers the dark trees with white plumes, the hills like swans. She could have watched them unmoving all the morning. But the bell rang; and walking up the corridor she felt the mask of horrid and impotent authority impose itself already on her face. Like ice and lead the books and her fingers froze together.

Prue was sitting on the windowsill above the class; she was saying, 'Well, I know it's rot. It's only what my mother thinks. I mean, she does know about that sort of thing so she ought to know what she's talking about, but she must have had a sort of fit or something. No, but I mean, if she was so absolutely ravishing we could all *see*, or couldn't we?' IVa were enchanted with sensation, united against Prue's mother, yet pleasingly racked with doubt; they said, 'Oh, Prue, her hair's *straight*; Prue, there must have been something funny about the light; well, your mother must have been looking at someone else; well, we can't all be off our rockers; I mean, she looks like nothing on earth; Prue, are you *sure* it was . . .'

From the corridor, Miss Maurer heard the murmur, the scuffle, the 'Shut up, she's coming'; feebled with apprehension, her fingers burning with cold stuck to the handle, but she went in to a profound silence. Thirty-four eyes were frozen on her face, and Miss Maurer was quite terrified. Oh, heaven, she thought, oh, what are they going to do today? But in this awful vacuum of calm they sat quiet at their desks, not whispering, not scraping, not sawing, only fixing their eyes on her, staring, gazing, as intent as owls. Too unnerved to have more than the dimmest notion of what she was saying, Miss Maurer began at random on the subjunctive mood, but her mind was quite taken up with what in heaven's name they could be staring at. Nothing odd about her clothes, which were the same as yesterday; her skirt was fastened, her suspenders held, both her shoes were black; and, in any case, the eyes all focused on her face. She ran fingers over her hair; it fell on her neck in some disorder of darkness, but not more than usual. It can only be, Miss Maurer said to herself, a very large smut or a smear; but if it is that, why don't they laugh? She turned away from the temptation to leave them and go and look in the staffroom mirror. She went on talking about the subjunctive mood and they went on staring in silence.

The lesson dragged itself in tedium round the clock; but towards its end there was a gradual stirring among the class, as though it had slept and was slowly wakening. Miss Maurer, in her shell of fear and apprehension, watched it with the beginning of relief. When her questions were answered with a touch of impertinence, when Prue leaned from her desk and whispered to Helen, when heads turned inattentively to look out of the window, she was almost happy; at the first sign of insolence, she smiled. Oh, they're unbearable, Miss Maurer said to herself, but now they are back to normal I nearly like them; anything, anything rather than that shattering stare. And still smiling she looked over their heads to the first patches of green on the white hills, the first melting of the snow.

'Oh, Prue,' said IVa after the lesson, 'do you think your mother was pulling your leg? Oh, Prue, you *don't*!' 'Well, I can see what she means, too.' 'Gosh, Susan, well, you must be cracked.' 'Helen, I'm *not* cracked.' 'Well, you must say, Anna, when she smiled –' 'But I mean, her hair's . . .'

Miss Maurer stood in front of the staffroom mirror, still holding her books in both hands; without expression, her face looked back at her, nothing about it was different. Her eyes, her pallor, the disorder of her hair were those she saw every morning and night, disinterested, in her glass; only her eyes remembered the staring, her mouth the relief of its relaxation; and lifting her shoulders, shaking her head in the conviction she would never know, she moved across to the window and stood looking out at the trees and hills darkening and melting with the thaw.

THE LOTTERY

Shirley Jackson

(1948)

The morning of June 27th was clear and sunny, with the fresh warmth of a full-summer day; the flowers were blossoming profusely and the grass was richly green. The people of the village began to gather in the square, between the post office and the bank, around ten o'clock; in some towns there were so many people that the lottery took two days and had to be started on June 26th. but in this village, where there were only about three hundred people, the whole lottery took less than two hours, so it could begin at ten o'clock in the morning and still be through in time to allow the villagers to get home for noon dinner.

The children assembled first, of course. School was recently over for the summer, and the feeling of liberty sat uneasily on most of them; they tended to gather together quietly for a while before they broke into boisterous play, and their talk was still of the classroom and the teacher, of books and reprimands. Bobby Martin had already stuffed his pockets full of stones, and the other boys soon followed his example, selecting the smoothest and roundest stones; Bobby and Harry Jones and Dickie Delacroix – the villagers pronounced this name 'Dellacroy' – eventually made a great pile of stones in one corner of the square and guarded it against the raids of the other boys. The girls stood aside, talking among themselves, looking over their shoulders at the boys, and the very small children rolled in the dust or clung to the hands of their older brothers or sisters.

Soon the men began to gather, surveying their own children, speaking of planting and rain, tractors and taxes. They stood together, away from the pile of stones in the corner, and their jokes were quiet and they smiled rather than laughed. The women, wearing faded house dresses and sweaters, came shortly after their menfolk. They greeted one another and exchanged bits of gossip as they went to join their husbands. Soon the women, standing by their husbands, began to call to their children, and the children came reluctantly, having to be called four or five times. Bobby Martin ducked under his mother's grasping hand and ran, laughing, back to the pile of stones. His father spoke up sharply, and Bobby came quickly and took his place between his father and his oldest brother.

The lottery was conducted – as were the square dances, the teen club, the Halloween programme – by Mr Summers, who had time and energy to devote to civic activities. He was a round-faced, jovial man and he ran the coal business, and people were sorry for him because he had no children and his wife was a scold. When he arrived in the square, carrying the black wooden box, there was a murmur of conversation among the villagers, and he waved and called, 'Little late today, folks.' The postmaster, Mr Graves, followed him, carrying a three-legged stool, and the stool was put in the centre of the square and Mr Summers set the black box down on it. The villagers kept their distance, leaving a space between themselves and the stool, and when Mr Summers said, 'Some of you fellows want to give me a hand?' there was a hesitation before two men, Mr Martin and his oldest son, Baxter, came forward to hold the box steady on the stool while Mr Summers stirred up the papers inside it.

The original paraphernalia for the lottery had been lost long ago, and the black box now resting on the stool had been put into use even before Old Man Warner, the oldest man in town, was born. Mr Summers spoke frequently to the villagers about making a new box, but no one liked to upset even as much tradition as was represented by the black box. There was a story that the present box had been made with some pieces of the box that had preceded it, the one that had been constructed when the first people settled down to make a village here. Every year, after the lottery, Mr Summers began talking again about a new box, but every year the subject was allowed to fade off without anything being done. The black box grew shabbier each year: by now it was no longer completely black but splintered badly along one side to show the original wood colour, and in some places faded or stained.

Mr Martin and his oldest son, Baxter, held the black box securely on the stool until Mr Summers had stirred the papers thoroughly with his hand. Because so much of the ritual had been forgotten or discarded, Mr Summers had been successful in having slips of paper substituted for the chips of wood that had been used for generations. Chips of wood, Mr Summers had argued, had been all very well when the village was tiny, but now that the population was more than three hundred and likely to keep on growing, it was necessary to use something that would fit more easily into the black box. The night before the lottery, Mr Summers and Mr Graves made up the slips of paper and put them in the box, and it was then taken to the safe of Mr Summers's coal company and locked up until Mr Summers was ready to take it to the square next morning. The rest of the year, the box was put away, sometimes one place, sometimes another; it had spent one year in Mr Graves's barn and another year underfoot in the post office; and sometimes it was set on a shelf in the Martin grocery and left there.

There was a great deal of fussing to be done before Mr Summers declared the lottery open. There were the lists to make up – of heads of families, heads of households in each family, members of each household in each family. There was the proper swearing-in of Mr Summers by the postmaster, as the official of the lottery; at one time, some people remembered, there had been a recital of some sort, performed by the official of the lottery, a perfunctory, tuneless chant that had been rattled off duly each year; some people believed that the official of the lottery used to stand just so when he said or sang it, others believed that he was supposed to walk among the people, but years and years ago this part of the ritual had been allowed to lapse. There had been, also, a ritual salute, which the official of the lottery had had to use in addressing each person who came up to draw from the box, but this also had changed with time, until now it was felt necessary only for the official to speak to each person approaching. Mr Summers was very good at all this; in his clean white shirt and blue jeans, with one hand resting carelessly on the black box, he seemed very proper and important as he talked interminably to Mr Graves and the Martins.

Just as Mr Summers finally left off talking and turned to the assembled villagers, Mrs Hutchinson came hurriedly along the path to the square, her sweater thrown over her shoulders, and slid into place in the back of the crowd. 'Clean forgot what day it was,' she said to Mrs Delacroix, who stood next to her, and they both laughed softly. 'Thought my old man was out back stacking wood,' Mrs Hutchinson went on, 'and then I looked out the window and the kids was gone, and then I remembered it was the twenty-seventh and came a-running.' She dried her hands on her apron, and Mrs Delacroix said, 'You're in time, though. They're still talking away up there.'

Mrs Hutchinson craned her neck to see through the crowd and found her husband and children standing near the front. She tapped Mrs Delacroix on the arm as a farewell and began to make her way through the crowd. The people separated good-humouredly to let her through; two or three people said, in voices just loud enough to be heard across the crowd, 'Here comes your Missus, Hutchinson,' and 'Bill, she made it after all.' Mrs Hutchinson reached her husband, and Mr Summers, who had been waiting, said cheerfully,

'Thought we were going to have to get on without you, Tessie.' Mrs Hutchinson said, grinning, 'Wouldn't have me leave m'dishes in the sink, now, would you, Joe?' and soft laughter ran through the crowd as the people stirred back into position after Mrs Hutchinson's arrival.

'Well, now,' Mr Summers said soberly, 'guess we better get started, get this over with, so's we can go back to work. Anybody ain't here?'

'Dunbar,' several people said. 'Dunbar, Dunbar.'

Mr Summers consulted his list. 'Clyde Dunbar,' he said. 'That's right. He's broke his leg, hasn't he? Who's drawing for him?'

'Me, I guess,' a woman said, and Mr Summers turned to look at her.

'Wife draws for her husband,' Mr Summers said. 'Don't you have a grown boy to do it for you, Janey?' Although Mr Summers and everyone else in the village knew the answer perfectly well, it was the business of the official of the lottery to ask such questions formally. Mr Summers waited with an expression of polite interest while Mrs Dunbar answered.

'Horace's not but sixteen yet,' Mrs Dunbar said regretfully. 'Guess I gotta fill in for the old man this year.'

'Right,' Mr Summers said. He made a note on the list he was holding. Then he asked, 'Watson boy drawing this year?'

A tall boy in the crowd raised his hand. 'Here,' he said. 'I'm drawing for m'mother and me.' He blinked his eyes nervously and ducked his head as several voices in the crowd said things like 'Good fellow, Jack,' and 'Glad to see your mother's got a man to do it.'

‘Well,’ Mr Summers said, ‘guess that’s everyone. Old Man Warner make it?’

‘Here,’ a voice said, and Mr Summers nodded.

A sudden hush fell on the crowd as Mr Summers cleared his throat and looked at the list. ‘All ready?’ he called. ‘Now, I’ll read the names – heads of families first – and the men come up and take a paper out of the box. Keep the paper folded in your hand without looking at it until everyone has had a turn. Everything clear?’

The people had done it so many times that they only half listened to the directions; most of them were quiet, wetting their lips, not looking around. Then Mr Summers raised one hand high and said, ‘Adams.’ A man disengaged himself from the crowd and came forward. ‘Hi, Steve,’ Mr Summers said, and Mr Adams said, ‘Hi, Joe.’ They grinned at one another humourlessly and nervously. Then Mr Adams reached into the black box and took out a folded paper. He held it firmly by one corner as he turned and went hastily back to his place in the crowd, where he stood a little apart from his family, not looking down at his hand.

‘Allen,’ Mr Summers said. ‘Anderson. . . . Bentham.’

‘Seems like there’s no time at all between lotteries any more,’ Mrs Delacroix said to Mrs Graves in the back row. ‘Seems like we got through with the last one only last week.’

‘Time sure goes fast,’ Mrs Graves said.

‘Clark. . . . Delacroix.’

‘There goes my old man,’ Mrs Delacroix said. She held her breath while her husband went forward.

'Dunbar,' Mr Summers said, and Mrs Dunbar went steadily to the box while one of the women said, 'Go on, Janey,' and another said, 'There she goes.'

'We're next,' Mrs Graves said. She watched while Mr Graves came around from the side of the box, greeted Mr Summers gravely and selected a slip of paper from the box. By now, all through the crowd there were men holding the small folded papers in their large hands, turning them over and over nervously. Mrs Dunbar and her two sons stood together, Mrs Dunbar holding the slip of paper.

'Harburt. . . . Hutchinson.'

'Get up there, Bill,' Mrs Hutchinson said, and the people near her laughed.

'Jones.'

'They do say,' Mr Adams said to Old Man Warner, who stood next to him, 'that over in the north village they're talking of giving up the lottery.'

Old Man Warner snorted, 'Pack of crazy fools,' he said. 'Listening to the young folks, nothing's good enough for *them*. Next thing you know, they'll be wanting to go back to living in caves, nobody work any more, live *that* way for a while. Used to be a saying about "Lottery in June, corn be heavy soon." First thing you know, we'd all be eating stewed chickweed and acorns. There's always been a lottery,' he added petulantly. 'Bad enough to see young Joe Summers up there joking with everybody.'

'Some places have already quit lotteries,' Mrs Adams said.

'Nothing but trouble in *that*,' Old Man Warner said stoutly. 'Pack of young fools.'

'Martin.' And Bobby Martin watched his father go forward. 'Overdyke. . . . Percy.'

'I wish they'd hurry,' Mrs Dunbar said to her older son. 'I wish they'd hurry.'

'They're almost through,' her son said.

'You get ready to run tell Dad,' Mrs Dunbar said.

Mr Summers called his own name and then stepped forward precisely and selected a slip from the box. Then he called, 'Warner.'

'Seventy-seventh year I been in the lottery,' Old Man Warner said as he went through the crowd. 'Seventy-seventh time.'

'Watson.' The tall boy came awkwardly through the crowd. Someone said, 'Don't be nervous, Jack,' and Mr Summers said, 'Take your time, son.'

'Zanini.'

After that, there was a long pause, a breathless pause, until Mr Summers, holding his slip of paper in the air, said, 'All right, fellows.' For a minute, no one moved, and then all the slips of paper were opened. Suddenly, all the women began to speak at once, saying, 'Who is it?' 'Who's got it?' 'Is it the Dunbars?' 'Is it the Watsons?' Then the voices began to say, 'It's Hutchinson. It's Bill,' 'Bill Hutchinson's got it.'

'Go tell your father,' Mrs Dunbar said to her older son.

People began to look around to see the Hutchinsons. Bill Hutchinson was standing quiet, staring down at the paper in his hand. Suddenly, Tessie Hutchinson shouted to Mr Summers, 'You didn't give him time enough to take any paper he wanted. I saw you. It wasn't fair!'

‘Be a good sport, Tessie,’ Mrs Delacroix called, and Mrs Graves said, ‘All of us took the same chance.’

‘Shut up, Tessie,’ Bill Hutchinson said.

‘Well, everyone,’ Mr Summers said, ‘that was done pretty fast, and now we’ve got to be hurrying a little more to get done in time.’ He consulted his next list. ‘Bill,’ he said, ‘you draw for the Hutchinson family. You got any other households in the Hutchinsons?’

‘There’s Don and Eva,’ Mrs Hutchinson yelled. ‘Make *them* take their chance!’

‘Daughters draw with their husbands’ families, Tessie,’ Mr Summers said gently. ‘You know that as well as anyone else.’

‘It wasn’t *fair*,’ Tessie said.

‘I guess not, Joe,’ Bill Hutchinson said regretfully. ‘My daughter draws with her husband’s family, that’s only fair. And I’ve got no other family except the kids.’

‘Then, as far as drawing for families is concerned, it’s you,’ Mr Summers said in explanation, ‘and as far as drawing for households is concerned, that’s you, too. Right?’

‘Right,’ Bill Hutchinson said.

‘How many kids, Bill?’ Mr Summers asked formally.

‘Three,’ Bill Hutchinson said. ‘There’s Bill Jr, and Nancy, and little Dave. And Tessie and me.’

‘All right, then,’ Mr Summers said. ‘Harry, you got their tickets back?’

Mr Graves nodded and held up the slips of paper. ‘Put them in the box, then,’ Mr Summers directed. ‘Take Bill’s and put it in.’

'I think we ought to start over,' Mrs Hutchinson said, as quietly as she could. 'I tell you it wasn't *fair*. You didn't give him time enough to choose. *Every*body saw that.'

Mr Graves had selected the five slips and put them in the box, and he dropped all the papers but those onto the ground, where the breeze caught them and lifted them off.

'Listen, everybody,' Mrs Hutchinson was saying to the people around her.

'Ready, Bill?' Mr Summers asked, and Bill Hutchinson, with one quick glance around at his wife and children, nodded.

'Remember,' Mr Summers said, 'take the slips and keep them folded until each person has taken one. Harry, you help little Dave.' Mr Graves took the hand of the little boy, who came willingly with him up to the box. 'Take a paper out of the box, Davy,' Mr Summers said. Davy put his hand into the box and laughed. 'Take just *one* paper,' Mr Summers said. 'Harry, you hold it for him.' Mr Graves took the child's hand and removed the folded paper from the tight fist and held it while little Dave stood next to him and looked up at him wonderingly.

'Nancy next,' Mr Summers said. Nancy was twelve, and her schoolfriends breathed heavily as she went forward, switching her skirt, and took a slip daintily from the box. 'Bill Jr,' Mr Summers said, and Billy, his face red and his feet over-large, nearly knocked the box over as he got a paper out. 'Tessie,' Mr Summers said. She hesitated for a minute, looking around defiantly, and then set her lips and went up to the box. She snatched a paper out and held it behind her.

'Bill,' Mr Summers said, and Bill Hutchinson reached into the box and felt around, bringing his hand out at last with the slip of paper in it.

The crowd was quiet. A girl whispered, 'I hope it's not Nancy,' and the sound of the whisper reached the edges of the crowd.

'It's not the way it used to be,' Old Man Warner said clearly. 'People ain't the way they used to be.'

'All right,' Mr Summers said. 'Open the papers. Harry, you open little Dave's.'

Mr Graves opened the slip of paper and there was a general sigh through the crowd as he held it up and everyone could see that it was blank. Nancy and Bill Jr opened theirs at the same time, and both beamed and laughed, turning around to the crowd and holding their slips of paper above their heads.

'Tessie,' Mr Summers said. There was a pause, and then Mr Summers looked at Bill Hutchinson, and Bill unfolded his paper and showed it. It was blank.

'It's Tessie,' Mr Summers said, and his voice was hushed. 'Show us her paper, Bill.'

Bill Hutchinson went over to his wife and forced the slip of paper out of her hand. It had a black spot on it, the black spot Mr Summers had made the night before with the heavy pencil in the coal company office. Bill Hutchinson held it up, and there was a stir in the crowd.

'All right, folks,' Mr Summers said. 'Let's finish quickly.'

Although the villagers had forgotten the ritual and lost the original black box, they still remembered to use stones.

The pile of stones the boys had made earlier was ready; there were stones on the ground with the blowing scraps of paper that had come out of the box. Mrs Delacroix selected a stone so large she had to pick it up with both hands and turned to Mrs Dunbar. 'Come on,' she said. 'Hurry up.'

Mrs Dunbar had small stones in both hands, and she said, gasping for breath, 'I can't run at all. You'll have to go ahead and I'll catch up with you.'

The children had stones already, and someone gave little Davy Hutchinson a few pebbles.

Tessie Hutchinson was in the centre of a cleared space by now, and she held her hands out desperately as the villagers moved in on her. 'It isn't fair,' she said. A stone hit her on the side of the head.

Old Man Warner was saying, 'Come on, come on, everyone.' Steve Adams was in the front of the crowd of villagers, with Mrs Graves beside him.

'It isn't fair, it isn't right,' Mrs Hutchinson screamed, and then they were upon her.

A VIEW OF EXMOOR

Sylvia Townsend Warner

(1948)

From Bath, where Mr Finch was taking the waters, the Finches travelled by car into Devonshire to attend the wedding of Mrs Finch's niece, Arminella Blount. This was in 1936, when weddings could be garish. The Finches made a very creditable family contribution – Mrs Finch in green moiré, Cordelia and Clara in their bridesmaids' dresses copied from the Gainsborough portrait of an earlier Arminella Blount in the Character of Flora, Mr Finch in, as his wife said, his black-and-grey. Arden Finch in an Eton suit would have looked like any normal twelve year old boy in an Eton suit if measles had not left him preternaturally thin, pale, and owl-eyed.

All these fine feathers, plus two top hats, an Indian shawl to wrap around Arden in case it turned cold, and a picnic basket in case anyone felt hungry, made the car seem unusually full during the drive to Devonshire. On the return journey it was even fuller, because the Finches were bringing back Arminella's piping bullfinch and the music box that was needed to continue its education, as well as the bridesmaids' bouquets. It was borne in on Mr Finch that other travellers along the main road were noticing his car and its contents more than they needed to, and this impression was confirmed when the passengers in two successive charabancs cheered and waved. Mr Finch, the soul of consideration, turned in to a side road to spare his wife and daughters the embarrassment of these public acclamations.

'"Pember and South Pigworthy,"' Mrs Finch read aloud from a signpost. 'The doctor who took out my tonsils was called Pember. It's so nice to find a name one knows.'

Mr Finch replied that he was taking an alternative way home. After a while, he stopped and looked for his road map, but couldn't find it. He drove on.

'Father,' said Cordelia a little later, 'we've been through this village before. Don't you think we had better ask?'

'Is *that* all it is?' said Mrs Finch. 'What a relief. I thought I was having one of those mysterious delusions when one half of my brain mislays the other half.'

Mr Finch continued to drive on. Arden, who had discovered that the bars of the bird cage gave out notes of varying pitch when he plucked them, was carrying out a systematic test with a view to being able to play 'Rule Britannia'. Cordelia and Clara and their mother discussed the wedding.

Suddenly, Mrs Finch exclaimed, 'Oh, Henry! Stop, stop! There's such a beautiful view of Exmoor!'

Ten-foot hedges rose on either side of the lane they were in, the lane went steeply uphill, and Mr Finch had hoped that he had put any views of Exmoor safely behind him. But with unusual mildness he stopped and backed the car till it was even with a gate. Beyond the gate was a falling meadow, a pillowy middle distance of woodland, and beyond that, pure and cold and unimpassioned, the silhouette of the moor.

'Why not,' Mr Finch said, taking the good the gods provided, 'why not stop and picnic?' It occurred to him that once the car was emptied, the road map might come to light.

The Finches sat down in the meadow and ate cucumber sandwiches. Arden wore the Indian shawl; the bullfinch in its cage was brought out of the car to have a little fresh air. Gazing at the view, Mrs Finch said that looking at Exmoor always reminded her of her Aunt Harriet's inexplicable boots.

'What boots, Mother?' Cordelia asked.

'She saw them on Exmoor,' Mrs Finch said. 'She and Uncle Lionel both saw them; they were children at the time. They were picking whortleberries – such a disappointing fruit! All these folkart fruits are much overrated. And nobody's ever been able to account for them.'

'But why should they have to be accounted for?' Clara asked. 'Were they sticking out of a bog?'

'They were in a cab.'

'Your Aunt Harriet –' Mr Finch began. For some reason, it angered him to hear of boots being in a cab while he was still in doubt as to whether the map was in the car.

'Of course,' Mrs Finch went on, 'in those days cabs were everywhere. But not on Exmoor, where there were no roads. It was a perfectly ordinary cab, one of the kind that open in hot weather. The driver was on the box, and the horse was waving its tail to keep the flies off. They looked as if they had been there quite a long time.'

‘Days and days?’ Arden asked.

‘I’m afraid not, dear. Decomposition had not set in. But as if they had been there long enough to get resigned to it. An hour or so.’

‘But how could Aunt Harriet tell how long –’

‘In those days, children were very different – nice and inhibited,’ Mrs Finch said. ‘So Aunt Harriet and Uncle Lionel observed the cab from a distance and walked on. Presently, they saw two figures – a man and a woman. The man was very pale and sulky, and the woman was rating him and crying her eyes out, but the most remarkable thing of all, even more remarkable than the cab, was that the woman wasn’t wearing a hat. In those days, no self-respecting woman could stir out without a hat. And on the ground was a pair of boots. While Harriet and Lionel were trying to get a little nearer without seeming inquisitive, the woman snatched up the boots and ran back to the cab. She ran right past the children; she was crying so bitterly she didn’t even notice them. She jumped into the cab, threw the boots onto the opposite seat, the driver whipped up his horse, and the cab went bumping and jolting away over the moor. As for the man, he walked off looking like murder. So what do you make of that?’

‘Well, I suppose they’d been wading, and then they quarrelled, and she drove away with his boots as a revenge,’ said Clara.

‘He was wearing boots,’ said Mrs Finch.

‘Perhaps they were eloping,’ Clara said, ‘and the boots were part of their luggage that he’d forgotten to pack, like Father, and she changed her mind in time.’

'Speed is essential to an elopement, and so is secrecy. To drive over Exmoor in an open cab would be inconsistent with either,' said Mr Finch.

'Perhaps the cab lost its way in a moor mist,' contributed Arden. 'Listen? I can do almost all the first line of "Rule Britannia" now.'

'But, Clara, why need it be an elopement?' Cordelia asked. 'Perhaps she was just a devoted wife who found a note from her husband saying he had lost his memory or committed a crime or something and was going out of her life, and she seized up a spare pair of boots, leaped hatless into a cab, and tracked him across Exmoor, to make sure he had a dry pair to change into. And when Harriet and Lionel saw them, he had just turned on her with a brutal oath.'

'If she had been such a devoted wife, she wouldn't have taken the boots away again,' Clara said.

'Yes, she would. It was the breaking point,' Cordelia said. 'Actually, though, I don't believe she was married to him at all. I think it was an assignation and she'd taken her husband's boots with her as a blind.'

'Then why did she take them out of the cab?' inquired Clara. 'And why didn't she wear a hat, like Mother said? No, Cordelia! I think your theory is artistically all right. It looks the boots straight in the face. But I've got a better one. I think they spent a guilty night together and, being a forgetful man, he put his boots out to be cleaned and in the morning she was hopelessly compromised, so she snatched up the boots and drove after him to give him a piece of her mind.'

'Yes, but he was wearing boots already,' Cordelia said.

'He would have had several pairs. At that date, a libertine would have had hundreds of boots, wouldn't he, Mother?'

'He might not have taken them with him wherever he went, dear,' said Mrs Finch.

Mr Finch said, 'You have both rushed off on an assumption. Because the lady drove away in the cab, you both assume that she arrived in it. Women always jump to conclusions. Why shouldn't the cab have brought the man? If she was hatless, she might have been an escaped lunatic and the man a keeper from the asylum, who came in search of her.'

'Why did he bring a pair of boots?' Cordelia asked.

'Ladies' boots,' said Mr Finch firmly.

'He can't have been much of a lunatic-keeper if he let her get away with his cab,' Clara said.

'I did not say he was a lunatic-keeper, Clara,' said Mr Finch. 'I was merely trying to point out to you and your sister that in cases like this one must examine the evidence from all sides.'

'Perhaps the cabdriver was a lunatic,' said Arden. 'Perhaps that's why he drove them onto Exmoor. Perhaps they were *his* boots, and the man and the woman were arguing as to which of them was to pay his fare. Perhaps –'

Interrupted by his father and both his sisters, all speaking at once, Arden returned to his rendering of 'Rule Britannia'. Mrs Finch removed some crumbs and a few caterpillars from her green moiré lap and looked at the view of Exmoor. Suddenly, a glissando passage on the bird cage was broken by a light twang, a flutter of wings, a cry from Arden. The cage door had flipped open and the bullfinch had flown out. Everybody said 'Oh!' and grabbed at it. The bullfinch flew to the gate, balanced there, flirted its tail, and flew on into the lane.

It flew in a surprised, incompetent way, making short flights, hurling itself from side to side of the lane. But though Cordelia and Clara leaped after it, trying to catch it in their broad-brimmed hats, and although Arden only just missed it by overbalancing on a bough, thereby falling out of the tree and making his nose bleed, and though Mr Finch walked after it, holding up the bird cage and crying 'Sweet, Sweet, Sweet' in a falsetto voice that trembled with feeling, the bullfinch remained at liberty and, with a little practice, flew better and better.

'Stop, all of you!' said Mrs Finch, who had been attending to Arden, wiping her bloodstained hands on the grass. 'You'll frighten it. Henry, do leave off saying "Sweet" – you'll only strain yourself. What we need is the music box. If it hears the music box, it will be reminded of its home and remember it's a tame bullfinch. Arden, dear, please keep your shawl on and look for some groundsel, if you aren't too weak from loss of blood.'

The music box weighed about fifty pounds. It was contained in an ebony case that looked like a baby's coffin, and at every movement it emitted reproachful chords. On one side, it had a handle; on the other side, the handle had fallen off, and by the time the Finches had got the box out of the car, they were flushed and breathless. His groans mingling with the reproachful chords, Mr Finch staggered up the lane in pursuit of the bullfinch, with the music box in his arms. Mrs Finch walked beside him, tenderly entreating him to be careful, for if anything happened to it, it would break Arminella's heart. Blithesome and cumberless, like the bird of the wilderness, the bullfinch flitted on ahead.

'I am not carrying this thing a step further,' said Mr Finch, setting down the music box at the side of the lane. 'Since you insist, Elinor, I will sit here and play it. The rest of you can walk on and turn the bird somehow and drive it back till the music reminds it of home.'

Clara said, 'I expect we shall go on for miles.'

Seeing his family vanish around a bend in the lane, Mr Finch found himself nursing a hope that Clara's expectation might be granted. He was devoted to music boxes. He sat down beside it and read the list of its repertory, which was written in a copperplate hand inside the lid: *Là Ci Darem la Mano; The Harp That Once Through Tara's Halls; The Prayer from 'Moïse'; The Copenhagen Waltz.* A very pleasant choice for an interval of repose, well-earned repose, in this leafy seclusion. He ran his finger over the prickled cylinder, he blew away a little dust, he wound the box up. Unfortunately, there were a great many midges, the inherent pest of leafy seclusions. He paused to light a cigar. Then he set off the music box. It chirruped through three and a half tunes and stopped, as music boxes do. Behind him, a voice said somewhat diffidently, 'I say. Can I be any help?'

Glancing from the corner of his eye, Mr Finch saw a young man whose bare ruined legs and rucksack suggested that he was on a walking tour.

'No, thank you,' Mr Finch said. Dismissingly, he rewound the music box and set it going again.

Around the bend of the lane came two replicas, in rather bad condition, of Gainsborough's well-known portrait of Arminella Blount in the Character of Flora, a cadaverous small boy draped in a bloodstained Indian shawl, and a middle-aged lady dressed in the height of fashion who carried a bird cage. Once again, Mr Finch was forced to admit the fact that the instant his family escaped from his supervision they somehow managed to make themselves conspicuous. Tripping nervously to the strains of 'The Copenhagen Waltz', the young man on a walking tour skirted around them and hurried on.

'We've got it!' cried Mrs Finch, brandishing the bird cage.

'Why the deuce couldn't you *explain* to that young man?' asked Mr Finch. 'Elinor, why couldn't you explain?'

'But why should I?' Mrs Finch asked. 'He looked so hot and careworn, and I expect he only gets a fortnight's holiday all the year through. Why should I spoil it for him? Why shouldn't he have something to look back on in his old age?'

THE WOMAN NOVELIST

Diana Gardner

(1950)

Madeleine finished dressing by the open window, looking down onto the garden. It was not yet seven, but she knew that the day was going to be hot, cloudless and unchanging, because of the vivid, almost unnatural green of the trees on the far edge of the dew-damp lawn. Nothing moved anywhere – except a blackbird, whose tail pitched like a see-saw as it alighted on a stone in the Flemish garden.

She paused, her hairbrush threaded into her dark, soft hair. The Flemish garden! It was bright yellow with charlock. Wykham should have tidied it – there were things that he had undertaken to do at weekends, and during his vacations from the law school – but he had not done so. There were, in fact, other things that he had not done.

He lay now, behind her in the room, in the bed nearest the wall. He still slept.

She felt suddenly despondent, although it was so early in the day. She often felt this nowadays, losing, as she did so, the glory of these summer mornings. Such small things, too, sent her skimming down. To keep the seven of them going – herself and Wykham, the three children, and the two old ladies, Wykham's mother and her mother, whose contributions barely covered the rent – allowed no chance for anyone to slip up on their job. If anyone did that, she could not then carry on with hers, and it was by her work that they lived. Including Wykham. His state grant on leaving the Army barely covered his expenses in London, where he was studying for the Bar.

This last week he had been on vacation, and had spent it reading in his 'study', the old morning-room – was he reading law books or those green and white paperbacks which later she found imbedded in dust in the garbage bin? – or visiting in the neighbourhood, which was remote enough to contain still a few of the orthodox, but ruined, and beginning to be faintly ridiculous, gentry, who made him feel – as he was handed a glass of brandy by a white-haired squire resembling his late father – that he counted somewhere in the world, that there was a place still for his 'type'. How he enjoyed this, Madeleine thought, softening. At those times, he would become vivid and alive, almost visibly becoming heavier – he was thin – and looking handsome in an old-fashioned way. She turned from the window and finished doing her hair. That was the sort of life Wykham ought always to live. He ought to have been born a hundred years before.

Her helplessness returned. She leaned one hand on the windowsill, her long, slim body twisted and drooping.

But then she thought of the book she was working on. Last week it had taken a new, interesting turn. It had come strongly to life. Her spirits rose. Those two and a half hours in the afternoon, when the children were at school, and the two old ladies, the mothers-in-law, were withdrawn, resting in their bedrooms, were hers – hers for herself. Some of the joy of those hours now came to her. Her oval, nearly beautiful face – it had a small twist to it, so that the centre of her slightly pointed chin was not in line with the middle of her forehead – which, when first she had gone to the mirror, had been pinched and pale, was now filled out and glowing. She could carry on – the family was secure – if she were certain of those two and a half precious hours.

She went out onto the landing. It seemed very empty, and was bright, whitely bright, as if in some way it had been gutted by the night. She went into the children's rooms. Only the younger boy was still asleep. Robert and Jenny were already sitting up in bed, looking at books. She told them to get up and dress. She then went downstairs to the large, cool kitchen, let out the tortoiseshell cat, lit the Calor stove, and put on the kettle. The daylight grew stronger, less ethereal and exquisite; the ordinary day proceeded to arrive. A tractor began to climb, as if in pain, up the short hill, which rose beyond the edge of the garden.

Madeleine then thought of Beryl, her twenty-year-old help from two miles away down the valley. At half-past eight she would come, as fresh-cheeked as if she had collected dew on the way, on her bicycle, and with her fair hair crisp and shining, and scarcely out of place. Madeleine thought of her with a gratitude, deep and tender, like love. It was love. For how could she have managed without her? And she was always capable, willing, reliable. She seemed to like working out here at the

White House – this old half-mansion among the untidy, farming acres.

As Madeleine made toast and fried the bacon, she heard her mother, Mrs Grinling, coming down the stairs – slowly, because of her rheumatics – to help. The tractor now turned at the bottom of the hill for a second ascent. What had the farmer planned for this morning, out there? Madeleine wondered, idly. It was too early for hay-making. Could it be ploughing? She scraped fat into the frying pan and went and joined her mother in the dining-room. Mrs Grinling always laid the breakfast table, but slowly and painfully, because of her stiff joints. The first child, Jenny, now came downstairs.

During the meal, the youngest, Timothy, spilt his milk; Jenny was gay and too talkative – she was taking anemones to her form mistress, with whom she was in love. Robert ate his bacon contentedly. Thank goodness, Madeleine thought, they could all now dress themselves. But what, she wondered, would their rooms be like?

Afterwards, she and the old, white-haired lady watched them ride off on their bicycles down the long, white, empty road. There was little traffic in that part of the world, even in the small country town containing the school, so that they could be fairly trusted. The two women then returned to the house – Mrs Grinling to the dining-room for her last, private cup of tea and a brief look at her son-in-law's newspaper, and Madeleine to the kitchen. The warm May wind came soothingly, freshly, through the window – open – above the stone sink. She would have liked to do nothing more in the house all that day, but to have gone out into the garden and to have sat under the beech trees, thinking about, and working out, her novel. But she had still much to do, to get through. Her next job was to prepare breakfast for the other old lady, Mrs Filmer, Wykham's mother.

She took it, with a letter, into the downstairs bedroom, which had once been the drawing-room of the house, and had an ornate, moulded ceiling. Mrs Filmer had furnished it with large, late-Georgian furniture from the country house where she had been born. The old lady, her hair a faint blue-white, in neat, flat waves under an invisible hairnet, was sitting up in her mahogany bed, holding in readiness a silver paper-knife.

'Good morning, my dear,' she said, brightly, 'I hope you slept well, and that the children have gone off safely.' She used the same words every morning.

'Yes, thank you, mama,' Madeleine answered, as usual.

She drew back the brocade curtains. On the path under the window a tricycle lay on its side over a crushed white, lidless shoe box and some old tennis balls. She ought to have put them away last night, and not left it to the children. On this side of the house, the garden was even more neglected. Her despondency returned. If only Wykham would fulfil his promises! She leaned on the windowsill, and looked through the foliage of the trees, at the cornfield beyond. Why, she mused, had this large white house been built right out here, in the first place? Whose vision had started it all off? They had heard of it – to let cheap – through an ex-Army friend of Wykham's. And how enormous it was! The rooms had been designed for large house parties, even balls: and yet it belonged to no especial period. She wondered how long they would be able to afford to live here. Her heaviness increased.

But once more she remembered her work, and the solace it brought her – as well as the money it earned. Again, she grew cheerful. Today she would work out in the conservatory, instead of, as was customary, in the dining-room. No one ever went there. She would be undisturbed. And the trees, having grown up round it, cooled it off. She would use the white painted bamboo table, and leave the door open so that, from time to time, she could look out onto the garden.

She turned back to her mother-in-law, whom she had almost forgotten.

The old lady smiled brilliantly, and said charmingly, but without sincerity – she was already returning to her letter – as she left the room: 'Now dear, you're to let me know if I can do anything to help you.'

Out in the sunny kitchen, Madeleine found Beryl putting on her snow-white overall. She was, as Madeleine had expected to see her, fresh, cheerful, neat – even elegant. She lived with her grandmother in a brick cottage beside the canal, in the nearby town.

'Good morning, Mrs Filmer.' Beryl's eyes were admiring and kind.

Together they cleared the breakfast table – except for Wykham's things, which were left for him to enjoy peacefully. While on vacation, he never came down before ten. Beryl then started the washing-up, while Madeleine went upstairs to tidy the children's rooms. Passing Wykham's and her bedroom, she went in. He lay on his back, wide awake, staring at the ceiling. He was unusually good-looking, with a square jaw, deep-set blue eyes, and black, curly hair. He smiled at her, showing his flawless teeth. She felt brighter. When he greeted her like this, she always felt warmed, soothed.

But then, through the window, as she turned her head, she saw once more the charlock choking the Flemish garden. She thought desperately: what a pity he has not cleared it, as he promised.

'I suppose I had better get up,' he muttered, feeling that she had accused him of lying in bed.

'And I must get on with my housework,' she said, flatly, going to the door.

He sat up and scratched his back with his thumbs, under his striped pyjama jacket. As she passed him she drew her hand lightly over his hair. He caught at her wrist, smiling.

She went to the children's rooms. As she had expected, they were in vivid, elemental disorder. The sun poured over them through the enormous square windows. Each child seemed to have left something of its own personality in all three rooms. Particularly Jenny. Madeleine could almost hear her high, eager and faintly irritating voice as she went in. How unconcerned they all were by their parents' struggle to feed and educate them! She collected up their soiled underclothing. Tomorrow she and Beryl would have a big wash-day. She then ran the Ewbank over the threadbare, almost paper-thin Oriental rugs, which Wykham's mother had once given them.

When, finally, she went downstairs, Beryl was already preparing the lunch. Peeled potatoes lay, transparent-looking, in a bowl of water; cabbage leaves glistened under the tap. Beryl had also thoroughly 'done out' the dining room, the hall, and the drawing room – where Mrs Grinling now sat at the desk, writing a letter. Old Mrs Filmer had not yet appeared. She did not usually arrive until lunchtime. Wykham must have gone already to his study.

Madeleine took a basket, and went out into the garden, to pick rhubarb, and a lettuce for salad. While out there she would transplant some of the young lettuces from the frame. She wished that Wykham could have been out there with her, that they could have had a little time alone together, as in the old days. But it would not have been right: she must not ask for it. She must do nothing to prevent him from one day getting to the Bar.

Wykham came and stood at the french window of the study, with his hands in his pockets. He found it almost impossible to concentrate these bright mornings. He wanted to go over again to see Colonel Clavering, at Place House. Would Madeleine mind; would the Colonel be in? He watched the white butterflies fluttering above the charlock in the Flemish garden. It was his mother who had called it the 'Flemish' garden. Very like her. Such big ideas still, when for so long she had possessed nothing more impressive than a downstairs bed-sitting room.

He supposed, he thought idly, that he ought to have cleared out that charlock weeks ago. Now that he remembered, hadn't he promised Madeleine that he would do so?

* * *

At twelve, Madeleine returned to the house. Beryl was rolling the pastry for the rhubarb pie. Together, they built up the lunch; fish for Mrs Filmer, salad for Mrs Grinling; 'solid' food for Wykham. The children took theirs at school. They worked silently and steadily. The kitchen felt peaceful, industrious. Once, Mrs Grinling came out to the kitchen for water for some flowers. Madeleine and she then laid the table for lunch.

When she heard the one o'clock time signal coming from the library Madeleine untied her apron, and went in there. Both the old ladies were there, trying to make conversation. At all other times of the day, they avoided each other. Wykham, in his new dark-grey flannel suit, was standing up reading aloud the label on a sherry bottle.

'I couldn't find the brown glasses, darling,' he said, to Madeleine, 'so I've used those.'

He pointed to a brandy glass on the spinet. With dismay, she saw that a ring of sherry had formed on the polished wood, showing white. Could it be removed? she wondered, anxiously.

But suddenly she decided that she would no longer mind so much about things like that. The most important thing was to get lunch over so that she could get to her novel. Was this progress: or was she growing old? She did not know. She sat down.

Wykham raised his glass. 'To all the Filmers,' he said, smiling.

Mrs Grinling tried, with a self-effacing smile, to feel included.

After lunch, Madeleine and Beryl washed up swiftly, for at half-past two Beryl had to go. They then prepared the children's tea, spreading it out on the great kitchen table. With every five minutes that passed, Madeleine's heart lifted: soon she would be working at her book.

At twenty-past two there were still a few small jobs to be done in the kitchen.

'I'll do them,' said Beryl. 'You go and get started, Mrs Filmer.'

Madeleine hesitated, but the determined understanding in the girl's clear eyes destroyed argument. She went to the dining-room, and collected her folder from the window-seat. An idea for the book's next sequence was already bubbling, like a fountain under pressure: clear images were waiting to be fixed on paper. But she must hurry. She was almost perspiring.

On her way through the hall, she met Wykham, standing, undecided, at the front door.

'Thought I might do a bit in the garden,' he said, vaguely. He hoped that she would make up his mind for him. He was still wondering whether or not to go over to Colonel Clavering. If he gardened, he would have to change his clothes.

'It's very hot,' she said, 'if you do, perhaps you ought to wear a hat.'

He half-barred her way, about to put his arm round her, but she would not stop. At this moment, she could give no more time to anyone.

She walked round the great, pale house – to the conservatory, which looked out onto a deserted part of the garden.

The door was jammed. She pushed it hard, and it ground open, scraping over the tiled floor. Inside, it was hot and airless. For thirty years nothing had been cultivated there and the heating grills were rusted through. Entering, she felt as if she had stepped into another, earlier time.

She pulled the bamboo table up to the open door, so that, while working, she could feel the summer air on her bare arms. She sat down swiftly, and opened out her folder.

* * *

Wykham decided, in the end, to clear the Flemish garden. He turned up his trousers at the ankles. They'd be all right like that, surely! He then went out to the garage, to fetch a fork. If only he'd tackled the job a fortnight ago, when the ground was softer. Today, he'd probably break the fork.

The garage was crammed. Under a dust-sheet was a car, wheel-less, blocked-up. He had bought it with the idea of one day making it go. On all sides were garden tools and children's toys. He had to climb over a pile of tomato boxes, to get at the fork.

He then saw Beryl's bicycle against the wall. Like herself, it was gleaming, bright, new, and he felt a sudden surge of admiration, envy, for her, which came to him now frequently, when he saw her. Whatever she did, she did so well. Success for her seemed certain. He sought for the fork in a group of rusted garden tools.

Just after half-past two, Beryl came out. She had folded up her white overall to put in the bicycle basket. She did not see Wykham deep in the garage, watching her. He kept very still.

How fresh and clean she is, he thought. More like a smart dentist's assistant, than a house-help.

He half-lent against the covered car, to watch her better. Without meaning to, he moved a bucket.

She started.

'I didn't know you were there, sir.'

Without speaking, still watching her, he came forward, climbing slowly over the tomato boxes. Again he was thinking: How fresh she is.

She stood, seeing his approach, as if transfixed.

He was now very near her. Suddenly, thoughtlessly, he leaned forward and gently took hold of her wrist. She was surprised, looking at him in the eyes. Slowly and deliberately, he bent and kissed her on the mouth.

She stepped back, her blue eyes steady and reproving.

'No, Mr Filmer,' she said. 'Not that. I'm not here for that. I'm here to help Mrs Filmer.'

He looked down, foolishly.

'You ought not to do that, you know,' she went on, as if speaking to a child.

He now spoke quickly: 'I'm extremely sorry. I can't think what came over me.'

'That's all right then,' she answered, stern, still reproving.

Under his thick, rather pale skin he looked hot, awkward. He helped her wheel her bicycle out of the garage. He watched her get up on it.

'Goodbye, sir.'

'Goodbye, Beryl,' he said.

She rode out into the lane.

He turned back nervously, to get the fork.

He was suddenly deeply worried. Supposing that Beryl, after this, gave notice? What, then, would happen to them? Madeleine depended on Beryl – or else she could not write – and the rest of them, including himself, depended on Madeleine, and Madeleine's writing. He must do nothing, must never do anything that might make Beryl not want to come to the house. He ought to have thought of this before.

And when, he wondered, would he be able to earn enough to support this family of his and Madeleine's? Fear cut through him. He felt small, young, doomed. During the war he had felt like this sometimes.

He searched among the tools. He had better hurry up and clear the charlock from the Flemish garden.

* * *

On the far side of the house, everything was deeply still; the conservatory was enfolded by silence. In that detached, blazing hour after lunch even the birds were withdrawn, not moving, or visible, and the tractor which, all morning, had droned on the hill was now quiet.

Madeleine looked at her manuscript. This next section was going to be the most difficult and involved, and the most significant. How would her two central characters – the man and the woman – come together again? If she could get this next part to go right, the rest would follow. Surely she could do it; surely she had the power? The answer was very near the surface of her mind. She must let her mind go free, so that she could pick it up.

She looked up, letting her gaze wander out on the garden. Her thoughts then left the book and she unexpectedly thought of Wykham and Beryl. She believed that Wykham liked Beryl. He often grew quiet when he joined them in the kitchen, and stood, staring at her, his blue eyes dense and dark. She knew his tendency to admire twenty-year-olds, she thought wryly. Was this likely to grow less, or to develop? she wondered. But out here, she was without anxiety about the idea. She could review it calmly. Yet what would happen if Wykham were to make a pass at Beryl? What would Beryl do? She felt then, almost instantly, as she looked down at the white sheet of paper in front of her, that she had such trust in Beryl, and the girl's commonsense – that Beryl, apart from her loyalty to her, Madeleine, had some plan in life which would not be deflected by the passing advances of the husband of her employer – that she could not feel anxious about this. It was more likely that Beryl would leave, if Wykham got fresh. She was only out here because she liked it, and liked working for Madeleine. But if Beryl were no longer here to help her, the fat would be in the fire. Then her troubles would really start. For it was almost impossible to get help so far out. What would she do? For a moment, she felt helpless, lost, almost trembling. She wondered how she would be able to go on with her book.

And for all she knew, Wykham might at this very moment be making those passes at Beryl. They were alone on that side of the house. She had left him, half-amorous, at the door. What a risk she had taken!

But she looked again at her work, at the open folder and the white page, and her old strength came back. She always had this – to earn money, to keep the family going. Somehow they would survive by it, whatever happened. Even if Wykham did not get to the Bar for years. Even if Beryl went away. She could cope – if she had this.

She heard then a bee humming against the glass in the depths of the conservatory, and got up to lift it in her handkerchief, and let it go free through the door. It flew off, vivid with relief. She returned to her bamboo chair, and sat down – its creaking was the only sound in the silence. She knew now how to go on; how to link up her characters. Yes, this was right. Such and such would follow; and so on. She took up her pen and began to write swiftly, without pausing.

A beam of sunlight, striking through a break in the clouded glass above her head, struck across the white page.

WHAT A LOVELY SURPRISE

Penelope Mortimer

(1957)

Paul Lawrence came back from work early. Jill lost count of the pile of shirts she was checking and impatiently started again, cramming each shirt into the laundry basket and muttering: 'One . . . two . . . three . . . four . . .' By the time she had captured them all and written them down in the book, he had shouted for the children and, after a great deal of rustling and whispering, they had shut themselves in the sitting-room.

With desperate speed, she began to count sheets. Louisa, their twelve year-old daughter, came two steps at a time up the stairs, stopped short on the landing and said furiously, 'Oh. There you are. Can't you move?'

'But I'm in the middle of doing the laundry.'

'Well, we've got to bring something upstairs. Can't you just go away for a minute?'

Jill dropped her armful of sheets; she had already forgotten how many there were. 'All right,' she said, trying to look pleased. 'I suppose so.'

She went and sat on her bed. She was tired, and there was nothing to do in the bedroom, so she just sat on the bed and waited. In a few moments she heard them coming up the stairs, the crackle of new, stiff brown paper, her husband swearing as he stumbled over the laundry basket.

'Where shall we put them?'

'Up in the attic, stupid.'

'Won't she go up to the attic?'

'Of course she won't.'

'Well how do you know she won't?'

'Oh, do be quiet . . .'

They creaked on up the stairs. She gave them another couple of minutes, then crept out of the bedroom and began counting the sheets again.

Paul came down from the attic hitting the dust off his suit and looking exhausted.

'Hallo,' he said. 'What on earth are you doing?'

'I should have thought it was obvious,' she said, writing down six sheets.

'Isn't it rather a peculiar time to be doing the laundry?'

'Well, it goes tomorrow.'

'Oh. I see.'

He realised, of course, that she couldn't do the laundry tomorrow. He sat down heavily on the stairs, watching her.

'There's an awful lot of it,' he said gloomily. 'Couldn't we cut down on it a bit?'

She realised that he had spent too much money today and was regretting it. She scooped up three pairs of his pyjamas and pushed them into the corners of the basket.

'If you'd wear drip-dry shirts,' she said, 'like everyone else.'

'But I loathe all that nylon and terylene and stuff.'

'Well, then. Eight shirts at one and sevenpence each. Pyjamas are one and ten. No one else sends any clothes to the laundry. Why don't you buy a washing machine?' At last she had the whole lot battened down. She straightened herself, pushing the hair out of her eyes. 'You could have bought me one for my birthday, come to think of it.'

He was alarmed. 'Really? Would you have liked a washing machine? I didn't think of it.'

'No,' she said. 'I wouldn't.'

'I could have got one on hire purchase,' he insisted. 'But I didn't think of it.'

'But I don't want one!' she said, smiling desperately.

'Then why did you say – ?'

The children came out of the attic and peered down over the banisters. 'Are you going to stay there all night?' Louisa asked. 'We want to bring something down.'

'All right,' Jill said, dragging the laundry basket across the landing and bumping it down the stairs. 'I'm just going.'

She had prepared, as far as possible, for tomorrow. Her birthday cake, with one deceitful candle, was ready in the larder; she had washed the kitchen floor and bought groceries for two days and checked that the tin opener and the cork-screw were both in the drawer. She took a pile of mending and sat down on the window seat in the sitting-room. The sun was misty, the small, narrow gardens littered with disorderly September flowers, leaning stacks of Michaelmas daisies, chrysanthemums like spilled copper, Aaron's rod and seedy willowherb, slovenly splashes of dahlia against the grey brick walls. Somewhere somebody was already burning leaves. The clock in the hall chimed and struck the hour.

As she counted the strokes, one hand gloved in her husband's sock, she was momentarily caught by a sharp, composite memory of all her birthdays. She could actually feel anticipation, even pleasure, flash through her, as though tomorrow really contained a mystery; as though she might unwrap something – a doll, the shrouded bulk of a new bicycle – which would really be a surprise, an astonishing happiness. It had left her before the clock had finished striking. If only, she thought, stabbing the hard heel of the sock with the needle, it was all over.

'We want the scissors,' Jane announced, bursting through the door. Her round, seven year-old face was stern. 'We are very busy.'

'Bring them back,' Jill said. 'And be careful.'

The door slammed, the child pounded upstairs. Two minutes later she was back again.

'Where's the string?'

'I don't think,' Jill said brightly, 'we've got any string.'

Dismay threatened. 'What shall we do, then?'

Jill pulled her hand out of the sock, lifted the pile of mending off her knee and began to look for the string. She groped in the back of shelves, hunted through the drawer of the desk which contained bits of sealing wax,dried-up bottles of marking ink, three or four unidentified keys, two pipes, various bits of broken china, an old toothbrush and some lighter flints, but no string. Jane sat down patiently and looked at a magazine. Jill looked systematically through the broom cupboard and kitchen drawers and produced at last a roll of green garden twine and six yards of new pink ribbon intended for reviving someone's party dress. 'You'll have to manage with this,' she said.

Jane looked at it critically. 'All right,' she said. 'I suppose it'll do.'

She went off, and Jill sat down again, lifting back the mending. She decided not to bother with the sock, but to do something restful, like changing all the buttons on Louisa's overcoat. They hadn't brought back the scissors, so she gnawed and pulled at the buttons for a while and then gave up, folding the overcoat neatly over the back of the chair and waiting.

Becky, the middle one, was the next to come down. She put her sharp little face, weighted with horn-rimmed glasses and topped with a scrub of chopped red hair, round the door and asked, 'Daddy says, where's the glue?'

'There might be some in the cupboard.'

Becky was ten and had just finished a two-year-long impersonation of Roy Rogers. The change had been sudden and extreme. The checked shirt, the patched jeans, the stringy neck scarf were still in a heap on her bedroom floor. She now wore one of Louisa's petticoats trailing its grubby frill two inches below a velvet skirt she had salvaged from the dressing-up box. She also wore ballet pumps and a large broderie anglaise blouse which Jill remembered putting away to give, in another three or four years' time, to Louisa. Round her neck, instead of the scarf, she wore a broken necklace of plastic beads, cunningly mended with fuse wire. She looked as though she had just been converted by a visiting missionary.

'Becky –' Jill began.

'Yes?' The huge spectacles, which the child had mistakenly been allowed to choose for herself, flashed innocently.

'Oh,nothing. It should be in the bottom shelf.'

'I've got it. By the way, how old will you be tomorrow?'

'A hundred and ninety-five.'

'No. Really.'

'Thirty-nine.' But she couldn't help adding, 'I think.'

'Gosh. Daddy didn't know.' She wandered to the door. 'I asked him,' she explained. 'He said, oh, about thirty-five or something.'

Jill smiled. Her face was already beginning to ache a little.

'We need to know, you see, for the play.'

'Do you mean to say there's going to be a play?' There was always a play. It took up, mercifully in some ways, most of the afternoon. 'Really?' she asked incredulously.

'Perhaps I shouldn't have told you. Oh dear.'

'It's all right. I'll just pretend I don't know.'

In a little while her husband came down.

'Well,' he asked in a distraught way, 'and how's the birthday girl?'

She looked at him imploringly. She had the absurd idea that she could ask him to abandon the whole thing.

'The children are working so hard,' he said.

'How sweet of them.' She smiled quickly.

'Looking forward to your day off?'

'Oh yes. Of course I am.'

‘That’s good.’

He settled himself in an armchair and closed his eyes. The expression on his face was that of a man doggedly resting before a battle that might well be his last.

Next morning she woke, opened her eyes, took in the grey square of window and the sound of rain, snapped her eyes shut again. Thirty-nine, she thought. It didn’t mean anything. She was relieved and, turning cautiously over, settled to sleep again.

In five minutes the alarm began to ring. Her husband had, of course, taken the day off. However, being her birthday, the alarm rang half an hour earlier than usual. He groaned and humped about the bed a little, then got up. She heard him putting on his dressing gown and shuffling out of the room.

‘Honestly,’ she heard before the door closed, ‘we’ve been up for *hours* . . .’

She got quickly out of bed and brushed her hair, peering at herself in the damp mirror with the superstitious feeling that overnight her hair should have gone grey, the wrinkles multiplied. However, she looked much the same, except for the anxious smile that already seemed to be driven into her face. She shut the window and switched on the fire, then got back into bed and folded her hands calmly over her stomach. The great thing, she told herself, is to relax. Just relax, and it may all be quite painless.

The door opened and the three clear, sturdy voices struck up:

‘Happy Birthday to you,

'Happy Birthday to you,

'Happy Birthday' – Paul joined in rather haphazardly – 'dear Mother,

'Happy Birthday to you!'

'Oh,' she said. 'What a lovely surprise.'

They filed in, business-like, serious, dumped their packages on the bed, kissed her and stood back. Paul followed with the teatray and kissed her and wished her a happy birthday.

'Well,' she said. 'I don't know where to start.'

They glanced at each other and giggled shortly. She began untying the pink ribbon.

'Oh,' she said, 'what a beautiful card! Did you make it, Becky?'

Becky nodded. 'I made up the poem too.'

'Let's read it, then.

Thirty-nine is not such a very great age to be
Think how you'd feel if today you were ninety-three.

There was a moment's silence.

'Well,' Jill said, 'I think it's perfectly lovely. And a blotter, too! Just what I wanted. *Thank* you, darling.' She kissed Becky, who blushed almost purple.

'Open mine now,' Jane said.

'But it's a needle case! And you made it all by yourself! *Thank you*, darling.'

While Jill was kissing Jane, Louisa, who thought her youngest sister a frightful show-off, looked distantly out of the window. 'Now,' Jill said, 'whatever can this be?' She unwrapped, with caution, two quilted coat-hangers. 'Oh!' she breathed. 'And another poem!'

'It's not much good,' Louisa muttered.

'I'm sure it's brilliant.

You're Thirty-nine today,
So Happy Birthday, Mum.
You may feel rather old,
But to us you're still
Twenty-one!

Paul choked over his tea. The tray nearly upset and, helped by this distraction, Jill kissed Louisa warmly. The worst was over.

The remaining presents were from Paul. The sweater, a size bigger than last year's, would be quite possible if she took the collar off and had it dyed. She said it was lovely, and the perfume was lovely and the Braque print – she nervously turned it the right way up – was really lovely.

'I think it's perfectly ghastly,' Louisa said.

'Oh well,' Jill was amazed to hear herself saying, 'we can't all have the same tastes, can we? And it's awfully cheerful.' She kissed her husband gratefully. 'I don't know how to thank you,' she said. 'Such wonderful presents.'

Something was wrong, her tone of voice or what she said: there ought to be more. They waited, and she kept smiling, and at last Paul said, 'Well, you'd all better go off and get dressed or something. I'll go down and get breakfast.'

'I really don't want any,' Jill said. 'Please don't –'

'But you always have breakfast in bed on your birthday!' Louisa blazed. 'You always do!'

'Oh well, then. All right. Thank you,' she said humbly.

Left alone, she wound up all the pink ribbon which, if ironed, might still do for the party dress. She folded the wrapping paper and arranged the cards on the mantelpiece and got back into bed. A faint smell of burning crept up from the kitchen. How wonderful it is, she told herself sharply, to be loved.

The rule of her birthday was that she was not allowed to do anything. This had started when Louisa was about four. It had impressed Louisa, if no one else, as a wonderful idea and she had never allowed it to be forgotten. She was a highly organised child, very good at giving orders. Combined with remarkable beauty this made her, at twelve, rather formidable.

Unhappily dressed in the new sweater, Jill sidled downstairs at about ten o'clock. Louisa was vacuuming the sitting room.

'Why didn't you stay in bed?' she asked. 'And rest?'

'Oh well . . .' Jill said.

'It's a pity, because if it was a nice day you could sit in the garden.'

'Yes,' Jill said.

'Well, do you mind moving, because I want to hoover over there?'

Jill went back to the bedroom and did her nails. When they were dry she thought of tidying her drawers and this reminded her that she had, for weeks, been meaning to move the chest of drawers over to the other side of the room where it would not only look better but hide a small patch of damp on the wall. She resolutely put this idea out of her head and went downstairs again. Louisa was dusting, Becky finishing the washing up. They both seemed disappointed to see her, so she went and stood in the dining room for a little while, looking with interest at the rain, until Jane burst in and said, 'Oh. *You're* here. We're going to lay the table now.'

'But it's not nearly lunch time!'

'Well, that's what Louisa told me to do. Couldn't you,' she suggested sympathetically, 'go for a walk or something?'

Jill went upstairs again and looked at the chest of drawers. She closed the door and cautiously pulled out the drawers, balancing them on the bed. Then she pulled the heavy chest carefully, inch by inch, across the room. One of its feet got caught in the carpet, so she lay down on her stomach, lifting up the chest with one hand while niftily tucking the carpet down under its foot with the other. She was lying half under the bed and had just got the carpet straightened out when Louisa came in.

'I brought you some coffee,' Louisa said, and then, 'oh! What are you *doing*?'

Jill got up and took the cup without looking at her. 'Thank you,' she said. 'I was just moving the chest of drawers.'

'But why?' Louisa wailed. 'On your birthday?'

'Oh, don't be so silly,' Jill snapped. 'Why shouldn't I move the chest of drawers on my birthday if I want to?'

'But you're meant to be resting.'

‘But I don’t want to rest!’

They glared at each other and slowly, painfully, Louisa’s eyes filled with tears. Jill held out her hands, but the child turned her head away and ran down the stairs. Nobody, Jill remembered hopelessly, cried on her birthday. She knelt down and heaved savagely at the chest, upsetting the cup of coffee which poured, a scalding christening, over her new sweater.

‘Louisa’s thoroughly upset,’ Paul said from the doorway. ‘I do think you might – what on *earth* are you doing?’

‘I’m trying,’ she said, getting up slowly, ‘to move the chest of drawers. It isn’t a crime. It isn’t hurting anybody. It isn’t spoiling anyone’s fun.’

‘Look at that sweater.’

‘I know.’

‘It’s ruined. When I think what it cost –’

‘Don’t tell me,’ she said. ‘I can always have it dyed.’

‘Why can’t you rise to the occasion a bit? You’ve thoroughly upset Louisa.’

‘Is it Louisa’s birthday,’ she snapped suddenly, ‘or mine?’

‘Everyone’s trying their damnedest to please you.’

‘Oh, really. If that’s your attitude.’

‘Good God, if you can’t appreciate it, I’m sorry.’

‘Oh. . .’ She hung her head, watching the pale grey coffee dripping on to the carpet. ‘Of course I appreciate it, Paul.’

‘Well, then. Now where do you want this chest of drawers?’

‘Over there,’ she said humbly.

He picked it up, carried it across the room and dumped it against the wall.

'Now,' he said, 'why don't you go downstairs and look at a magazine or something?'

'All right.' It struck her that they were behaving in the most curious way. He looked shifty and sick and it suddenly occurred to her that he really hated her birthday, hated her growing older. That, in fact, he was ashamed. She was certain of it. He was ashamed because he could no longer avoid knowing that she was middle aged.

'Paul –' she began.

'Well?' He had his back to her, pushing in the drawers.

She couldn't think what to say. 'Do you love me?'

'Of course. You might just have a word with Louisa. She tries hard on your birthday.'

'I know,' she said. 'You all do.'

'Well, then. I'll go and get the lunch. You just relax. You know – relax a bit.'

'Yes,' she said. 'All right.'

He went heavily downstairs. She sat down on the bed and began pulling the fluff off the blanket, rolling it between her finger and thumb.

The play, this year, concerned two princes captured by a wicked wizard and saved in the nick of time by a benevolent fairy aged thirty-nine. Last year it had been two princesses captured by a wicked witch and saved in the nick of time by a benevolent fairy aged thirty-eight. Jane and Becky played the princes and Louisa doubled for the other parts. It was full of 'Oho!' and 'By my troth!' and 'Whither away?' After each scene Jane applauded loudly and was scolded by Louisa. In the interval, while Louisa was bringing up the birthday cake and ice cream, Jane and Becky danced to a long- playing record of Sidney Bechet. As time wore on their faces became grimmer and their breathing louder, but they continued to lollop bravely about and never moved their eyes from the audience, which kept smiles of appreciation clamped firmly on both their faces. At last the record ended, Jill cut the cake and remembered to wish.

'What did you wish?' Jane asked.

'Don't be silly. She can't tell. Come on, we've got to do the second scene now.'

They hurried busily away.

'It's a lovely play,' Jill said timidly. 'Are you all right?'

Her husband nodded. He was absolutely exhausted and had put down four dry martinis before lunch in order to nerve himself for the washing up. Jill had changed into a dress and made up her face with great care. In spite of this, she had begun to feel slightly hysterical. It was not surely necessary for the fairy to grow so old?

'Gadzooks!' Louisa cried, looking evil, 'those princes will make me a jolly fine supper . . .'

At the end of the play the entire cast sang God Save The Queen and Happy Birthday To You. Then the curtains were drawn back and Jane inexplicably burst into tears. Becky, too, hung about looking moistly through her enormous glasses.

'They're tired,' Jill muttered, patting them hopelessly, 'I'll put them to bed.'

'You can't,' Louisa said, looking disgusted under her

benevolent fairy's crown. 'It's your birthday. You're going out. I'll put them, if they're such babies.'

'But I'm sure there's time –'

'You wouldn't want Mummy to bath you, would you? On her birthday?'

Dumb, guilty, swamped in tears, Jane shook her head.

'Then come on.' A tinsel and muslin wardress, she pushed them out of the room. 'And if you're good,' Jill heard her saying, 'you can watch television for half an hour but, mind you, not a minute longer.' Their voices, like the voices of tired, nattering old women, retreated up the stairs.

Jill tidied the sitting room and poured herself a drink. The day weighed heavily on her, like some expensive mistake, a lapse of good taste which, once paid for, is irrevocable. The bonfire had been extinguished by the day's rain. Some of the leaves on the laburnum had turned yellow overnight, but this was the only sign of autumn. The air had become clear and watery as spring and birds were twittering and fussing in the tall, grimy trees. The year, yesterday so mellow, had become petrified in a grey, damp evening.

'Well, shall we go?'

She turned reluctantly. Paul had changed his suit, but not his expression. He went straight over to the decanter and poured himself a triple whisky.

'Yes,' she said. 'When you're ready.'

'I'm ready now.'

'All right, then. Let's go.'

'Well, what do you mean, when I'm ready?'

'Nothing. Where are we going?'

'Where do we always go on your birthday? Pierre's, of course.'

'How silly of me,' she said. 'I should have known.'

They came home, rather unsteadily and in silence, about eleven. The children were all asleep. The house felt surprisingly normal, freed from tension. There was even a banana skin in the sitting room grate which Louisa hadn't tidied away. They climbed slowly upstairs, not speaking, yawned and sighed in the cold bedroom. It's over, they both thought, pulling off their shoes. Weariness, apathy, drowned them. They moved about the room as languidly and pointlessly as fish in a small tank. When, at last, she had turned down the coverlet, put his pyjamas ready on the pillow, opened the window, turned off the main light, he was still standing in his shirt looking vaguely about the room. She had already forgotten about her birthday. Her face, after an enormous yawn, settled back, lax and unsmiling.

'Do hurry,' she said. 'I'm dropping.'

He picked up his pyjamas, looked at them with distaste and let them fall in a heap on the floor. Then he wandered to the cupboard, took out a clean pair of pyjamas and began, with laborious concentration, to undo the buttons.

In one movement she sat upright. Her whole body was stiff and trembling. 'You can't,' she said, 'wear clean pyjamas.'

He lowered towards her, his head stuck forward. 'Why not?'

'You had clean pyjamas last night.'

'And is there any reason,' he inquired, skidding a little over the words, 'why I shouldn't have clean pyjamas tonight as well?'

'Of course there is!' She was desolate, outraged. 'We can't afford the laundry! You said so yourself! We can't afford the laundry!'

At last he let fly. 'Then why don't you wash them yourself instead of fooling around all day moving the furniture?'

'Why should I wash your horrible pyjamas? Why should I?'

'Don't shout,' he said. 'I cannot stand you shouting.'

'Why shouldn't I shout?'

'Because,' he said, 'you are too old.'

They stared at each other. All sound, even the sound of breathing, had stopped. He went out of the room, carrying the clean pyjamas. He went downstairs. She heard the sitting room door close.

He had drunk too much, of course. It had been a strain. She had only been trying to save him the expense of the laundry. He was overtired. He would soon come back and apologise. She turned off the bedside light and lay on her back, staring at the patterns of the street lamp on the ceiling. The clock chimed and began to strike midnight. Next year, she realised, I shall be forty. She lay waiting, the little smile of gratitude fixed on her face, a distant welcome.

THE REAL THING

Diana Athill

(1958)

I went to the dance with Thomas Toofat. It's Toogood really, but he *is* too fat, with frizzy hair and flat feet. We never meant to let him know we call him that, but the week before, at the Turners' picnic, Sally said without thinking, 'And this is Thomas Toofat. . . .' Oh, it was utterly withering.

On the night of the dance, no sooner had he come than he said might he go upstairs to wash his hands – he would. My father is always talking about putting in a lavatory downstairs and I shall die if he doesn't – we're the *only* people without one – but I'm sure he never will. Sally and Richard had arrived first and we were standing about in the drawing-room, and I began to wish it wasn't happening, it was such a let-down after the bliss of getting dressed. But when old Toofat came back into the room it got better again because he looked better than usual in his dinner jacket (his own, not his father's). And at least he is old enough to drive a car.

Although Sally and Richard are brother and sister they like dancing together. They are so good, now, from practising, that they despise dancing with other people and that's why Toofat was mostly mine that evening. I had never been to a dance with a man in a dinner jacket. Nine till two, it was, and my latest until then had been eight till twelve.

'Come on children,' said my mother. 'We must start dinner if you don't want to be late.'

She had put candles on the dining-room table, and the little silver dishes for chocolates afterwards, but when I had asked if we could have sherry first she had just laughed. It was utterly mortifying. Toofat's only been at Cambridge for two terms, but he must have thought it positively nursery to be offered no drink at all.

'You look very smashing,' said my father. 'Sally and Lucinda will be the belles of the ball.' He doesn't usually speak in a hearty voice but he seemed to think he ought to then. There's nothing more withering than dinner with grown-ups before a dance, I couldn't *look* at them and I couldn't look at Toofat or Richard either. Sally was wonderful, she talked to my parents about a million things, and Richard talked to my father about sailing and Toofat held forth about being at Cambridge – he's very pompous since he's been there even though he is only a medical student and Sally and I have decided that they don't count as proper undergraduates.

It was easy for the others to behave normally, it wasn't their parents – I'm quite good with Sally's, come to that. But if I talk naturally to my friends in front of my mother and father it doesn't sound natural to my mother and father. 'No one likes an affected girl,' my mother said the other day ('affected' is her *worst* word) – and I hadn't been, I'd only forgotten for a minute that she was there and told someone I'd rather die than read Proust in translation (and I would, too. I know I got stuck in the first volume, but after I have been to France I shall be able to do it).

Anyway, dinner was hateful but I had known it would be. I just sat and felt my skirt round my legs and my hair on my bare shoulders, and waited for the dance. The truth is I wouldn't mind going to a dance with a *baboon*. Once the lights and music and dancing begin it's so fabulous that you don't need anything extra, though now I rather think I shall when I fall in love.

They made us go in our car because Toofat's looks fast though it isn't really, it would fall to pieces if it went over sixty. And there was a lot of fuss about 'Drive carefully' and 'Don't be too late', but we got away at last and Sally and Richard and I started singing in close harmony like we do. If I hadn't known them so well and if the other man hadn't been Toofat it would have been like doing something that other people do, and perhaps as we drove through villages the people who saw us thought we *were* other people: just a flash of black and white they'd have seen of the boys, and Sally and me with our chiffon stoles over our heads and the roses my father had cut for us pinned to our shoulder straps (because we'd taken off our coats once we were out of sight). By the time we got there I was beginning to feel it myself.

A long time ago, when I was twelve, I heard my mother and Aunt Molly saying how glad they were that they had got out of going to some dance. At that time I only thought it was a bit odd but now I think it was the most tragic thing I ever heard, because if you're so old that you don't even *want* to dance I can't see that you can want to do anything; and if you don't want to do anything you might as well be dead. I told Sally about it while we were putting on lipstick (her mother won't let her use it so I agreed not to use mine either until we got there, so that she wouldn't feel silly at dinner. Mine lets me, for parties). We agreed that we would pray to God to let us die before we got as old as that.

Toofat just shuffles from side to side and turns at the corners, but in spite of his flat feet he has a good sense of rhythm – it's not exciting to dance with him but it's not withering – and when we had been twice round the floor he said in his patronising voice, 'You dance very well.' Luckily he's taller than I am. It was easy to look down and hide the fact that I blushed, which of course I did at once. I wasn't blushing because I'd had a compliment. I was doing it because as soon as I have a compliment I think quickly, 'I mustn't blush,' and that makes me. I have always thought that I shall die if I don't grow out of it soon, but later that evening something happened which changed things.

There were plenty of people there who Sally and Richard knew, and Toofat as well, of course, because he gets asked to lots of parties, being a spare man. I knew them too, in a way, but they hadn't got round to thinking of me as someone to meet at a grown-up dance. When we began to mix in with them I could feel sometimes that boys asked me to dance because they felt they had to. They did ask me, though, and I didn't mind much who they were or what they were thinking so long as they danced well, which some of them did. I was in a sort of dream, almost, because it was so beautiful. I danced several times with Toofat, and twice with Richard, and about five times with other people, and then I somehow got attached to the party which the Morgans had brought and somebody introduced me to this extraordinary man.

I didn't hear his name. He was quite old and he came from London. It wasn't so much that he was good-looking, but he had light grey eyes with very black lashes and his nose was thin and crooked so that he looked witty – I thought the minute I saw him that he was probably the most intelligent person there besides me, but because he was so much older I couldn't see how to show him that I was intelligent too. When we began dancing he said: 'Do you like to talk when you dance, or do you prefer to keep it for afterwards?' which was a great relief. Of course I said afterwards. We had a fabulous dance – one of those when my feet can do all kinds of things I didn't know they knew: a floating dance. Afterwards he got me an ice and we sat on a sofa and he said: 'Now. Do you prefer to be flattered, or amused, or disconcerted?'

I *was* disconcerted, of course, but I didn't show it. What I said – and I still think it was very good – was: 'What I really like best is to be enraptured.'

'That's a tall order,' he said. 'You must give me a clue to what sort of thing enraptures you – traveller's tales? Poetry? This season's collections? Visions of eternity?'

'Well,' I said, 'not visions of eternity, because as a matter of fact I'm an atheist' – and I had never told anyone that before, not even Sally, but the way he danced and the way he looked had made me feel very odd.

‘A real, thorough-paced atheist?’ he asked. ‘Not just an agnostic?’

‘I *think* I’m a real atheist,’ I said.

‘That’s pretty dashing,’ he said, and then I saw that he was laughing at me but to my great surprise I didn’t mind at all.

‘And I’m a Socialist too,’ I told him. ‘It’s not at all easy to be an atheist and a Socialist where I live, everyone else is fabulously conventional.’

‘What are you going to do about it?’ he asked. ‘Have a one-girl revolution?’

So I told him about going to Oxford when I get back from France, and it turned out that he had been there too, ages ago, about five years I think. He said that the smart thing now was to be a Young Conservative and a Catholic, but he was teasing, and then he told me things I would do at Oxford, quite different from the things Miss Montague told me when she was coaching me for the entrance exam, and much more the kind of things I would like. He said I would go to tea with a different man every day of the week and be a nervous wreck at the end of each term, trying to decide which of them to be seduced by.

Now when he said that about being seduced I was not at all shocked – of course I *shall* be seduced (only that’s a silly word) as soon as I want to be – but the word sort of startled me, in connection with myself, and what did I do but start to blush, a really bad one right to the top of my head. I thought it was going to be the most withering moment in my whole life. But instead of pretending not to notice, which is what most people do, this man said in an ordinary voice: ‘Do you find that you blush very easily at nothing? I used to do it too and it was utter misery.'

It was an enormous relief to hear him say that, in such a natural way, and I felt better at once. I told him all about what a terrible mortification my blushing is to me.

'It will stop quite suddenly,' he said. 'Mine did.'

'How old were you when it stopped?' I asked, being naturally very interested.

'I suppose I was about nineteen and a half,' he said.

'Help!' I said. 'That means I've still got nearly three more years of it.' (Which was the silliest thing to say, because I look quite nineteen in that frock and I didn't want him to know I wasn't.)

'But I don't see why you worry,' he said.

'You've just said yourself how much you hated it.'

'Yes, but I was a gawky boy and you're a very pretty girl. If a girl is very pretty she can carry off anything, even blushing. Hasn't anyone ever told you that you look enchanting when your face is pink?'

For about one second I didn't take it in, I truly didn't, but then it dawned on me that I'd just had the most fabulous compliment of my whole life. Of course my parents sometimes say, 'You look pretty in that colour,' and people have told me I dance well, and a boy said to me last year that he liked my hair, and I can see for myself that I haven't got a face like an old boot, but this was different. When I was much younger I used to imagine myself becoming a new person when I grew up – a raving beauty with chestnut-coloured hair – but I realised long ago that people don't change all that much, and since then I've just supposed that I was all right. I never thought that I was *very pretty*. I was so astounded to hear him say it that I didn't blush again, in fact I think I may even have gone pale.

'Did you actually *mean* that?' I asked, and he told me he did. Then he said: 'Bother. There's my next partner adrift by the door – I must go and do my stuff. We must dance again later,' and he looked at me and crinkled his eyes and went off to dance with someone beautiful in a black dress. As a matter of fact I think they were in love with each other because I saw them later dancing with their cheeks touching and their eyes shut, and he didn't ask me again, but after that wonderful conversation I could hardly expect any more.

I ran upstairs to look at myself, and it *did* seem to me that I was very pretty even though my face was quite pink again by then. When I came down I was feeling dreamier than ever and Toofat happened to be at the bottom of the stairs and just put his arm round me and whirled me into the room for a waltz, which he did pretty well. He talked all the time about how, although he despises games, he has decided to take up a sport because he believes that everyone should exercise his will power by doing some things he hates. He wanted to know whether I thought cricket or rugger would be best. I told him cricket because I guess that's easier – he would be very bad at either, you should see his tennis. But wanting to exercise your will power is something I admire, so I decided to stop calling him Toofat, even to myself – and even more so when he went on to say that his favourite occupation is writing poetry. Last term he actually had a poem published in a Cambridge magazine. Really published, in print. I never dreamt I would get to know a poet so soon.

I asked him to tell me his poem but he said it was too complex, it had to be read slowly and that he would explain it to me and give me a signed copy of the magazine. He always talks to me in this patronising way but it seemed almost justified after his revelation. Then I told him a little about my poems and he offered to read them and say if they were any good. A few minutes earlier I would have thought, 'Pompous ass, what a nerve!' but now I felt quite grateful. We began to have a very interesting conversation about poetry. If he didn't talk in such a pompous way which sounds silly coming from someone so fat and pink, he would be a most interesting man, I believe. Also if he didn't sniff so often.

But I must never again be horrible about Toofat – Thomas, I mean – because the next fabulous thing which happened to me that evening happened because of him.

It had got very hot and they had opened the French windows. 'Let's go into the garden for a breath of air,' he said. In the middle of the lawn there was an enormous mulberry tree on which they had strung millions of fairy lights, and the grass where the windows shone on it was brilliant and the night was black with a terrific smell of honeysuckle. It was terribly romantic. We walked past the tree into the shadowy part of the lawn where you couldn't see anything but a few pale dresses floating here and there, and shirt fronts, and the white flowers in the border, just dimly. We were walking along slowly, still talking about poetry and sort of bumping into each other occasionally, when Thomas did an unexpected thing. He put his arm round me.

He didn't say anything special, went on booming about John Donne as though nothing were happening – but his arm was round me and his hand was on my waist. I wasn't sure whether he had done it absent-mindedly or on purpose, but there it was, his hand on my waist, and it gave me the most extraordinary feelings. First I felt as though I were a girl in a film with a man's arm around her, graceful, with my waist swaying towards him – *me*, doing that! And then I felt as though my bones had gone soft and as though his hand wasn't just touching my dress but was sending rays right down into me – the feeling went right through into my stomach. It was quite different from when someone puts his arm round you for dancing. I almost began to feel sick but it was vital not to show how surprised I was, so I went on saying yes and no to old Toofat in an ordinary voice, while all the time my body was absolutely full of this extraordinary feeling of that hand on my waist, and my mind was full of how this was really happening.

'I suppose we should go back,' he said, when we got to the fence at the end of the lawn, and he squeezed his arm tighter as he turned me round. And then it became even more marvellous. He said in a funny voice, 'You're a very sweet child,' and before I knew what was happening he bent down and kissed me.

His lips were cold and rather sticky from the hock cup he had been drinking. Some people might have been pretty disappointed by that kiss, but luckily for me I read the whole of Thomas Hardy when I was much too young to appreciate it and I have always remembered one thing out of one of his books – I forget which book. A man and a girl are walking together and he kisses her for the first time and it is disappointing, but Thomas Hardy says that *first kisses always are*. So although in a *way* I had always imagined my first real kiss from a man would be tremendously warm and soft and faint-making, I did actually know that it might not be, and after one second I remembered this. You have to *learn* about lovemaking like you do about dancing – look how I hadn't known about the hand feeling – but I expect some people learn more easily than others and I'm sure I'm going to be one of those.

I stood quite still while Toofat was kissing me – it didn't take long – and I was doing a lot of things all at once: thinking 'This is *me*, being kissed'; remembering Thomas Hardy; noticing the tree with the lights and the green grass outside the windows; listening to the music from the house; smelling the honeysuckle; thinking that I must fix every bit of it in my mind for ever. Then the kiss stopped and we went indoors, still talking as though nothing had happened. And the next time I'm kissed it will be by someone like the man with the crooked nose.

A BAD COLD

Elizabeth Spencer

(1967)

The grated window overlooked a not very busy street, full this noon with weakened sunlight. He stood looking out of it to avoid looking at his two children, who kept coming in and out of the living room. He could not stand to look at them because, as he often remarked to his wife, 'Each of those children is actually smoking forty cigarettes a day, the air pollution is so bad. Do you realise it? It's been medically ascertained that everybody in this city is doing that, just by breathing. You don't even have to light a match. You don't even have to think of tobacco. Since I learned that, every time I see them they seem to be chain-smoking.' This impression was especially bad by daylight; at night, smoking himself, with enough to drink inside his head, he forgot it. Anyway, at night you seldom got the full impact of air pollution, because you did not have to see the sunlight being diluted by it. Now he was at home with a cold, and he further imagined that the air pollution was making the cold worse.

He did not want anything but soup. If some was already open, he would take that. His son, Henry, stood by the refrigerator door, having just put out one of those invisible cigarettes, and asked what he was looking for.

'Some soup,' he said. 'Leftover will do.'

'It's in that,' said Henry, pointing to a small covered dish.

'Get away from me,' said his father. 'I've got this awful cold.'

'It's past time for catching it,' said Henry, and began to swing on the chrome door handle. 'Mother said so.'

'That doesn't make it true,' he said.

'Oh yes, it does,' said Henry.

Henry was a stout soul. When he asserted something of a sincere emotional nature, his father never argued.

'Yesterday a balloon flew by the window,' said Henry.

'What colour was it?' he asked.

'Brown.'

'I never heard of a brown balloon.'

Henry did not reply. He had been right about the location of the soup, which was leftover vegetable alphabet. His father dumped it in a small saucepan and flicked on the gas. He stirred it so it wouldn't stick. In a minute, he began to smell it, the first smell in two days.

The phone rang in the hall. He heard his wife come out of the far recesses of the apartment, from a small back room she had fitted out as an office, and hasten toward it. It was much nearer to him, and he would have reached it first, but the soup was beginning to boil. He had to watch it or turn it off. So she completed her dash, catching up the receiver just after the third ring.

She had been back there typing. Every few days, she got little packages of dictated tapes to type, brought to the door by messenger. This occupation was paid for by the typed word and earned her a substantial sum each month. No sound of this ever came to the children or to him. The tape was unpackaged and fitted into a smart grey-and-blue metal tape recorder made in West Germany. It talked directly into her ears through tiny wired earphones. Even her electric typewriter was almost soundless, and could never be heard through the door. This highly insulated and completely impersonal arrangement worked two ways. She could not be disturbed by the usual humdrum, unextraordinary sounds the children made, but could hear them shouting if they were in some crisis that needed her attention. She could also hear the doorbell or the telephone.

She needn't have run, he thought. Probably she forgot I'm here. He switched off the gas under the soup and heard her say, 'I'm awfully sorry . . . Yes, I know. . . . It's just that Pete's at home sick.'

'Who was that?' he shouted at once. 'Your lover?'

She did not answer, but hurried back down the hall, heels going clack-clack, and clacked shut the door. She's paying me no attention, he thought, and decided to torment her. He went in after her with the soup in a cup, eating it with a teaspoon. Having closed the door, he began to gnaw at her neck. He said he wanted to make love.

She shut off the tape recorder, switched off the typewriter, and took the little earphones out one at a time. They were different colours, for left and right ear. 'You what?' she asked.

He repeated it, and she replied, 'That's what I thought you said.' They looked rather tipsily at one another. 'At high noon, with the children every which way?'

'It would be better for them than all that mechanical world you keep on dealing with. And don't tell me I have a bad cold. Anyway, colds always make me feel sexy. They dull certain senses and sharpen others. I feel definitely like reclining luxuriously. And not alone!' He growled the words in a sidelong, wolfish fashion.

She broke out laughing.

'Besides,' he said, 'the children are both busy smoking. They have to get through their two packs a day.'

'They are not,' she said. 'They want their lunch, I bet. What have you got in that cup?'

'Vegetable alphabet soup. Who was that on the phone?'

'Mavis.'

'In town again? But she just left for that trip.'

'It didn't work out. Bermuda isn't very warm. She was disappointed and came back. Bad weather, to boot.'

'I think it was your lover. Otherwise, why did you make a break for the phone with me only three feet away from it?'

'I forgot you were here. It was reflex action. You're never at home.'

'But that's the first thing you said. You didn't forget at all. "Pete's home," you said. "Pete's home!" Why, pray, would Pete being home keep you from talking to Mavis about the weather in Bermuda?'

'I didn't have time to talk to her, that's all. If you hadn't been here, I would have said – well, something else. Like

“Mavis, I’d love to talk, but I have to call you back. I have a whole set of company promotion-announcement letters to type up, plus letters regretfully accepting the resignation of – oh, of people nobody knows.’

He glared at her. ‘I don’t believe it. Men get their regular secretaries to do work like that.’

‘I sometimes get work like this when they’re short-staffed. I work for an agency. I told you a hundred times.’

‘I don’t believe it this time. Let me hear. Put the little anodes in my ears.’

‘Oh, stop it. You’re just acting dreadful. I do have to finish things today.’

‘If you won’t let me hear what’s on those tapes and you won’t let me answer the telephone and you won’t let me make love to you, what can I do?’

‘You can finish your soup. It must be getting cold.’

‘I think it is your lover who writes passionate letters to you, has them tape-recorded, and sends them to you by messenger. He is wealthy. The messenger is his servant in disguise. You sit back here with the typewriter, all hooked up to that thing, pretending to type up routine letters, and all the time your soul is drinking from fresh fountains. Every few days he sends you more.’

‘When do I meet him?’

‘Not often. You can let several weeks go by: you like it this way. He objects. He calls on the phone at noon. It is his words you lust for. This whole set-up is completely phoney. You take money from him not because you want it but to make me think that you are really working. If I am not right, why won’t you let me answer the telephone, why won't you let me play the tape recorder?'

'You are trying your best to give me that cold,' she said. 'You have been from the first sneeze.'

'No one can catch a cold after the incubation period. Henry said so.'

'Henry can be wrong.'

'In this case he isn't. Where is Phyllis?'

'Sewing. On that funny miniature electric sewing machine you gave her for Christmas.'

'What does she make?'

'Different things for dolls. She's fascinated with it now, but I guess she'll soon get tired of it. Do you know, Pete, you can go to stores to get supplies for that little machine – all sorts of tiny parts, little patterns for doll dresses. It's all worked out, down to the last detail.'

He took the rest of his soup and sat on the day bed, first carefully moving aside the sheets of neatly typed letters. 'I wonder why I'm happy,' he said.

'You're happily married. You have two fine children, who are healthy and well cared for. You have a good job, which interests you. You have a quick mind, which invents amusing things, so you're never bored. You know, you're never really boring, Pete. I mean, even when you *are* boring, it still has something coming up in it, something interesting is cooking in what you say.'

'That isn't why I'm happy. The other day, when I was getting this cold, I was walking down in the West Forties somewhere, because I had to go over three blocks to another drugstore to get some 4-Way Cold Tablets, because the one I went to first was out of them. On the way, I passed a sort of run-down seafood restaurant, and there were some run-down lobsters in the window. At first I thought they were made of red wax, like artificial flowers, and then I thought, Holy cow, they're real but stone dead, and who would go in that place wanting ptomaine poison in addition to a bad cold? And then I saw one move. Just a little groping movement with one poor old claw. God, it was sad. Do you know why it was especially sad to me? Because I knew what the lobster was saying. Whether the lobster knew it or not, whether anybody would pass and think of it or not, I knew. It was saying, "Where is my world? Oh, where is my world, my own true world?" Over and over. On and on. How can I think about that poor damned lobster and still be happy?'

She came right out and told him. 'OK, I'll tell you. You're happy because of me.'

'And why are *you* happy? Don't think I don't know. It's because of what comes out of that machine.'

Exasperated, she snatched up a handful of equipment; red, black, and pink plastic wires dangled in an abstract pattern from her fingers. 'Do you actually want to hear what is really on those tapes? Do you? Just listen, then. Go right ahead!'

'Of course I won't. Do you take me for an eavesdropper, a keyhole watcher, a happiness killer? Do you think I'm destructive?'

Hunched over his cup and spoon, he devoured the last of the soup, smiling through a provoking haze of headache, sore throat, bleared eyesight, and severe nasal congestion.

WORLDS APART

Penelope Fitzgerald

(1983)

Hester told her daughter that she ought to try and make Mr Bergen feel more at home.'

'He's not at home,' said Tilly. 'He's in our house.'

At two years old, Tilly had been sympathetic to the whole world, a perpetual angel of mercy, keeping the whole house hushed in case her poor sick teddy bear should be disturbed. Now that she was six years old, where had this calm severity come from?

'He's only in one room,' Hester persisted. 'The things he has there are probably all he has in the world. I only meant you ought to make him think he's at home.'

'That would be deceitful,' said Tilly.

Hester knew what the other mothers (all of them neighbours and her good friends, but still the other mothers) thought, and probably said: that Tilly had become hardened since her father left them. Hester, however, knew that Tilly never mentioned Rod, that he hadn't left them but simply stayed away by agreement, that all was well and safely over, and about such things it was impossible to be mistaken. Probably it was a natural process. Probably time hardened women between the ages of two and six, just as it certainly did between twenty-five and thirty; that's to say, during those years you get much harder on yourself.

Mr Bergen was no trouble. Indeed, having made her point quite clear, Tilly added, as she sorted out her school case, 'He's no trouble.' The room was no trouble either. It was quite separate, having been built on, long before they came, over the little kitchen, which was itself built out into the back garden.

Tilly took some faded wild flowers out of the case.

'You can put some of these in his room, if you like. You know, you have to paste them on to pieces of brown paper, and write the proper name clearly under each one.'

'I don't go into his room while he's out,' said Hester indignantly.

Mr Bergen had been 'got', though indirectly, through the Red Cross. Hester had a secretarial job for three mornings a week, and did some typing for the Red Cross Centre on Fridays. It wasn't, she thought, wanting to be honest in all things, that she deeply cared about the work, but that she didn't like to feel guilty about not caring.

She really would have liked to have volunteered out of sheer good nature, like Maisie Meade, whom she had met there, and who had evidently escaped any kind of hardening process. Shapeless, or rather not bothered by her shape, Maisie went everywhere with three large bags: one for shopping; one containing 'my life', as she called it – keys, addresses, lists, and so on; one in case she should be given something which had to be taken to somebody else.

'Your spare room, Hester dear . . . I know you don't have to let it . . .'

'If I did have to, it wouldn't worry me,' said Hester. 'I don't mind talking about money.'

Now she had been sharp with Maisie, which was not forgivable. 'Of course I'll help out, Maisie.'

'He's from Poland, dear, and he'll be out every day. He has a job, to do with refugee families over here in fact, but it's so difficult to find anywhere for him that's not too expensive . . .'

'What's his name?'

'Ernst or Ernest Bergen, I'm not absolutely sure which . . .'

'What am I going to call him then?'

'I thought you might say his name rather quickly and quietly dear, so that it might be either . . .'

Ernst paid the rent punctiliously. He cleaned the room and took his washing to the launderette, where Hester glimpsed him once or twice, sitting in quiet correctness, watching the shirts and a recurrent two pairs of dark socks as they whirled round in foaming circles before him. He always had a book in his hand.

It wasn't as though he had no friends, or nothing to do. He appeared to have both, and went out often in the evenings, and always on Sundays, as he told her to 'gatherings'. These gatherings seemed to be at the place where he worked, and to consist of the people he worked with, which struck Hester almost as a definition of loneliness.

She showed him the shelf in the passage where Rod used to keep a few things. In fact there were probably one or two of them left. It would have been ludicrous to clear everything away, as though there'd been a death in the house.

'You can use that if you like, Ernst. There isn't much space upstairs, I know, if you've got a lot of books.'

He had to stretch to reach the shelf. It was summer, he had taken off his jacket and, as he reached up, a little of his white shirt pulled out of his trousers, but was replaced so neatly that it was almost magical, as though he had the gift of never making an awkward gesture.

'Your husband must have been taller than I am,' he said, with the rueful smile of the less tall.

Tilly came through the passage, walking as though in a dream, with each foot exactly in line, the toe of one track shoe touching the heel of the other. She was singing to herself as she passed on into the kitchen.

'What is she doing?' Ernst asked.

'Oh, they're all walking about like that at her school. You know how it is, it'll be something else in a week or so. Do you have a family?' But that struck her as not quite the right question. 'I mean, back in Poland?' That was worse. Where else, after all, could his family be?

'If I had had a family, I should not have left them behind me,' he said. If that's meant as a reproach I shan't like it, Hester thought. But it could hardly have been one, because he was still smiling.

'I was only wondering if you had any plans . . . that's to say, if you had any idea how long you will be staying here?'

‘I’m afraid I can’t say. It is possible that I may be able to arrange a re-entry permit.’

‘And then you’ll go home?’

He looked puzzled. ‘I shall go back.’

There was a silence, and then he went on more urgently, ‘Unless that is – if you wish me to go. I don’t want to be of the slightest nuisance to you. If you prefer it I could look for another room.’

Of course he could. Diligently he could go through the small ads in the local paper, underlining them with his silver pencil, or he could ask the resettlement agency where he worked, or indeed, Maisie Meade. But they were not, of course, talking about rooms.

No one could have missed the appeal in his voice, made with dignity and even pride – pride, as she well knew, being a useful protective habit: ‘I could leave tomorrow, if you find my presence inconvenient.’

As at so many important moments (but why, in heaven’s name, should this be an important moment?) Hester seemed – most unwillingly – to hear the reproachful voice of her elder sister: Go on, why can’t you say something kind? And surely Hester could; it wouldn’t be difficult. If Ernst was something more than far from home, if he was making a nakedly human appeal, there was nothing embarrassing about that for a sensible woman. Everyone thought of her as someone who conducted her life sensibly, and took people on their own terms. So surely she could say something kind. But she could do nothing of the sort.

Are there other women like me? Is there one single other

woman, thought Hester, standing there and feeling the warm gusts of air through the open door from the summer garden, one single other person who knows exactly what they're going to do and then does the opposite? Even Tilly managed better than she did, walking in again, backwards this time, and asking Mr Bergen whether or not he could swim.

'I can,' he replied gravely.

'How many strokes?'

He didn't know but told her that he would count next time. The strain of the moment evaporated into the air of the late afternoon.

Neither of them referred again to his going away, or, indeed, to his staying put. Ernst continued to travel punctually to and from his work with his briefcase and silver pencil. He took no holiday, having nowhere in particular to go. Hester and Tilly went for three weeks to the seaside – to Hester's sister and her husband at Whitstable.

Here the great charm, for Tilly at least, was the beach hut. Suffocatingly warm, smelly, and close, with an ill-tempered butane gas stove on which a large tin kettle slowly came to the boil, it was not really much of a place to be, but Tilly reigned there as hostess and much preferred it to her aunt's comfortable house. She was up early every morning, asking, 'When do we go to the beach hut?'

School, however, still imposed its tasks. Twelve natural objects had to be collected and brought back from the beach, so that they could be drawn and written about next term.

‘Can’t we just enjoy ourselves?’ Hester asked her. ‘And not worry about the natural objects till just before we go?’

She loved her daughter. In the evening both of them emptied their shoes out onto the bedroom windowsill, creating a small heap of warm dry sand. If it didn’t rain, the pile of sand gradually got higher and higher. ‘Do you remember we used to do that?’ she said to her sister.

‘You’re losing weight,’ her sister told her. ‘There are problems about managing by yourself. If you find there are difficulties you can’t cope with, you should get advice you can trust.’

‘Well, I can trust myself,’ said Hester.

She went to the library, which she never seemed to have time to do at home. She looked up the history of Poland, and felt in her bones what it must be like to live in a flat, spreading country, rolling away over countless miles to a white-skied horizon without sight of the sea, with Russia on one border, Germany on the other, both ready to roll their forces forward with nothing in all that flatness to stop them. Perhaps she ought to have known more about it before, but you can’t know everything. Everyone knows something that nobody else does.

They were back in the last week of August. Ernst was at work when they got home, but he had neatly arranged the letters which had come for them, and the numerous bright folders offering five pence off their next purchases. The tiny bit of grass in the back garden was closely mown. Tilly went out to tea immediately with her next-door friend, to compare their collections of twelve natural objects. Hester got out her bike to go up to the cleaners, to fetch their winter raincoats.

'Could I have a word, dear?'

Hester put her foot on the kerb and then had to lift her bike on to the pavement as an old Mini drew up closely beside her and Maisie's urgent face appeared at the rolled down window.

'Such an awkward place to talk . . . but I just wanted to ask you . . .'

'Yes?'

'It's just about your Mr Burger . . .'

Why couldn't Maisie get his name straight? In a moment she'd be calling him Frankfurter.

'That's all working out all right, is it, dear?'

After all, Maisie had always had the greatest difficulty in remembering anyone's name.

'Yes, it's fine. I don't know yet how long he'll be staying, but it's fine.'

'And your little girl, she gets on with him?'

'She hardly notices him, he's no trouble.'

'It's just that I wondered, dear, if you could tell me where you got him from, I mean, how you heard about him in the first place . . . I try to keep a sort of list . . . people are so good . . .'

Hester began to speak, then checked herself. 'I was told about him by a very kind friend.'

The traffic urged Maisie's car forward, and carried her away, still waving and speaking rapidly. Now, thought Hester, who is Ernst Bergen? One support after another has been lost to him and even Maisie Meade, who presumably must once have known who he was, doesn't know now. He has no family, otherwise he would not have left them behind. He is noiseless; everyone who dropped in said they wouldn't have known he was there. What was his claim to identity?

In October the pavement's rank of trees dripped and dropped, and Tilly's new assignment was to make a selection of autumn leaves, Hester couldn't remember of how many different kinds.

The houses, which had stood amiably open all summer, with neighbours and children running in and out, drew back into themselves and, brightly lit behind their drawn curtains, covered their private worlds, well protected from the dank streets.

Tilly, arranging her leaves, looked tranquil and absorbed. She had never been the worrying kind. Hester, on the other hand, was unaccountably melancholic, but determined not to be. I want something or somebody to tell me what's wrong, she thought, about to pick up the phone and ring her sister. No, I don't really want to be told what's wrong.

The mornings were now hazy and chilly. 'Mr Bergen has a black suit on,' said Tilly.

It was quite true, and neither of them had ever seen it before. Punctual as always, he was just shutting the gate on his way out, and they could see from the rear his sober, rather dusty-looking black jacket, with overlapping seams, like the seams on Levi's, never to be found on an English suit. He wore black, perhaps, to mark one of the sadly-remembered dates in

Poland's long history. Or, it might simply be, Hester suggested, that the suit was thick and he was wearing it because he was feeling cold.

'His shoulders are bowed,' said Tilly.

Hester thought this nonsense, indeed Ernst walked off briskly enough into the damp. Just before he got to the corner, the familiar Mini overtook him. Maisie opened the left-hand door and shouted a friendly invitation which seemed, while he politely raised his hat, to draw him into the car as though by suction.

He'll be too early for work now, and he won't like that, Hester thought. But this idea by no means accounted for the piercing resentment which was so strange a feeling that, not having known it for years, she wasn't able at first to recognise it for what it was. She couldn't, surely, be jealous of Maisie Meade. It couldn't be jealousy, could it?

It was jealousy, but of a peculiar kind. It was this: that until Hester could get things straight and see them clearly, it wasn't bearable that anyone but herself should be allowed to be with Ernst, or to speak to him. There was something that had to be settled between the two of them that had nothing to do with anyone else on earth, except perhaps Tilly.

She didn't even want Maisie to remember – as presumably she was doing at this very moment – who Ernst was. Because when the Mini's door slammed, like a sharp echo of separation, Hester's mind had been jolted in a flash into images of Ernst which had been there for how long? She saw, rather than knew, that she wanted to sleep and wake in the dark beside his darkness and preciseness and warmth, the preciseness of a man who never made an awkward gesture.

Well, she would tell him so. There was no reason not to. She had plenty of time to think exactly how to put it, since Tilly's class was going on an all-day visit to a Road Safety Exhibition. There was no mystery about Ernst Bergen's movements. He was back always, even if he was going out again, at twenty minutes to seven.

Hester sat down to the kind of lunch that mothers eat when their children are on an all-day outing. It consisted of the last triangle of cheese from a cardboard box, and a cold potato which had been in the fridge for some days. At a quarter past one, Ernst, in his black suit, came back. He didn't go upstairs, but walked into the kitchen, took off his hat and drew from his briefcase a bottle wrapped in paper.

Hester was surprised to the point of fear. 'What are you doing here?'

'I am taking a half-day,' Ernst replied. 'I have earned one, it is quite in order.'

It was a bottle of white wine, and Hester recognised the label immediately.

She had seen it in a tub at the cash-out at the supermarket: a Special Drink at a Special Price for Special Occasions.

'I have come to bring you this,' said Ernst, 'because I know that you need to raise your spirits.'

Perhaps they were both going mad.

'I wanted to come back and bring you some kind of comfort and consolation, because I know that today is the anniversary of your great loss.'

Hester stared at him as he gravely took a folding corkscrew out of his top pocket.

'Tilly told me, you see, that it was today, October 25th, that you lost your husband.'

'Tilly? But how could she? When did she tell you?'

'She mentioned it to me yesterday evening. We were speaking when I returned from work.'

'But she can't have done! She doesn't remember what day it was! For that matter, I don't remember what day it was either!'

Now she was furious. It was betrayal. Not even to her did Tilly ever say a word about such things. She knew it was betrayal, she knew by the wound she felt.

'Tilly doesn't know anything at all about it!'

Ernst looked graver still.

'She does not know that her father is dead?'

'He's not dead!' Hester shouted. 'He's perfectly well, as far as I know. He's married and living in Huddersfield. It's all over and done with long ago.'

She was standing with her hands flat on the kitchen table trembling, and more wretched still, because now that she had said, as she certainly hadn't intended to do, that her marriage was over, why couldn't he show that it was important to him? Why didn't he say something kind?

But he stood there entirely sombre in his black suit.

'I don't know what we're talking about!'

'I can see I have displeased you. That is the only thing that matters.'

Immediately he uncorked the wine and poured it down the sink. It was terrible to see the pale golden level of the wine tilt up and escape in great throbs, while through the glass of the emptying bottle the kitchen taps behind it appeared, bit by bit. Quietly he put the bottle down, and just as he had come in, he walked out.

She wasted time looking for her showerproof, and then when she found it and ran out after him the rain was coming down heavily and soaked her through in a moment. She took the bottle with her. That seemed to her at the time quite clearly necessary, to prove to him that she had not been displeased. She must take something with her to prove that.

So from one house after another, along the street, Hester, who was known to be sensible and conduct her life sensibly, could be seen pelting along with her hair hanging in damp streaks, and waving an empty bottle.

She caught up with him at the corner, too out of breath to speak clearly. She held up the bottle.

'Waste!'

He clicked his tongue slightly in distress, took it from her, and put it carefully into a bin. Then he smoothed her wet hair.

'Ernst, what are we going to do?'

Mr Bergen replied that he was going to take her home.

A FEW PROBLEMS IN THE DAY CASE UNIT

Georgina Hammick

(1986)

My name is Lettice Pomfrey and I am thirty-four years old. I am sitting in the gynaecologist's waiting room waiting to see the gynaecologist. I tell you this now, at the beginning, in case gynaecology is not the subject for you; in case you find some aspects of it distasteful; in case you would rather be somewhere else than in this waiting room on a hot and sunny July afternoon.

I don't want to be here; I've a high failure rate in gynaecologists. The first one I saw was a misogynist and an extortionist, the second a lecher. The third one might have been all right, I can't positively say he wasn't, but we moved house before I had a chance to find out. The fourth one, Mr Gamble, I haven't yet met. He's been recommended by my doctor and by several people I know who variously say he's sympathetic, attractive, dishy. A surgeon's wife I share the school run with told me Mr G is the envy of his colleagues, who've had to watch him sweep the gynaecological board, not just of the county's childbearers, but of the menopausal. They seek him out, according to her, for hysterectomies, for removal of ovarian cysts and ovaries, and for Hormone Replacement Therapy. This is enough to put me off him, but I'm telling myself to keep an open mind.

The waiting room is in the consulting rooms an ENT man, a paediatrician and Mr Gamble share. They see their private patients here, and their NHS patients at the Infirmary. I'd have been quite happy, not being on BUPA, to see Mr G at the NHS clinic he holds on Tuesdays, but my doctor explained that because of the consultants' dispute, and as I can't be called an urgent case, it'd mean tagging on to the end of a long waiting list. Impossible to say when I'd get an appointment. It could be years, not months. Centuries even, my doctor said, with one of his occasional flashes of humour. Millenniums.

The waiting room is very smart. Its colour scheme is white and fawn and chocolate brown. The ceiling is white, the walls fawn, the carpet fawn with a chocolate Greek key pattern round the edge. The chairs are white tubular with chocolate wool seats. There are two rubber plants, one either side of the fireplace, standing in white, square jardinières. In front of the plate-glass window is a large table with a glass top, and on this are magazines. They've been arranged like a game of giant clock patience, but in the centre, where the king of hearts or spades should be, is an enormous ashtray, square and glass to match the table. I would like a cigarette at this moment, but don't want to be caught smoking. Also it seems common courtesy to keep my breath sweet for Mr Gamble, even if my mouth is not the part of me he'll be seeing most of.

Apart from the furniture, the waiting room is empty. I walk up and down, try out different chairs and angles, tidy a thumbnail, sniff the magazines. These are new, or recent, issues of glossy monthlies; no stimulating reads here, no *Diver* or *Motorcycling Weekly* or *Aircraft Modeller*; no *Exchange & Mart*. The only mag on this table that could be called specialist is *Horse and Hound*. The number I've got hold of contains a round-up of last year's hunting season, with copious photographs. A Good Day Out With The Whitemore Vale, I read. Colonel Jim Vane-Fitzpatrick, joint master, shows hounds –

Mrs Pomfrey, ready for you now.

The nurse who's come for me is a dark girl, and pretty except for some serious and disconcerting spots (no matter how often you come across them, spotty nurses, like dentists with bad breath and hairdressers with hacked hair, are always somehow shocking). I follow her to a little room where I am weighed, and where my blood pressure is taken. As she pumps me up I squinny to see the reading, but she's too quick for me. That's fine, she says grimly, unwinding the black mackintosh from my arm.

Mrs Pomfrey for you, Mr Gamble, she says, opening a connecting door. Mr Gamble gets up from behind his desk and comes forward and shakes my hand. Then he squeezes my shoulder, a gentle pressure that encourages me to sit down on the chair my side of the desk and facing his chair. When he has returned to his place he leans towards me on his elbows.

Well, Mrs Pomfrey, he says, well now.

Mr Gamble is a good-looking man; he may even be attractive. Somebody told me he's a bit like James Stewart, and he is, about the mouth and chin. His eyes aren't blue though, they're brown. They're kind eyes, and the expression in them of sympathy and concern is intensified by the furrows in his brow. They cannot be a misogynist's eyes, I'm sure. And there's no hint of lechery in them.

Mr G begins to ask me questions – my date of birth; my husband's date of birth; the dates of birth and sexes of our four children, etc – the answers to which he jots down with a fountain pen on a sheet of unlined A4. I wonder why he bothers with this: most of the information must be in the letter from my doctor I can see on his desk, or in the file containing my medical notes, ditto. Perhaps he hasn't read the letter or had time to glance through the notes; or perhaps he prefers to do his own spadework in what for him is new ground, in what for me is old ground, dug over many times before.

How old was I, Mr G wants to know, when I had my first period? Can I give him a brief account of the births of my children? Am I a smoker? Do I have any problems at all with bowels or waterworks?

Mr G lays his pen on the paper. Would I like to tell him, and I can take my time, about the various methods of birth control I and my husband have tried during the course of our marriage? We started off with my using a cap, I tell him, and Mr G picks up his pen and writes Diaphragm on the sheet of paper. Then we started a baby – on purpose, I explain, and then after the baby was born I went on the pill. Oral C, Mr G writes down. And how did that suit? he asks, leaning forward again.

The truth is it made me sick and fat and gave me headaches, and I tell him this. Mr G writes, Usual side effects and something else I can't read. Sounds as though you should have been on a low dose pill, he says. I was, I assure him, on the lowest dose available at the time. And after the second baby? After our second baby I tried a Coil. IUD, Mr G writes. Will I describe for him, if I can, this Coil? It looked like a firework, I tell him, you know, a squib. Ah, I *see*, Mr G says, rubbing his chin, How did that work for you? Were you happy with it? I hesitate – but what is the point of mincing words? He's asking me, after all; he wants to know. I got the curse very badly, I tell him, every ten days. And I had a dragging, stitching pain, low down. Heavy loss, Mr G writes, Discomfort. And after the third baby? Another pill, same side effects. And after the fourth (which I've already told him was a mistake, and which he has decided was unplanned)? Another Coil, a different sort, with the same results only more so. It became embedded, I explain, and for them to remove it I had to spend a day in hospital and have a general anaesthetic. . . .

You don't seem to have much luck, do you? Mr G still sounds concerned, but at the same time ever so slightly disbelieving, just the teeniest bit resentful. Has he decided I'm a difficult patient? So, he says, looking down at his hands, so what's the score at the moment? What method are you using now?

I must think about this. I can't say French letter to *him*. But the official words, the words I know I ought to use, stick in the throat. My husband is taking precautions, I say. Mr Gamble writes down Sheath, and asks if it's satisfactory for us, me and my husband.

Pictures float into my head; my husband groping in his bedside drawer, having knocked the lamp over; me lying in the dark with nothing to do and going off the boil, if I was ever on it; our children wandering round our bedroom before breakfast while I'm getting dressed or putting my face on, touching things, picking up things, opening drawers. What are these, Mum? What are they *for*? Not just pictures. Some man once told me that doing it in a French letter is like sucking a sweet with the wrapper on.

It's not ideal, I say to Mr G.

No, it's not, Mr G says. It's not much fun for your husband, I can promise you that. Even more important, perhaps, it's not really *safe*. The accident rate is high. Have the two of you ever considered – he pauses, he presses the tips of his fingers together, and then pushes them apart – sterilisation? A vasectomy? I tell him we have, but one of us might, you never know, die of a heart attack or get run over by a bus, and the other might then remarry someone who hadn't had children and who wanted some.

Mr G glances at his watch. Let's re-cap, he says. Which method you've tried was, d'you think, if not entirely satisfactory, then on balance the best for you, the best for both of you? Remembering, of course, that no method – apart from sterilisation, and we've ruled that out – is a hundred per cent?

The Coil, I say. Because it has to be the Coil. At least with the Coil you know it's there, and you don't have to remember to swallow anything; or coat something with sperm-killing cream and stick it up yourself. And remember to take it out afterwards (but not too soon, not before the sperm-killers have had a chance to be effective), and wash it and dry it and dust it with talcum powder; and not leave it on the basin when the telephone rings.

Mr Gamble, looking at me, opens a drawer in his desk and places what he finds there on the surface between us. He pushes at it with his forefinger. This is the Copper Coil, he says, triumphantly, like a conjuror at the end of a difficult trick, and I think we should give it a try.

The Copper Coil is very small. It is not shaped like a coil; it is a piece of bent fusewire; half a hairpin; a shorthand character; a rest in music. How could it possibly prevent a baby?

We're not exactly sure, Mr G admits, still pushing the wire around with his finger, but we know it does. Of course there's bound to be some failure rate, but it's a low one as these things go. Right then – Mr G leans back in his chair and pushes at the desk as though he's trying to get rid of it – I think we'd better have a little peep at you. If you'd like to pop up on the day bed over there. Just remove your tights and pants and bra, but keep your slip on if you're wearing one.

We get up together. My skirt is sticking to my bottom and to the backs of my knees. Am I supposed to take my bag with me, or leave it on the floor by my chair? I walk to the curtained-off corner where the day bed waits, Mr G to the cabinet where, presumably, his disposable gloves and his instruments are.

It's dark behind the curtain. I take off my shirt, my skirt, my shoes, my tights, my pants. With difficulty and without removing my petticoat – for although it's a hot day I am wearing one, I knew I should need it – I unhook my bra. I fold all these things on a chair, covering my underclothes with my outer clothes. I clamber onto the day bed, which is high. It has a hard flat pillow and draw-sheet, across which has been laid a square of linen the size of a baby's cot sheet. Am I meant to lie on top of this or under it? I lie under it, or rather arrange it to cover as much of my lower half as it will. My feet are turned out; my heels are resting on a length of cellophane that crackles when I move them.

A light snaps on above me. The curtains rattle back. It's Mr G who does this. He is just going to examine my breasts, he says, he is sorry if his hands are cold, he's washed them, can I slip my shoulder straps down for him please!

If people can be divided into those who look better, and more themselves, naked, and those who look better, and more themselves, wearing clothes, I must come into the second category. My mammary glands, in particular, don't stand up to scrutiny. They aren't, alas they never were, composed of two firm and perfectly moulded hillocks from which twin rosy budlets spring. They fall, when I lie on my back, flatly away from the breastbone and sag either side of the ribcage like two badly-filled shopping bags. An exaggeration? My bosom is a sad sight; if I allow myself to think about it, I weep; if I glimpse it in the bathroom glass, I turn my back. Were it not that my husband professes, once every five years, to be fond of my bosom, I should have cut my throat long ago.

I stare at the ceiling and tell myself he has seen worse sights than this, while, with the flat of his hands, Mr Gamble goes over the part of me I've just described. Do you do this at home? he asks, as he squeezes prods and cups. You should, you know, at least once a month, in front of the mirror. That's fine, he says (How does he know it's fine? How, with all these lumps and bumps, could he tell if any of them were unusual?) He pulls the cot sheet up over my top half, so that my lower half is now exposed. He presses the folds of my stomach, he pushes his fingers in hard at the sides, just above the groin. Any tenderness here? Or here? Relax. Let yourself go limp. Now, now I'd like you to roll over onto your side and draw your knees up for me as high as you can.

I roll over on my side to the wall and draw my knees up, just a little. Higher, if you can, Mr G says. He tucks my petticoat out of the way; he tweaks the cot sheet from my shoulders and removes it all together. I grip the edge of the mattress. I screw my eyes tight shut – for doing so I may be able to blot out from the my imagination the terrible view Mr G now has of me: the spots on my bottom I tried to disguise with talcum powder before I set out; the corrugated skin in the groove below my coccyx; the –

Try not to tense yourself, Mr G says, as his gloved hands part me. One of these hands, the left hand, stays on my left *buttock*; the other hand, the right hand, bypasses my (now what would he call it? *Anus? The opening of the alimentary canal?*) bum hole; enters somewhere below this. Excavates. Explores. Probes. La la la, I sing to myself, la la la, to shut out the sound (of old men drinking soup, of gumboots being pulled from a bog) that accompanies the withdrawal of this hand. La la la la.

You may feel this a little, Mr G says. No, don't tense, let yourself go. La la la la, porn, porn, porn, porn, let yourself go, I sing to myself, as the plunger, or whatever it is, twists in deeper and deeper, to my very core, centre, kernel, essence, nucleus, thesaurus. *The*saurus? Or the*sau*rus? Which should it be? If in danger, cross your legs; if you can't be good be careful; if sex is inevitable, relax and enjoy it; if –

All done, all finished, Mr G says, you can get dressed again now.

I suppose I'll bleed a bit, I say to Mr G. when I am dressed again and back in my chair. (I'm an old hand at this; I seem to remember a bloody aftermath to Coil insertions.)

I see no reason for that, Mr G says. He looks puzzled. Oh I see – I should have made myself clearer. What you've had was merely a routine smear test, long overdue. If all's in order in that department, you'll get an appointment card from the Infirmary. Until very recently, he confides, I did Coil insertions here, in the Consulting Rooms, but it's safer and more hygienic in Theatre, where everything's to hand. It's better for the patient. More comfortable.

I've never had it done in a hospital before, I say. (I'm not at all sure.) I'm not sure –

There's absolutely nothing to worry about, believe me – Mr G stretches a pinstriped arm across the desk and pats my hand – Feeling all right now, dear?

We get up. Mr G walks with me to the door, one arm lightly around my shoulder. There's nothing sinister about this, I'm certain. I'm quite sure this is the way he dismisses all his patients.

* * *

And now it is evening, our children tucked in their beds, what's left of the fish pie back in the larder. My husband is sitting in an armchair, reading a book. I am sitting in an identical chair, cobbling a seam in a pair of my son's jeans. There was no blue cotton in the sewing box, so I am making do with green.

I went to see the gynae today, I say to my husband.

My husband turns two pages at once of his book, Alan Moorehead's *Gallipoli*. He has read it before, a long time ago, but is looking something up.

What? Oh yes. How did it go? Is he a good egg, d'you think, your Mr Whatsisname?

I don't know. I think he may be. He took a lot of trouble (for it's true; he did take a lot of trouble). His name is Gamble.

Ho ho, my husband says, going back to the index. You'd think he'd change it. He runs his finger down the page. Can't seem to find it, damn, he says.

He's giving me another Coil, I say. I've got to have it done in the Infirmary.

Why's that? What for? my husband asks, his eye still on the index. What does that mean exactly? *In nuce*, mind you, not verbatim, says my husband who is a Latin tag man, a man for whom all invoices are, *per se* and *ipso facto*, (if *a priori*) *pro forma*, all payments *ex gratia*, all evidence *prima facie*, all quids *pro quo*.

It's safer and more hygienic in hospital, in Theatre, Mr Gamble says.

That makes sense, my husband murmurs to the index, that makes sense.

I'm not too keen on the idea of Theatre, I say. I'd rather have it done in the Consulting Rooms, or the Clinic, like last time.

Don't then, my husband says. He takes off his spectacles and puts them back on again. You're the customer, I'm paying for this, remember. Do what you want to do. Have it done where you want.

But Mr Gamble doesn't do it in the Consulting Rooms any more. He said –

You told me what he said, and it makes sense to me, my husband says. He clearly has a *causa movens*. Stop worrying, he says, *nil desperandum*.

There is silence for a while. My husband leaves the room and returns with the whisky bottle, which is nearly empty. We must have clobbered it before supper, he says.

I had to have an internal examination today, I tell him.

I'm sure you did, my husband says. He sips his whisky. Poor you, he says, how horrid for you, poor you.

When we were newly married my husband came with me on my first visit to a gynaecologist. I wasn't sure I wanted him as a matter of fact, but he insisted. He was very distressed. I cannot bear the idea of another man touching you, even looking at you, he said as we drew up outside the surgery. I cannot bear it, you are mine – and he thumped the steering wheel in despair. When I came out an hour later I found him hunched in the driving seat, and when I got in beside him he clung to me. My baby, he said, his eyes full of tears, my precious, precious baby. I imagine that my husband, who is a positive, forward-looking man and, Latin tags and military campaigns apart, never one to dwell on the past, has long since forgotten this incident.

I bite off the end of my cotton and take another item from the mending pile at my feet. Emerald green will not do for the rip in Angelica's scarlet party dress, but there's a reel of crimson Sylko in my lap which will have to.

* * *

The queue in Reception is very long, and I join the end of it. I'm annoyed by this queue because it wasn't easy getting here on time. I had to organise, which means beg, someone else to do the school run; we had to have breakfast before seven; I had to drive my husband to the station, get back, make sandwiches for two school lunch boxes, put the dustbins out, and then walk the dogs – because who knows how long they're going to be shut up for. All this so I could leave the house by ten to eight, so I could be here by half-past.

There's a telephone on the Reception desk. It rings and rings. It rings all the time I'm waiting, all the time I'm inching up the queue. No less than three people to deal with appointments and enquiries, and yet none of them can answer this telephone. None of them so much as looks at it, and it's odd. I know I couldn't work at a desk where a telephone was ringing without doing something about it, without at least taking it off the hook, or shouting at it.

Follow the sign to B2, the Receptionist says when I hand

her my card, and she jerks her head to her right. Your telephone is ringing, by the way, I tell her. Card please, she says to the person next in line.

I follow the signs to B2. Left from the desk through swing doors, right at the end of the corridor, up two levels in the lift, more swing doors, B2. A nurse is heading towards me. She's going fast, and when I accost her she has to brake, so that her black shoes squeak on the lino. I tell her my name and what I'm here for, and she turns back the way she's come and points to a door on the right. Go in there, she says, take off your clothes and put on a theatre gown and a dressing gown, and I'll be back in a jiff.

In the room there's a cupboard, partitioned down the middle: theatre gowns on the left, dressing gowns on the right. I take off my clothes and put on a theatre gown. It is like a high-necked apron with sleeves, and it fastens at the back with tapes, one of which is missing. I bend my head into the cupboard and sniff the dressing gowns to see if they've been worn, but they smell of nothing. I put one on. It is voluminous. Its sleeves come down over my hands, its skirts trail over the floor. I hitch it at the waist, and blouse and bag it over the tie-belt. I don't like these clothes, and the nothing smell of them. I want to pee. I want to go home.

I sit on the bed and swing my legs and wait for the nurse. She doesn't come. I've got time to consider what I don't want to consider, the question I meant to ask, and didn't ask, Mr Gamble, the problem I meant to discuss, and didn't discuss, with my husband, namely this: is it all right to have a Coil? Is it all right to put a foreign body, a *piece of wire* (even if copper wire) in the womb? Does the womb like it? Is it dangerous in any way? To the womb? To me in general? Last time, and the time before, I bled like a, like a *stuck pig*. I was a social embarrassment. I had to leave dinner parties in a hurry. I mean, is it okay to have a Coil? Is the Coil an okay thing to have?

I get off the bed and shuffle to the window. Far below two tiny figures in navy capes are being blown along a concrete walkway. They weave in and out of the buildings, disappear, reappear beside a grove of sapling poplars, vanish into Pathology, a shack like all the other shacks. Angelica's classroom is a shack. She will be in it now – arithmetic, first period after prayers. She didn't want to go to school today. She didn't feel well, she said. She had a headache and a tummy ache, she felt *sick*. She says this, or something like it, every morning. Every morning I want to keep her at home and let her mess up the kitchen table with paint-water and scissors and gummed squares; every morning I send her to school.

I go out into the corridor. There's a cleaner with a hovercraft outside my door. She shows me where the lavatory is, just in time.

I am back on the bed, curled up, reading the mail that came as I was leaving the house. My mail is one postcard, from a friend who's on holiday in Kenya (was on holiday, I should say. I saw her in Tesco yesterday, at the cheese counter. She was busy, I was busy, we pretended not to see each other). The card is addressed to Memsahib Pomfrey. It says Jambo! Habari? We are having a fantastic time. See you soonest, Love V & C. I turn it over. The picture side has a hippo with its mouth open, half submerged in a pool, surrounded by smaller hippos.

A man's head appears round the door of my room. I've come to take you to Theatre, he says. Leave your handbag and your clothes in the locker – and your watch if you're wearing one.

Are you a nurse? I ask the man when we are in the lift together, descending to G level. The man has his arms folded across his chest and is staring at the ceiling the way people tend to in lifts. I know I do, because it's the only way to avoid eyeball to eyeball confrontation with strangers. He uncrosses his arms and points to a badge on his overall which says Porter, green letters on white.

At G Level we follow signs to X-Ray and Haematology, but at the last moment bypass these and make now for Pharmacy, Outpatients Surgical, Gynaecology and Shop. We walk out through plastic swing doors, Emergency Exit 2, and I lift my skirts, costume drama style, onto covered concrete, uncovered concrete, covered concrete, through swing doors, into lino corridor, where we stop. Put on a pair of overshoes, the porter says, and take a seat here.

Against the wall are two chairs and a row of see-through galoshes, all the same size; it doesn't matter which pair I choose. I take a seat in the corridor. On my left side are the shut double doors of Theatre 1 and Theatre 2, and opposite to me on the wall is a notice in red: This a No Smoking Zone. I look from the notice to the doors and back again. Zone. It's an odd word; the longer I stare at it, the odder it is. Zone. *Zone*. What does it mean? Does it mean anything? No. No such number, no such zone. (This time I'm gonna take it myself, and put it right in her hand, and if it comes back the vurry next day, *then* I'll understand the writing on it) –

The doors of Theatre 2 open, a stretcher trolley shoots out, swings round, one person behind it pushing, another in front steering, holding the drip steady. I keep my head down as they trundle past at a trot, but I see because I want to see, because I have to, because I must: a white face, a dead face, surely, chin tipped up, mouth hugely open, a tube in the nose – or was it the mouth? Gone.

How long have I been here? Ten minutes? Twenty? I keep checking, but on my left wrist, printed across unbleached hairs and a mole, is only the ghost of my watch. Where is Mr G? Why doesn't Mr G come?

Ready for you in theatre now, dear.

It isn't Mr G, it's a nurse, in green, masked and gowned, who leads me, clopping in my overshoes, out of the darkness of the corridor into the light of Theatre 1.

It is very bright in Theatre. Interval time. The house lights are up and there's a party going on. It's a tea party, I can tell, because the six or seven people wandering about chatting have cups and saucers in their hands. It's surprising really, all this activity and chat and tea drinking, because you tend to think of hospital theatres as sterile, hygienic places, as Mr G. said, places (or areas, or zones) you can only enter if you're wearing overshoes.

Someone comes forward and helps me out of my dressing gown. Someone asks me to take off my overshoes and my shoes. This same person gives me a hand onto the stage. (No, not a stage, a table. An operating table, for operations.) I lie down on my back, feet together, arms by my sides. Lift your tail, please. And at once, when I comply, the theatre gown is rolled back, up over my knees and thighs, and then folded above my waist. My legs are separated into a V. My right leg is carried up and away and placed in a sling and strapped; my left leg is carried up and away and placed in a sling and strapped. I raise my head. The slings are attached to a contraption suspended from the ceiling. It's like a Big Top up there: lights, wires, machinery, all the gear for tightropes and trapeze.

My bottom, my *tail,* is no longer on the table. Somebody slips a pillow underneath me, wedges it into the small of my back.

And that's all. Nothing else happens. I am on my back, with no knickers on, my legs wide apart and in the air – and nothing happens. The tea party is still going on, to be sure, all round me I can hear chatter and laughter and cups being returned to saucers – but I'm not part of it somehow, no one offers me a cup, no one chats to me.

This is not the first time I've been in this position; our second daughter, in no hurry to be born, had to be induced. But that time there were only two people in the Treatment Room – me, and the hospital doctor (Brown? Yes, Brown) who explained nothing, who said nothing, as he strapped up my legs. I remember the pain when he *ruptured the membranes*; I remember thinking it must be blood that gushed out and ran back underneath me and soaked the hospital gown and the sheets; I remember the ward sister in the corridor who, as I staggered out into it, took one look and snapped her fingers: Nurse! That girl needs some pethadine! I can think of all this, and concentrate on the detail and the pain because nothing that happens today, nothing that Mr G has got up his sleeve, can be as bad as that.

Or can it? At least last time there was an end-product, a baby, to be born, at least there was someone to look forward to. What Mr G is going to do (why doesn't he do it?) is prevent a baby being born; and at the same time rob me (when I am tired or cross, or simply not in the mood for love) of the best, the most convincing, the least hurtful, of my nocturnal excuses: D'you think we should, darling, when we know it isn't *safe*?

There's a game I used to play with my brothers, that I dare say everyone plays with their brothers – or sisters – if they have them: the Would You Rather Game. Would you rather be (here describe the worst horror you are capable of inventing) or go to bed with (here name the most repellent specimen, of either sex, known to you all). Would you rather be on your back under a searchlight with your legs apart and no knickers on in the middle of a tea party, or . . .

All right, Mrs Pomfrey, dear? I'm afraid you will feel this, it will be a bit painful. But if you can relax and just allow yourself to go floppy, it will make it easier for you. It's Mr G's voice. It's Mr G's face, bending over mine, I recognise his eyes. He has pulled his mask down, below his chin, so that he can speak to me. I can see the bristles on his top lip and the hairs, wonderfully luxuriant hairs, in his nose. Has he been here all the time?

There is less chatter now, no chinking of cups. But no one has left the Theatre; I'm certain of this because if I roll my head to the right I can see the doors, and even if I couldn't see, even if I were blind, I'd feel the draught. Mr G prepares to insert the Coil. While he does so, he gives a commentary, an *ex tempore* lecture, my husband would say, to the throng at the end of the table because, yes, that is where the tea party is now assembled. They are students, of course they are! And I am the demonstration model. Watch closely, Mr G says, I'm just going to lubricate the vagina prior to insertion. Can you tell us about the relative safety and efficiency of this Coil? a male voice, eager beaver, enquires. How does this Coil, the copper Coil, compare with other intrauterine devices currently available?

All over, Mr G says at last, all done. Good girl.

My legs are unstrapped, removed from their slings and returned to me. I am helped down from the table. An S2, please, Mr G says, and someone springs forward with a cellophane packet which, snipped open, contains two sanitary towels, individually and hygienically wrapped. You will have a period now, Mr G promises, placing one of the sanitary towels between my thighs, but if the loss is unduly heavy don't hesitate to give us a ring. Take two aspirin four-hourly if there's any discomfort.

Dressing gown on, shoes on, overshoes on. Out of theatre. A six-yard stumble on cardboard legs. Overshoes off. And here is the porter, come to take me back to my clothes.

There are some questions I forgot to ask Mr G and the tea party in Theatre 1. How do you hold a sanitary towel in place when you haven't been given a belt or a pair of pants? How do you keep up with a porter in a hurry when your legs refuse to function properly, and when you're trying to glue your thighs together so that your ST won't leak or land on the floor? When your dressing gown was designed for a giant and is intent on tripping you up? When your insides are falling out, when your eyes are blurred and you can't see where you're going, when the pain is so bad you will surely faint, if not actually die?

In the lift, ascending to B2, a trickle – hot, sticky, but which cannot be amniotic fluid, not today – descends the inside of my right thigh, circumnavigates the knee muscle, finds a route down the calf, steers between the ankle and heel, arrives in my shoe, collects there.

Outside my door the porter and I part company. Here we are then, he says, the first words he's spoken since we left the theatre, and he goes. I reach out for the door handle of my sanctuary, and then I notice it, a red-black splash on the beige lino at my feet, the size of a coin, a little ragged around the edge. I turn, and look, there are more of them, all down the corridor back the way we've come, dark two-penny pieces, regularly spaced, as far as the eye can see. I've left a trail, like Hansel and Gretel did in the forest! Supposing, just supposing, I wanted to go back to Theatre now, I wouldn't need a porter to show me the way.

* * *

Afterword 1: The Letters
Unposted letter to Mr Gamble.

Dear Mr Gamble,

A week after my experience in the Infirmary I wrote you a letter.

I decided to write to you for two reasons: a) because I felt you should know what it was like to be on the receiving end of your lack of attention, and b) because I thought it incumbent on me, being articulate, to suggest ways of improving your set-up.

I took trouble over my letter. The first two drafts were too emotional (you mustn't be allowed to excuse yourself on the grounds that you were dealing with an hysteric); the third too rude. In the end my letter was polite, neither sarcastic nor acrimonious. I gave you a matter-of-fact account of what happened to me. I said I thought you'd want to know about it, so that the experience couldn't be repeated for anyone else. I suggested a few things (a female nurse to take the patient to and from Theatre; fewer people, if possible, present in Theatre; the provision of a sanitary belt or pants afterwards) to make it less of an ordeal for other women in future. Yours sincerely, etc, etc.

Nineteen days later I got your reply: seven typewritten lines, sincerely regretting 'the problems you encountered in the Day Case Unit', hoping the Coil was 'proving satisfactory' – signed in your absence by your secretary, and enclosing your bill.

Could you please tell me, because it wasn't quite clear, which part of the Infirmary was the Day Case Unit?

Afterword 2: The Titles

I had difficulty deciding on a title for this story. I hope I chose the right one (the right one, that is, for the story, and also for you). It cannot be said to mislead, although it may be on the dull side. If you did find it dull, you might be interested to see, in case there's one here you prefer, the other titles I rejected in favour of it. Before I list them, I'd like to tell you my reason for discarding them. It's that, when I typed them out, I saw they could all be construed as containing bitter little ironies; they all seemed to smack of, if not quite feminist, women's or alternative writing.

I was worried they might,if you're a man, put you off. Here they are, then, in order of invention, not merit:

1) The Would You Rather Game
2) That's Enough Gynaecology – Ed.
3) *Volenti Non Fit Injuria**
4) How to Make Your Man Happy in Bed.

* Which is what Lettice's husband said, not unsympathctically and among other things, when she told him what happened in Theatre. It seemed quite neat for a while, perhaps the best of the bunch, I nearly settled for it; but not everyone appreciates Latin tags, some people consider them a joke or pretentious, not everyone understands them.

AUTHOR BIOGRAPHIES

SUSAN GLASPELL (1876–1948) was born of pioneer stock in Iowa. Having been a society reporter she turned to political journalism, wrote magazine stories and spent time in Chicago and Paris. After her marriage to George 'Jig' Cram Cook she moved to Massachusetts and co-founded the Provincetown Players. Her plays included the classic *Trifles* (1916) and the Pulitzer Prize-winning *Alison's House* (1931); her novels include Persephone book No. 4 *Fidelity* (1915) and Persephone book No. 26 *Brook Evans* (1928).

KATHERINE MANSFIELD (1888–1923) was born in New Zealand and moved to London in 1908; she married the writer John Middleton Murry in 1918. The short story volumes published in her lifetime were *In a German Pension* (1911), *Bliss and Other Stories* (1920) and *The Garden Party and Other Stories* (1922). Persephone book No. 25 *The Montana Stories* collects everything she wrote during her last few months in Switzerland. Persephone book No. 69 is her posthumously edited *Journal*.

PAULINE SMITH (1882–1959) grew up in rural South Africa. In 1898, after her father died, she returned to England and went with her mother and sister to live in Dorset, although she often went back to South Africa. In 1909 she met Arnold Bennett, who became a close friend and encouraged her writing. Her short story collection *The Little Karoo* appeared in 1925 and her only novel, *The Beadle*, a year later.

E M DELAFIELD (1890–1943) was born to Count Henry de la Pasture and his novelist wife in Hove, Sussex. When she was 21 she entered a convent in Belgium and wrote about this in *Consequences* (1919), Persephone book No. 13. She was a VAD during WWI and afterwards married Major Paul Dashwood; from 1923 they lived in rural Devon, where she wrote over thirty novels including *The Diary of a Provincial Lady* (1930).

MALACHI WHITAKER (1895–1976) was born Marjorie Taylor in Bradford. The 'Bradford Chekhov', as she was known, published nearly a hundred short stories in several periodicals and in four collections; after the publication of her memoir *And So Did I* in 1939 she announced that she was giving up writing.

DOROTHY PARKER (1893–1967) was born Dorothy Rothschild in Long Branch, New Jersey. She sold her first poem to *Vanity Fair* in 1914, wrote for *Vogue*, *The New Yorker* and *Life* and was a founding member of the Algonquin Round Table. She published several volumes of poetry, many book reviews and two collections of short stories; later she was a screenwriter in Hollywood, but was blacklisted in the 1950s for her pro-Left views.

DOROTHY WHIPPLE (1893–1966) was born in Blackburn and lived for much of her life with her husband in Nottingham, where she wrote nine extremely successful novels including Persephone books No. 85 *High Wages* (1930), No. 95 *Greenbanks* (1932), No. 19 *They Knew Mr Knight* (1934), No. 40 *The Priory* (1939), No. 56 *They Were Sisters* (1943) and No. 3 *Someone at a Distance* (1953). Three collections of short stories were published in her lifetime: Persephone book No. 74, *The Closed Door and Other Stories* is a selection from these.

EDITH WHARTON (1862–1937) was born in New York, to Lucretia Stevens Rhinelander and George Frederic Jones, about whose family the phrase 'keeping up with the Joneses' is said to refer. Between 1900 and 1938 she wrote nearly a hundred short stories and more than twenty novels, most famously *The House of Mirth* (1905) and *The Age of Innocence* (1920), for which she won the Pulitzer Prize – the first woman to do so.

IRÈNE NÉMIROVSKY (1903–42) was born in Kiev, but after the Russian Revolution fled with her family to Paris. She attended courses at the Sorbonne and, writing in French, published ten novels and over forty short stories. Her most famous work is the unfinished *Suite Francaise* (published posthumously in 2004), two linked novellas (five were planned) written and set just after the fall of France. A selection of her stories, *Dimanche and Other Stories*, is Persephone book No. 87.

PHYLLIS BENTLEY (1894–1977) was born and lived for much of her life in Halifax. She went to London University, then worked as a teacher, as a munitions clerk and as a librarian; during WWII she worked for the Ministry of Information. She began writing in the early 1920s and in all published more than fifteen novels; her most successful books were the Yorkshire family chronicles, *Inheritance* (1932) and its sequels.

BETTY MILLER (1910–65) was born Elizabeth Bergson Spiro in Cork to a Lithuanian father and Swedish mother. Her husband was the psychiatrist Emanuel Miller; her son is the director Jonathan Miller. She wrote seven novels, short stories, and a biography of Robert Browning. *Farewell Leicester Square* is Persephone book No.14.

DOROTHY CANFIELD FISHER (1879–1958) was born in Kansas but spent most of her adult life in Vermont, where she wrote her twenty-two novels; she also wrote eighteen works of non-fiction, including two books on the Montessori method, and sat on the editorial board of the Book of the Month Club from 1925-51. Eleanor Roosevelt called her one of the ten most influential women in America. Her 1924 novel *The Home-Maker* is Persephone book No. 7.

NORAH HOULT (1898–1984) was born in Dublin, but was sent to England after the death of her parents. In 1928 she published a collection of five short stories to considerable critical acclaim. After working as a journalist and writing several novels she returned to Ireland, but eventually settled in Kensington where her neighbour Violet Hunt was the inspiration for Claire Temple in Persephone book No. 59, *There Were No Windows* (1944).

ANGELICA GIBBS (1908–55), the younger sister of the humorist and theatre critic Wolcott Gibbs, was born in New York. She went to Vassar and wrote for *McCall's* and other magazines; from 1931 onwards she was on the staff of *The New Yorker* writing short stories, poetry, theatre reviews, profiles and essays. She was married to Robert Canfield and had two children.

HELEN HULL (1888–1971) was born in Michigan, attended a liberal arts college and taught at Wellesley College in Massachusetts. Here she met Mabel Louise Robinson; for fifty years they lived together, in New York and in Maine. A forty-year teaching career at Columbia began in 1916. The first of her seventeen novels was published in 1922, her last in 1963. Her stories appeared regularly in magazines and were collected in two volumes.

KAY BOYLE (1902–92) grew up in Cincinnati, studied architecture and music and then moved to New York to work on a magazine. In England in the mid-1920s she wrote poems and short stories, and while living in Paris published several novels. She returned to the US in 1940; as well as being a well-known novelist and short story writer, she was Paris correspondent for *The New Yorker* from 1946-53; she then taught creative writing at San Francisco State University.

MOLLIE PANTER-DOWNES (1906–97) published her first, bestselling novel when she was just 17. In 1927 she married and moved to a C15th house near Haslemere in Surrey; after the birth of her two daughters she began writing 'Letters from London' and short stories for *The New Yorker*. She also wrote biographies, and another novel, *One Fine Day* (1947). Two volumes of her short stories are in print, *Good Evening, Mrs Craven* (Persephone book No. 8) and *Minnie's Room* (Persephone book No. 34).

ELIZABETH BERRIDGE (1919–2009), born in a London suburb, worked for the Bank of England and for a photographic agency. She published her first short story in 1941, just before moving to Wales with her husband; here she wrote more short stories, published in 1947 as *Selected Stories* (and reprinted as Persephone book No. 15, *Tell It To a Stranger*). She wrote nine novels, and was a fiction reviewer for the *Daily Telegraph* for many years.

FRANCES TOWERS (1885–1948) was born in Calcutta and from 1905–31 worked at the Bank of England, first as a clerk then as Assistant to the Supervisor. Her first short story was published in 1929. In the late 1930s she began teaching. She wrote most of her short stories during the late 1940s, but died suddenly of pneumonia on New Year's Day 1948, the year before the publication of her only book *Tea with Mr Rochester*, later reprinted as Persephone book No. 44.

MARGARET BONHAM (1913–91) was born in London and educated at Wimbledon High School for Girls. She was married three times, had four children and lived variously in homes in Wales, Oxfordshire and Devon. Her short stories were published in magazines and collected as *The Casino* (1948), later Persephone book No. 48. Her only novel came out in 1951.

SHIRLEY JACKSON (1916–65) was born in San Francisco. After her graduation from Syracuse University she married Stanley Edgar Hyman; they moved first to New York and then to Bennington, Vermont where she brought up their four children while writing numerous magazine articles, novels and short stories. *The Haunting of Hill House* (1959) was called 'the greatest haunted-house story ever written'.

SYLVIA TOWNSEND WARNER (1893–1978), whose father taught history at Harrow School, worked as a musicologist but soon began writing: her first collection of poetry was published in 1925 and her first novel a year later. In 1938 she met the poet Valentine Ackland and subsequently lived with her in Dorset. She published numerous short stories in *The New Yorker*, wrote several more novels, and maintained a large correspondence, famously with the novelist William Maxwell.

DIANA GARDNER (1913–97) went to Bedford High School and Westminster School of Art, after which she worked as a wood engraver and book illustrator. During WWII she lived with her father in Rodmell in Sussex where she was a neighbour of Leonard and Virginia Woolf. Her first short story was published in *Horizon* in 1940; *Halfway Down the Cliff* (1946), republished as *The Woman Novelist and Other Stories* (Persephone book No. 64), is a collection of her stories. Her only novel was published in 1954, and thereafter she became a full-time painter.

PENELOPE MORTIMER (1918–99) briefly studied journalism in London, married when she was 19 and had four children. In 1949 she married the writer and barrister John Mortimer and had two more children; meanwhile she wrote short stories for *The New Yorker* and was an agony aunt at the *Daily Mail*. From 1947–83 she wrote nine novels including Persephone book No. 77 *Daddy's Gone A-Hunting* (1958) and *The Pumpkin Eater* (1962), later a much-acclaimed film.

DIANA ATHILL was born in 1917 in Norfolk and went to Oxford; during WWII she worked as a news researcher for the BBC and from 1946-93 she was an extremely successful editor at André Deutsch Ltd. In 1962 she published a volume of short stories, some of which were republished as Persephone book No. 92 *Midsummer Night in the Workhouse* (2011); *Instead of a Letter*, her first volume of memoirs, came out in 1963; *Somewhere Towards the End* won the Costa Book Award in 2009.

ELIZABETH SPENCER was born in 1921 in Mississippi. After university in Tennessee she was a teacher until, in 1953, a Guggenheim Fellowship enabled her to go to Italy to write. Her 1960 novella *The Light in the Piazza* was made into a film in 1962 and, in 2005, into a Broadway musical. She and her husband moved first to Montreal and then to North Carolina. She has written nine novels, seven collections of short stories, a memoir and a play.

PENELOPE FITZGERALD (1916–2000) had a literary upbringing in Hampstead, went to Wycombe Abbey School and won a scholarship to Oxford. In 1941 she married an Irish soldier, Desmond Fitzgerald; her first novel was written to entertain him in his last illness. She went on to publish several more novels and biographies, including *The Knox Brothers* (1977) about her family. In 1979, she won the Booker Prize for her novel *Offshore*.

GEORGINA HAMMICK was born in Hampshire in 1939. Her first published work was poetry and throughout the 1970s her poems appeared in magazines and anthologies. Her first collection of stories, *People for Lunch*, appeared in 1987 and her second, *Spoilt*, in 1992. She has written two novels, *The Arizona Game* (1996), shortlisted for the Whitbread First Novel Prize, and *Green Man Running* (2002). She has three children.

PUBLICATION HISTORY

'From A to Z' was published in 1909 in *American 65* and reprinted in *Lifted Masks* in 1912;

'The Black Cap' was published in *New Age* in 1917 and reprinted in *Something Childish* in 1924;

'The Pain' was published in *The Adelphi* in 1923 and reprinted in *The Little Karoo* in 1925;

'Holiday Group' was published in *The Entertainment and Other Stories* in 1927;

'The Music Box' was published in *Frost in April* in 1929;

'Here We Are' was published in *Cosmopolitan* in 1931 and reprinted in *After Such Pleasures* in 1933;

'A Lovely Time' was published in *The Adelphi* in 1933 and reprinted in *On Approval* (1935);

'Roman Fever' was published in *Liberty* in 1934 and reprinted in *The World Over* (1936);

'Dimanche' was published in *La Revue de Paris* in 1934 and reprinted in *Dimanche et autres nouvelles* in 2000 and in *Dimanche and Other Stories* in 2010;

'The Photograph' was published in *The Whole of the Story* in 1935;

'The Exile' was published in *John O'London's Weekly* in 1935;

'The Rainy Day, the Good Mother and the Brown Suit' was published in *Fables for Parents* in 1937;

'Nine Years is a Long Time' was published in *Nine Years is a Long Time and other tales* in 1938 and in *Selected Stories* in 1946;

'The Test' was published in *The New Yorker* in 1940 and in *About Women* in 1943;

'It All Begins Again' was written in 1941 and published in *Octave* in 1947;

'Defeat' was published in *The New Yorker* in 1941 and in *Thirty Stories* in 1946;

'Good Evening, Mrs Craven' was published in *The New Yorker* in 1942 and in *Good Evening, Mrs Craven* in 1999;

'Subject for a Sermon' was published in *Selected Stories* in 1947 and in *Tell It to a Stranger* in 2000;

'Wednesday' was written in 1944 and published in *Wednesday and Other Stories* in 1961 and in *The Closed Door and Other Stories* in 2007;

'Spade Man from over the Water' was written in 1947 and first published in *Tea with Mr Rochester* in 1949, reprinted in 2003;

'Minnie's Room' was published in *The New Yorker* in 1947 and reprinted in *Minnie's Room* in 2002;

'The English Lesson' was published in *The Casino and Other Stories* in 1948;

'The Lottery' was first published in *The New Yorker* in 1948 and in *The Lottery,* or *The Adventures of James Harris* in 1949;

‘A View Of Exmoor’ was first published in *The New Yorker* in 1948;

‘The Woman Novelist’ was written in 1950 and was unpublished until 2006 when it appeared in *The Woman Novelist and other Stories*;

‘What a Lovely Surprise’ was first published in *The New Yorker* in 1957 and in *Saturday Lunch with the Brownings* in 1960;

‘The Real Thing’ was published in 1960 in *Glamour* magazine, in *An Unavoidable Delay* in 1962 and in *Midsummer Night in the Workhouse* in 2011;

‘A Bad Cold’ was first published in *The New Yorker* in 1967;

‘Worlds Apart’ was unpublished until 2008 when it appeared in the *Hudson Review*;

‘A Few Problems in the Day Case Unit’ was first published in the *Critical Quarterly* in 1986 and in *People for Lunch* in 1987.

Persephone Books publishes the following titles:

No. 1 *William – an Englishman* (1919) by Cicely Hamilton
No. 2 *Mariana* (1940) by Monica Dickens
No. 3 *Someone at a Distance* (1953) by Dorothy Whipple
No. 4 *Fidelity* (1915) by Susan Glaspell
No. 5 *An Interrupted Life: the Diaries and Letters of Etty Hillesum 1941–43*
No. 6 *The Victorian Chaise-longue* (1953) by Marghanita Laski
No. 7 *The Home-Maker* (1924) by Dorothy Canfield Fisher
No. 8 *Good Evening, Mrs. Craven: the Wartime Stories of Mollie Panter-Downes 1939–44*
No. 9 *Few Eggs and No Oranges: the Diaries of Vere Hodgson 1940–45*
No. 10 *Good Things in England* (1932) by Florence White
No. 11 *Julian Grenfell* (1976) by Nicholas Mosley
No. 12 *It's Hard to be Hip over Thirty and Other Tragedies of Married Life* (1968) by Judith Viorst
No. 13 *Consequences* (1919) by E. M. Delafield
No. 14 *Farewell Leicester Square* (1941) by Betty Miller
No. 15 *Tell It to a Stranger: Stories from the 1940s* by Elizabeth Berridge
No. 16 *Saplings* (1945) by Noel Streatfeild
No. 17 *Marjory Fleming* (1946) by Oriel Malet
No. 18 *Every Eye* (1956) by Isobel English
No. 19 *They Knew Mr. Knight* (1934) by Dorothy Whipple
No. 20 *A Woman's Place: 1910–1975* by Ruth Adam
No. 21 *Miss Pettigrew Lives for a Day* (1938) by Winifred Watson
No. 22 *Consider the Years 1938–1946* by Virginia Graham
No. 23 *Reuben Sachs* (1888) by Amy Levy
No. 24 *Family Roundabout* (1948) by Richmal Crompton
No. 25 *The Montana Stories* (1921) by Katherine Mansfield
No. 26 *Brook Evans* (1928) by Susan Glaspell
No. 27 *The Children Who Lived in a Barn* (1938) by Eleanor Graham
No. 28 *Little Boy Lost* (1949) by Marghanita Laski
No. 29 *The Making of a Marchioness* (1901) by Frances Hodgson Burnett
No. 30 *Kitchen Essays* (1922) by Agnes Jekyll
No. 31 *A House in the Country* (1944) by Jocelyn Playfair
No. 32 *The Carlyles at Home* (1965) by Thea Holme

No. 33 *The Far Cry* (1949) by Emma Smith
No. 34 *Minnie's Room: the Peacetime Stories of Mollie Panter-Downes 1947–65*
No. 35 *Greenery Street* (1925) by Denis Mackail
No. 36 *Lettice Delmer* (1958) by Susan Miles
No. 37 *The Runaway* (1872) by Elizabeth Anna Hart
No. 38 *Cheerful Weather for the Wedding* (1932) by Julia Strachey
No. 39 *Manja* (1939) by Anna Gmeyner
No. 40 *The Priory* (1939) by Dorothy Whipple
No. 41 *Hostages to Fortune* (1933) by Elizabeth Cambridge
No. 42 *The Blank Wall* (1947) by Elisabeth Sanxay Holding
No. 43 *The Wise Virgins* (1914) by Leonard Woolf
No. 44 *Tea with Mr Rochester* (1949) by Frances Towers
No. 45 *Good Food on the Aga* (1933) by Ambrose Heath
No. 46 *Miss Ranskill Comes Home* (1946) by Barbara Euphan Todd
No. 47 *The New House* (1936) by Lettice Cooper
No. 48 *The Casino* (1948) by Margaret Bonham
No. 49 *Bricks and Mortar* (1932) by Helen Ashton
No. 50 *The World that was Ours* (1967) by Hilda Bernstein
No. 51 *Operation Heartbreak* (1950) by Duff Cooper
No. 52 *The Village* (1952) by Marghanita Laski
No. 53 *Lady Rose and Mrs Memmary* (1937) by Ruby Ferguson
No. 54 *They Can't Ration These* (1940) by Vicomte de Mauduit
No. 55 *Flush* (1933) by Virginia Woolf
No. 56 *They Were Sisters* (1943) by Dorothy Whipple
No. 57 *The Hopkins Manuscript* (1939) by RC Sherriff
No. 58 *Hetty Dorval* (1947) by Ethel Wilson
No. 59 *There Were No Windows* (1944) by Norah Hoult
No. 60 *Doreen* (1946) by Barbara Noble
No. 61 *A London Child of the 1870s* (1934) by Molly Hughes
No. 62 *How to Run your Home without Help* (1949) by Kay Smallshaw
No. 63 *Princes in the Land* (1938) by Joanna Cannan
No. 64 *The Woman Novelist and Other Stories* (1946) by Diana Gardner
No. 65 *Alas, Poor Lady* (1937) by Rachel Ferguson
No. 66 *Gardener's Nightcap* (1938) by Muriel Stuart
No. 67 *The Fortnight in September* (1931) by RC Sherriff

No. 68 *The Expendable Man* (1963) by Dorothy B Hughes
No. 69 *Journal of Katherine Mansfield* (1927)
No. 70 *Plats du Jour* (1957) by Patience Gray and Primrose Boyd
No. 71 *The Shuttle* (1907) by Frances Hodgson Burnett
No. 72 *House-Bound* (1942) by Winifred Peck
No. 73 *The Young Pretenders* (1895) by Edith Henrietta Fowler
No. 74 *The Closed Door and Other Stories* by Dorothy Whipple
No. 75 *On the Other Side: Letters to my Children from Germany 1940–46* by Mathilde Wolff-Mönckeberg
No. 76 *The Crowded Street* (1924) by Winifred Holtby
No. 77 *Daddy's Gone A-Hunting* (1958) by Penelope Mortimer
No. 78 *A Very Great Profession: The Woman's Novel 1914–39* (1983) by Nicola Beauman
No. 79 *Round about a Pound a Week* (1913) by Maud Pember Reeves
No. 80 *The Country Housewife's Book* (1934) by Lucy H Yates
No. 81 *Miss Buncle's Book* (1934) by DE Stevenson
No. 82 *Amours de Voyage* (1849) by Arthur Hugh Clough
No. 83 *Making Conversation* (1931) by Christine Longford
No. 84 *A New System of Domestic Cookery* (1806) by Mrs Rundell
No. 85 *High Wages* (1930) by Dorothy Whipple
No. 86 *To Bed with Grand Music* (1946) by 'Sarah Russell' (Marghanita Laski)
No. 87 *Dimanche and Other Stories* (1934–41) by Irène Némirovsky
No. 88 *Still Missing* (1981) by Beth Gutcheon
No. 89 *The Mystery of Mrs Blencarrow* (1890) by Mrs Oliphant
No. 90 *The Winds of Heaven* (1955) by Monica Dickens
No. 91 *Miss Buncle Married* (1936) by DE Stevenson
No. 92 *Midsummer Night in the Workhouse* (1962) by Diana Athill
No. 93 *The Sack of Bath* (1973) by Adam Fergusson
No. 94 *No Surrender* (1911) by Constance Maud
No. 95 *Greenbanks* (1932) by Dorothy Whipple
No. 96 *Dinners for Beginners* (1934) by Rachel and Margaret Ryan
No. 97 *Harriet* (1934) by Elizabeth Jenkins,
No. 98 *A Writer's Diary* (1953) by Virginia Woolf,
No. 99 *Patience* (1953) by John Coates
No. 100 *The Persephone Book of Short Stories*

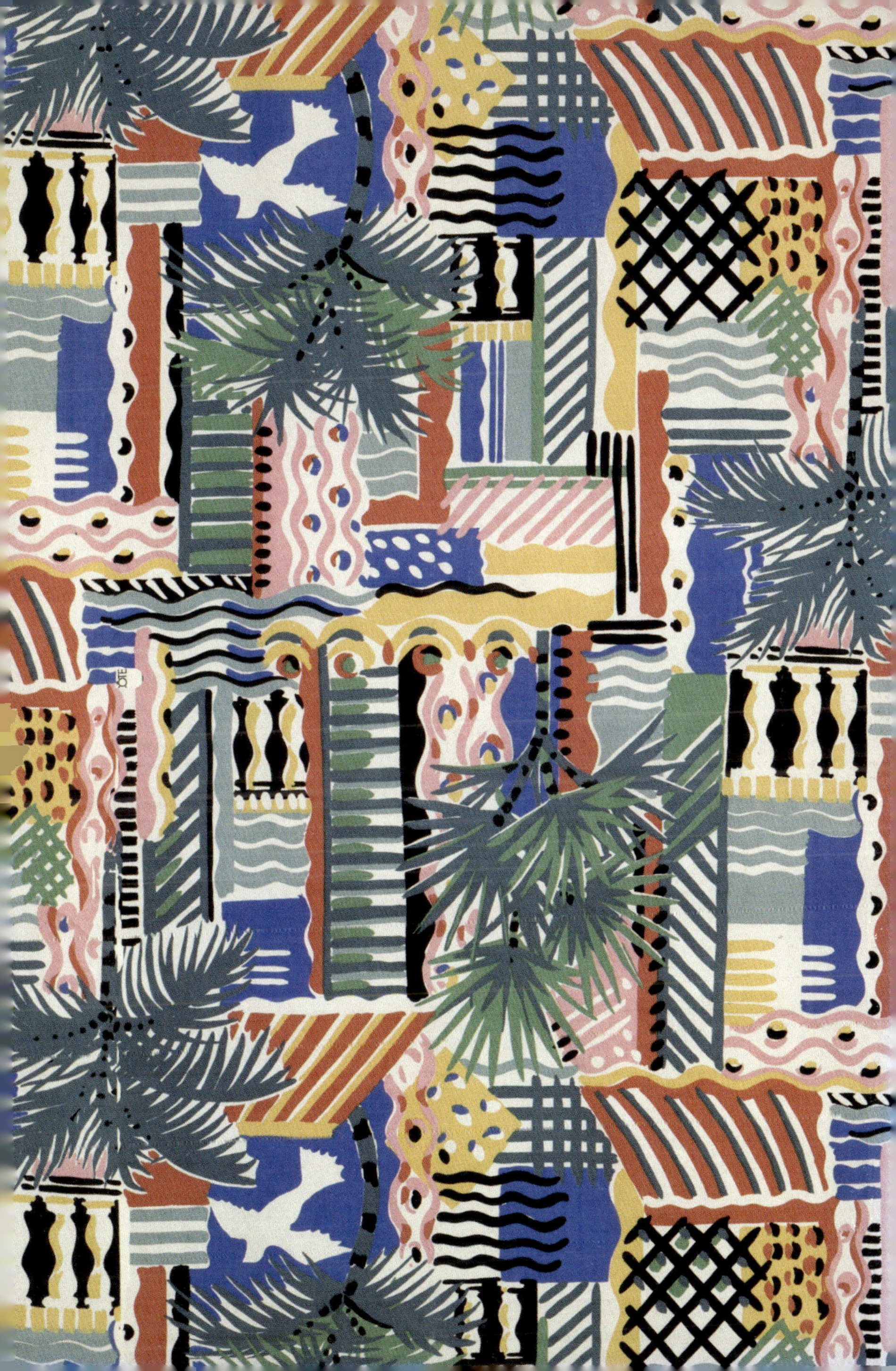